Algeri emerged from the rear door and headed straight for his car. He had just reached his Yukon, and opened the front door when he heard a voice from a few feet away.

The approaching man said something but Alex didn't quite catch it. "Hey, Paul," the guy might have said.

Before Alex had a chance to say that wasn't his name, five loud reports cut through the night. The sounds had come in rapid succession. All five bullets found their target. At point-blank range, Alex Algeri was a tough target to miss.

The bullets tore into Alex's neck and upper body. Lead slugs with a copper wash perforated his heart and both of his lungs. Bleeding profusely and choking on his own blood, he managed to stagger back into the gym. He collapsed to the floor and lay still. Blood flowed from his wounds and into the carpet near his back. Someone called 911 . . .

LETHAL
EMBRACE

Robert Mladinich and
Michael Benson

PINNACLE BOOKS
Kensington Publishing Corp.

http://www.kensingtonbooks.com

PINNACLE BOOKS are published by

Kensington Publishing Corp.
850 Third Avenue
New York, NY 10022

All Kensington Titles, Imprints, and Distributed Lines are available at special quantity discounts for bulk purchases for sales promotions, premiums, fund-raising, and educational or institutional use. Special book excerpts or customized printings can also be created to fit specific needs. For details, write or phone the office of the Kensington special sales manager: Kensington Publishing Corp., 850 Third Avenue, New York, NY 10022, attn: Special Sales Department, Phone: 1-800-221-2647.

Pinnacle and the P logo Reg. U.S. Pat. & TM Off.

First Printing: January 2007

10 9 8 7 6 5 4 3 2 1

Printed in the United States of America

This book is dedicated to my parents, Leon and Margot Mla-dinich. Although my father passed away in 2005, the love affair he had with my mother lasted fifty-five years and will continue on into eternity.

Acknowledgments

Many people contributed in some way, small or large, to this book. Some we can only thank personally. To those who requested anonymity, please know how grateful we are. To the others, we would like to thank you here:

Sal Algeri, for trusting us enough to share his thoughts and perspectives and for showing that a father's love for his children is eternal.

David Armanini, for showing that a father's love for his daughter knows no bounds.

Bruce Barket, for offering his insights into this emotionally charged case. As a former member of the law enforcement community, Barket is the kind of attorney we view as a thorn in the side, but there is no one we would rather have fighting for our freedom than this man.

Jay Salpeter, for showing why both active and retired NYPD detectives are universally regarded as the best in the world. If we were on the lam, we'd hate to have him on our tail.

Vincent McCrudden, for discussing so openly and honestly such a difficult chapter in his life.

Retired Suffolk County detective Christine O'Neill-Spady, for helping us with several logistical issues. Also to her father, Richard O'Neill, the onetime vice president of the New York City Patrolmen's Benevolent Association, for introducing us to her and for being such a good friend.

The New York City Sergeants Benevolent Association, especially President Ed Mullins and Treasurer Robert Johnson, for being so understanding and considerate during some very challenging times.

Giles Anderson and Jake Elwell, our respective literary

agents, for their support throughout this project as well as others.

Gary Goldstein, who is an old-school editor, blessed with the sensibility and enthusiasm of a beat writer.

Also thanks to driver extraordinaire Anne Darrigan, Erin Mainey, Grace Mainey, Cailin Murtha—and the Honorable Louis J. Ohlig, who sat on the bench for this most unusual trial.

Authors' Note

A married woman sent her bodybuilder boyfriend, a hood with ties to organized crime, to kill her estranged husband. The hood and his hapless sidekick set out to do the job, but—in a fatal mistake—shot and killed the husband's innocent business partner instead.

The hit went down in a dark parking lot behind a bodybuilding gym in the already infamous Long Island village of Amityville. Solid police work, consciences at work, and loose lips in a strip joint helped lead police to three arrests.

Emotions at the murder trials ran high, as they featured the presence of the intended victim, husband of one of the defendants. What unraveled was a tale that shocked Long Island and the nation. In *Lethal Embrace*, the complete story of Ralph Salierno, Lee Ann Riedel, and the murder of Alex Algeri—a story of bloodlust, of betrayal and blunder, of jealousy and drugs—is told for the first time.

In addition to a variety of other sources, such as police documents, notarized witness statements, court transcripts, and published reports, coauthor Mladinich attended the trial and the sentencing hearings.

Although this is a true story, some names will be changed to protect the privacy of the innocent. Pseudonyms will be noted upon their first usage. When possible, the spoken word has been quoted verbatim. However, when that is not possible, conversations have been reconstructed as closely as possible to reality based on the recollections of those that spoke and heard those words. In places, there has been slight editing of spoken words, but only to improve readability. The denotations and connotations of the words remain unaltered.

Chapter 1

The Parking-Lot Ambush

It was a cold winter evening in Amityville, Long Island, January 17, 2001. Even though it was only early evening, the days were noticeably short and twilight had given way to nightfall. Although it was only a few years ago, the world was a different place.

The attacks of 9/11 were still nine months away. Bill Clinton was serving his last few days as president and preparations were in full tilt for George W. Bush's inauguration on January 20. Dave Winfield and Kirby Puckett, baseball stars of the 1980s, had just been elected into the Hall of Fame. The New York Giants, with Kerry Collins at quarterback, had just defeated the Minnesota Vikings, 41–0, to earn the right to face the Baltimore Ravens in the Super Bowl.

Then, as now, however, power was often determined through violence, as was evidenced by the prior day's assassination of Laurent Kabila. The leader of the Congo had been shot and killed by his own bodyguard.

On that January night, entering Amityville, two men

drove in a white minivan, both dressed in zipper-up sweatshirts with hoods. Although the object of their visit was clear, they weren't entirely sure where they were.

They knew they weren't in Nassau County anymore. They'd just passed a sign that read: "Welcome to Suffolk County." Now they just had to figure out if they were on the right road. So much traffic, too much.

"Twenty-seven-A East. Where is Merrick Road?" the driver said, a cigarette hanging off his lower lip.

"There's a sign, this is Merrick Road," the other replied.

"What's the street number we're looking for?" the driver asked, even though he'd had the address memorized just minutes before.

"Eighty-eight."

"Right, right, right," the driver said, and then with a squint, uttered, "Shit, even numbers are on the left."

Merrick Road was a four-lane bustling major thoroughfare. There were red lights only at the major intersections. Turning across traffic was going to be a bitch. It was nighttime, but the road was well lit, both with streetlights and from the commercial establishments on either side. Plus, there was plenty of traffic providing light. Rush hour was over, but the road was still busy. One thing Long Island had plenty of was people.

They passed taverns, car washes, and a used-car lot. Before the pair had had a chance to see any other street number, their destination zoomed by on the left.

"That was it," the passenger said.

"Shit," the driver said, lighting one cigarette off another. The passenger had been teasing him about the chain-smoking. Pussy. The driver said he was nervous, hadn't done anything like this before. The passenger said relax, it was going to be a snap. Just drive the fucking car.

At the next red light the minivan turned around and headed back west. This time the driver was ready. They took a right and drove along the side of the building they needed to watch. As soon as they pulled off the main drag, the world got darker and quieter.

The place was a fitness club and it sat on the northeast corner of Merrick Road and Park Avenue. A little farther north, Park Avenue developed into the street that held the town's downtown drag, but down here, where the street started, was a quiet residential street that did not warrant its own traffic signal at Merrick Road.

This was the destination of a journey that had taken them northward, clear across the country. Now the goal was to take deep breaths, and, at least for the driver, try to keep his heart from beating clear out of his chest.

There was a parking lot in front of the club for customers, and a parking lot in the back for employees. The customer parking lot was bright and noisy. The rear parking lot was dark and quiet. The difference was dramatic, considering only one brick building separated the two.

Immediately next to the fitness club on the east was a large round-roofed building, which looked like it might have been an airplane hangar in another incarnation. The one-word sign on the front of the building read B-O-W-L-I-N-G in red neon lights.

The minivan made its second U-turn in a matter of minutes and creepy-crawled along the side of the road until it was just in front of the parking-lot entrance. Overshooting his mark, the driver threw the white vehicle into reverse and parked into place.

The view was perfect. The rear parking lot was accessible from Park Avenue only and the minivan stopped as close to the lot as it could get without actually pulling into the lot.

The lot was bordered on the south by the back of the fitness club, on the east by a screen fence separating it from the bowling-alley parking lot, on the north by an eight-foot wooden-plank fence protecting a private residence, and on the east by Park Avenue, where the minivan now sat and waited.

The back of the fitness club had five doors. Four appeared to be emergency exits and lacked doorknobs. These were painted the same dull yellow color as the rest of the back of the building.

The fifth door was made out of glass and had words painted on it. Maybe rules. Maybe the hours the club was open—something like that. They couldn't be read from the street in the dim light. Light from the inner hallway could be seen shining through the glass door. The glass door, they realized, was the one they had to keep their eye on.

They also had to look for a black Yukon. That was their man's vehicle. That wasn't hard to spot, either. The Yukon was parked with its nose pointed toward the rear of the club, just to the left of the glass door.

The Amityville branch of the Dolphin Fitness Clubs of Long Island was one of the largest. It was an L-shaped building, and among the services offered there—beyond the usual cardio- and strength-training equipment—were full-court basketball, racquetball courts, an inside running track, and steam rooms.

At that moment, inside the gym, the place was jumping, a beehive of activity. The co-owner of the place, thirty-two-year-old businessman Alexander Algeri, would have been out of the fitness-club business months before, if business hadn't been so damn good.

On this night Alex was standing behind the counter just inside the front entrance. Alex looked good. For that matter, so did just about everyone else. The gym, in every nook and cranny, celebrated beauty.

Womanly beauty. Manly beauty. Everyone was ripped and good-looking, The gym was a very hip spot. Customers were twenty-somethings. The music was usually hard rock, not the disco crap one got at a lot of places.

It was a friendly place, with a lot of chatting and laughter mixed in with the music and the grunts of exertion. There were regulars. Mostly regulars, in fact. To a large extent, the patrons of Dolphin's had melded their physical-fitness program and their social life into one.

Stacked on the counter in front of Alex were the gym's attractive pamphlets, which showed a muscular man bursting out of a blender, a visual tribute to a better-living-through-chemistry philosophy. It was chemistry under the guise of nutrition, but chemistry nonetheless.

The cover of the pamphlet read: "Dolphin Fitness Clubs Present Revolutionary Blendz." Inside the pamphlets were advertisements for Revolutionary Supplements, including power protein, weight gainer, whey protein, fat-burning protein, and creatine complex.

They also advertised Revolutionary Additions, which they encouraged to be added to one's "Blendz." They were nonfat yogurt, calcium, vitamin C, Turbo Charge, flaxseed oil, wheat bran, spirulina, rice bran, and oat bran.

The chemistry wasn't limited to superquick muscle-building nutrition combinations. Alongside the "menu" atop the gym's front desk was another leaflet, this one for "Glam Tan By Tiki," which involved bronzing the skin through the application of dihydroxyacetone.

According to the advertisement, the product "leaves a natural glowing look. Get that vacationed look without taking off of work. Stay healthy and glowing throughout the winter months."

Next to the tanning ad was a schedule of classes that could be attended. Just about every evening there was a class of some sort, earlier on weeknights, a little bit later on weekends. The classes had names like "Power Pilates with MaryAnn," "Abs with Nadia," "Yoga with David,"

"Body Sculpting with Lanya," and "Express Sculp with Eugenia." That night it was an aerobics class, and Alex could hear the instructor keeping up the banter of instruction, encouragement, and rhythm.

Alex was a social guy, so he left the front desk—one of his employees was working there anyway—and began to wander around chatting with folks, shouting out encouragement to the hardworking and sweaty customers.

He walked past the large flat-screen TV that was mounted on the wall. ESPN was usually on, a sporting event of some sort. On the left, Alex passed five rows of stationary bicycles, stepping machines, treadmills, and rowing machines. Almost all of them were being used. Yeah, he wanted to get out of the business, but . . . *kaching!* How could he unload a gold mine like this?

To the right of the desk was a cavernous room full of free weights. In the northeast corner of the gym, to the left of the weight room, was a huge circuit-training area.

Algeri was known to his friends and acquaintances as "Papa Smurf" because he was a gentle bear of a man, known for his kindness and affability. His dad, Sal, had once grown a white beard and was the first to be called "Papa Smurf." Later, the nickname was passed down to Alex.

As Alex passed the aerobics class, a female patron asked, "Hey, Alex, how about that CD you played last night for later? I got a great workout to that."

Alex remembered which CD she was talking about.

"It's in my car. I'll go get it," he replied cheerfully.

To retrieve the requested CD, Alex didn't bother to put on a coat. He was wearing a long-sleeved black knit shirt and tight-fitting jeans. Besides, he'd only be outside for a second or two. Even with his clothes on, there was no mistaking the fact that Alex was heavily muscled. He had a bodybuilder's physique.

His SUV was in the parking lot out back. The disc was

in the compartment between the front seats of his black GMC Yukon.

Algeri emerged from the rear door of the Dolphin Fitness Club. Since he took an immediate right, he probably did not notice that all of the vehicles behind the gym were empty except for one—the minivan parked on the street, which held two men. No one had noticed, even though the men had been there for some time, lying in wait.

Algeri was focused on his task and headed straight for his car. He had just reached his Yukon, and opened the front door so that the interior light had gone on, when he heard a voice from a few feet away.

The approaching man said something, but Alex didn't quite catch it. "Hey, Paul," the guy might have said.

Before Alex had a chance to say that that wasn't his name, five loud reports cut through the night. The sounds had come in rapid succession. All five bullets found their target. At point-blank range, Alex Algeri was a tough target to miss.

All five bullets tore into Alex's neck and upper body. Lead slugs with a copper wash perforated his heart and both of his lungs, but he was tough and he did not drop. Algeri, bleeding profusely and choking on his own blood, managed to stagger back into the gym. Once inside, with clients and employees already starting to gather to see what was wrong, he gasped, "I've been shot."

Then he collapsed to the floor and lay still. Blood flowed from his wounds and into the carpet near his shoulder and neck. Someone called 911 and summoned an ambulance. There were two clients in the gym that knew CPR. One was Peter Casserly, who at the time was a member of the Village of Amityville's Board of Trustees, the body that met on the second and fourth Mondays of the month to govern the seaside community. Casserly was a member of the Board of Trustee's Fire

Protection Committee. The other customer who knew CPR was a nurse who was never publicly identified.

An ambulance siren could be heard almost immediately. The emergency vehicle did not have far to go. It arrived at the gym minutes later. Painted on its side were the words AMITYVILLE RESCUE.

After the shooting, both men were once again inside the minivan. The urge was to tear out of the parking spot, and get the hell out of there as fast as possible. But that would tend to attract attention, and that was the last thing they wanted. Besides, the turn onto Merrick Road was only a few feet up ahead.

No point in peeling out and laying a patch if one is going to have to wait in the next five seconds to merge into traffic. The men turned left when they got to the road, and there must have been a solid reason. It would have been much easier to turn right, which didn't involve crossing traffic. Even though they did not want to draw attention to themselves, they also wanted to distance themselves as quickly as possible from the fitness club and the bleeding body they had just left there.

So maybe they turned right and then made a U-turn, or maybe they waited until there was a break in the action and turned left. Whichever, they were headed east. The next order of business was to get rid of the gun, preferably in a place where it would not be found for a very long time, if ever.

Right behind the ambulance pulling into the gym parking lot was an Amityville Village police car. Officers and paramedics arrived on the scene almost simultaneously. Paramedics worked on Alex for a moment or two; then he was loaded up and taken to Brunswick Hospital Center, less than a mile away.

The ambulance, like the minivan, had pulled onto Park Avenue, but they did not make a U-turn. Instead, after Alex was loaded in the back, the ambulance headed straight north on Park Avenue. At the point where it merged with Broadway, where the white gazebo was, Park Avenue changed and became Amityville's downtown drag. The large private houses, now at least partially converted for commercial use (an attorney, an optometrist, a florist, and a funeral home), gave way to downtown, where both sides of the street were lined with adjoining shops.

The ambulance raced under the Long Island Railroad overpass, and then took a left into the Brunswick Hospital grounds before taking an immediate right into the parking lot outside the emergency area and ambulance entrance. The ambulance had called ahead. The emergency room was alive with activity, ready for a patient with serious gunshot wounds.

Amityville Village police chief Woodrow Cromarty later said that when officers arrived at the scene, Algeri was still alive.

"He had a weak pulse," Chief Cromarty said. "He had been shot around the neck and head, but was still breathing."

It didn't take the doctors in the emergency room long to realize that there wasn't much they could do. There was no hope. Algeri was pronounced dead at the hospital. On his death certificate, the cause of death was listed as "multiple gunshot wounds."

As was true of all homicides, an immediate autopsy would be performed.

The minivan with its two adrenaline-jazzed occupants rolled east on Merrick Road, which was also Route 27A.

And, once one crossed the border ending the Village of Amityville, it stopped being called Merrick Road and became the Montauk Highway. If the men had stayed on that road heading east, they would have ended up at the easternmost tip of Long Island.

They passed a bank, an antique shop, and a series of white houses with long driveways leading to carports in the back. Some of those garages were visible from the road and looked like they had been converted from the original carriage houses.

Then came a strip mall, then a well-kept park with a small white monument of some sort. A little farther down the road, the van paused and pulled halfway onto the shoulder. The gun was hurled into a body of water that passed under the road.

Before the splash of the gun hitting the water could be heard, the van was back on the road and moving with the flow of traffic. They probably didn't notice it, and wouldn't have appreciated the irony if they had, but the next tavern they passed on their left was called the Jailhouse Inn.

As soon as the bleeding Alex Algeri was removed from the gym, the local Amityville police began to cordon off the area. It was no longer a place of business where patrons could monitor their heart rate while pumping away at a stationary bike. It was now a crime scene. Police had to control access.

No one in; no one out.

Was there a chance that the shooter was inside the club, that he had entered the club before the wounded victim and had blended in with the other customers? A witness outside, a young woman walking her dog, said the shooter got in a van and split. Still, cops needed to talk to everyone inside the gym. And contact information needed to be taken in case further conversation was required. The crowded conditions only complicated the process.

"There were a lot of people inside the club and we had to interview and take their names and addresses before they could leave the building," said Cromarty. "It was a couple of hours before we were done."

By that time the Suffolk County police were on the scene and had taken control of the investigation. Among those who responded were forensic scientists Robert Genna, Jeffrey Luber, and Debra Nelson.

The evidence found by the forensic team was not promising, but was carefully gathered nonetheless. There was a stain on the carpet in the rear hallway of the gym. Since this was where Alex collapsed, it was assumed that the blood belonged to the victim. However, there was always a chance that there were samples of the perp's blood as well, so it had to be tested. A swab was taken of the bloodstain.

An expended bullet had been found and was turned over to the forensic team in a plastic cup. Also found in the parking lot, just outside the rear door of the gym, were three cigarette butts. These were carefully picked up and labeled. Perhaps the killer had smoked one of these cigarettes and left DNA on the butt in the form of saliva.

The swab of blood from the carpet and the three cigarette butts were forwarded to the Serology Section of the Suffolk police. Serology is the study of serums, their reactions, and their properties. This was the division that handled the department's DNA testing. The slug in the plastic cup was turned over to the department's firearms section.

When the forensic scientists' work in the rear hallway of the gym and the parking lot was through, Alex's vehicle was moved to the Suffolk County Crime Laboratory garage, where further processing would take place the next day.

* * *

Salvatore Algeri, Alexander's father, had just gotten home from work. He and his wife, Maria, one of his sons, and his stepchildren were just about to sit down to dinner when the phone rang. Maria answered.

It was Vincent Sidoti (pseudonym), who was a friend of Alex and Paul's from down at the gym.

"Al's been shot," Vincent said.

Maria turned to Sal and said, "It's one of Al's friends. He said Al's been shot." Then, into the phone, she said, "How's he doing?"

Vincent said Alex had staggered in. Paramedics said he still had some vital signs, although they weren't as strong as they could be.

"Where is he?" Sal asked Maria, who relayed the question.

"They took him to Brunswick Hospital," Vincent said.

"Brunswick," Maria repeated.

"Tell him we're on our way," Sal said anxiously.

When Sal and Maria got to the hospital, they wouldn't let them in to see Alex. More than an hour passed before someone came out to tell the Algeris that Alex had died.

Also at the hospital at that moment were Alex's girlfriend, Jean, his brother Paul, and his sister, Christina. Later, Sal would come to believe that Al was gone before any of them had even gotten to the hospital.

Sal tried to tell Alex's mother, Lee Ferrari, but learned that she was out of the country on a cruise. Christina took charge of informing her mother of her brother's death. She got word to the ship through the cruise line. Christina was not, however, able to get in direct communication with her mother. A message was relayed. Apparently, cruise line personnel gave Alex's mom the bad news.

* * *

The morning after the crime, Detective Sergeant Edward Fandrey, of Suffolk County's homicide squad, made a public statement: "At about seven twenty-three last night, one of the owners of the Dolphin Fitness Club here at 88-92 Merrick Road, Amityville, stepped out back to get something out of his car. He is thirty-two-year-old Alexander Algeri. Moments after stepping outside, he came back into the gym, fell to the floor, and said he was shot." Fandrey said that an ambulance had taken the victim to Brunswick Hospital, where he was pronounced dead. Suffolk County police homicide detectives processed the murder scene thoroughly, but nothing encouraging developed. There had been no eyewitnesses to the shooting, but there were some people who saw and heard what happened just before and just after the crime.

One of the best witnesses was a woman who had been out walking her dog along Park Avenue in Amityville. Her name was Natalie Lynch (pseudonym). She told police that she'd seen a white van leave the scene. A pudgy white man had been driving.

On the outside there were two other eyewitnesses—at least they were *ear* witnesses. They were Diane Compitello and Jacki Kronemberg, who told police—and then the *Babylon Beacon,* the local newspaper—that they had been in the vicinity at the time of the shooting.

The young women agreed that they had heard seven shots. They said they recognized the reports as gunfire and rushed to the scene to find out what had happened.

On TV the next day they showed videotape of two male witnesses who were there when Algeri was shot. The first witness, apparently a patron of the fitness club, said, "One of the owners was shot here tonight. I was getting ready to leave. I walked around and saw that he'd fallen to the ground. Nobody knew what was happening. It was a little bit of a panic. He said before he fell that he'd been shot. I noticed three bullet wounds, one under his chin, one in the side of his neck, and one in his shoulder. He wasn't breathing. Very faint pulse. I administered CPR. There was a nurse and she was helping out. I think he was gone (dead) before he left here tonight."

The other witness, a carpenter who had been doing some work in the gym, then added, "He had a little blood on his chin and he said he was shot and he fell to the ground. We thought, he's an electrician. So we thought he said, 'I gotta shock.' We are here doing renovations and we thought he was doing electrical, and that's the first thing we thought. When he fell, we just thought he slipped or something. Then we just seen he wasn't breathing."

During the days and weeks following the shooting, the police used the local newspapers to beg the public for help: "Anyone with information is being asked to call Suffolk County Crime Stoppers unit," notices read. They gave out a special 1-800 number for crime tips, along with the main phone number for the homicide squad.

Chapter 2

Autopsy

Alex Algeri's autopsy was performed at ten o'clock the next morning by Suffolk County deputy medical examiner James C. Wilson, M.D. Dr. Wilson noted that there were signs that the victim had been a bodybuilder, beyond the fact that he had been a part owner of, and had been killed outside of, a fitness club.

Alex's body had "larger than typical amounts of skeletal muscle." Also, according to the medical examiner, the body hair on the chest and abdomen, as well as the upper pubic regions, had been shaved recently. The hair had just started to grow back. There was also evidence of shaving of the pubic hair in much of the genital region.

"With some regrowth," the medical examiner's report added.

The doctor noted that Alex had several tattoos. One, just above the middle of Alex's back, was a multicolored design. On the left arm was a tattoo of two hearts, an arrow piercing them, and the words "Mom and Dad" written in script. On the right arm was a tribal symbol.

On the outside of his left thigh was the head of a bull-dog and a collar. On the right thigh were images of a female warrior and two skeleton warriors. On his lower right leg was the cartoon character Wile E. Coyote, the one famous for chasing the Road Runner, who was shown in a cape and smoking a cigarette with a cigarette holder.

Although the body had been stripped of its clothing, part of Alex's shirt, which had been cut away at the hospital, was still beneath him. It was a long-sleeved knit shirt, mostly black in color. There were EKG lead patches on his torso that had been used to monitor the last few heartbeats of his life. A catheter and collection bag had been attached to collect Alex's urine.

Dr. Wilson started by counting the bullet holes. There were six. Five were entrance wounds and one was an exit wound. There were no other notable injuries. Alex's fingernails had been cut short and there was no evidence found beneath them.

The entrance wounds were all between .35 and .40 inches in diameter, which led the medical examiner immediately to speculate that they had been made by .38-caliber bullets. Predictably, the lone exit wound was larger, about three-quarters of an inch in diameter.

Dr. Wilson arbitrarily designated the bullet holes A through F. Wound A was on the right side at the base of the neck. As was true of all the wounds, there was no evidence of stippling. There was no soot or powder on the wound. That would mean that the gun was more than a few inches away from the victim when it was fired.

Wound B was the exit wound and was located in the right shoulder. Wound C was in the back of the left arm, where it met the shoulder. Wound D was in the right side of the back. Wound E was just below wound

D. Wound F was several inches below E, and wound F was several inches below that.

While looking at the body's left arm and shoulder, the medical examiner noted that there was something hard just beneath the skin. The lump was in the two-hearts portion of the "Mom and Dad" tattoo. He made an incision and found it to be a slightly deformed lead bullet. As he had earlier suspected, it was a .38. The slug had a lead core and a copper covering.

The doctor then traced the paths made by the bullet inside Alex's body. Wound A went from right to left and had passed through Alex's thyroid gland and his larynx.

Wound C went from left to right and probably would have been fatal even if it had been the only wound Alex sustained. This bullet fractured the sixth rib on the left side and the fourth rib on the right side. It had passed through both lungs and the heart. At the end of the bullet's path, Dr. Wilson found and removed the bullet. It was similar to the one found just under the skin in Alex's shoulder.

Wound D was the one that matched up with exit wound B. This bullet had entered the right shoulder, struck the scapula bone, and had exited from the same shoulder.

Wound E had put a groove in Alex's liver, gone through the right lung, and had struck the second rib on the right side before ending up in the soft tissues of the upper right side of the chest.

Although placing the wounds in chronological order was not necessary, or even desired, it could easily be determined that wound F was not the first wound caused. It fractured both left rib nine and twelve, and went through the left lung *after* it was already partially collapsed.

The "Report of Autopsy" from the Suffolk County

medical examiner would not be issued until a week later. Among its findings, Dr. Wilson listed "five gunshot wounds involving the torso and focally the neck with one exit wound on the body surface" and "bullet injuries to the heart, left and right lungs, liver and larynx." The report listed the cause of death as "gunshot wounds involving the torso and the neck."

Chapter 3

Processing Alex's Car

On the day after the murder Jeffrey H. Luber and Debra C. Nelson, two of the three forensic scientists who had reported to the murder scene the night before, went to work on Alex's vehicle, which had been moved to the Suffolk County Crime Laboratory garage.

The vehicle, according to their report, was a 1999 GMC Suburban. Everyone else agrees that the vehicle was a Yukon, but that's what the report read. It is possible that a "Suburban" was considered a generic term for a family SUV—much like Kleenex is often used as a synonym for facial tissue.

The forensic people looked in the console between the seats. Although the CD that Alex had been trying to retrieve when he was attacked was probably still there, the crime scene analysts were more interested in the familiar-looking pipe and Baggie combo they found.

Upon more careful inspection they found a second pipe. Without passing judgment, at least not in writing, they noted in the record that they had gathered from the vehicle two pipes and "plant material" from the console between the front seats. It was just a small amount of "plant material," a quantity of "plant material" typically meant for personal consumption. Instincts told the investigators that the Baggie and its minimal contents almost certainly did not have anything to do with the crime.

There was also something that appeared to be blood found in the car. A swab from an apparent bloodstain on the front passenger seat, over which the victim was leaning when he was accosted by his killer.

Also found, and probably insignificant, were a baseball cap with a Nike "Swoosh" logo on it, found in the foot well in front of the front passenger seat, and "trace material" near the backseat, the driver's-side front-door armrest, and near the front passenger seat.

Trace material can nail a killer who has come into contact with his victim. Analysts believe that each killer takes something of the crime scene away with him and leaves something of himself at the scene. This is particularly true in sex attacks, in which the victim and the attacker make contact and the perpetrator often leaves damning evidence in the form of DNA.

But these analysts knew that the evidence they were finding was far less promising. They correctly suspected that the criminal and the victim never came within more than a few feet of one another, that the killer never touched the car or looked inside the car.

It didn't look like a robbery. It looked like a hit.

The killer had left evidence all right, and it was in the form of bullets. That was about it. Four of the five bullets were recovered during the autopsy. The fifth was found at the crime scene. Still, they had to go over the vehicle thoroughly. There might be something in there that might betray the identity of Alex Algeri's killer.

The swab from the stain from the front passenger seat

was sent to the Serology Section, the trace material was sent to the Trace Evidence Section, and the plant material was sent to the Chemistry Section.

By the end of Thursday, January 18, George Krivosta, a forensic analyst with the Suffolk police, had received all five bullets for analysis. These included the four that had been recovered from the body during the autopsy, and the slug found at the scene. The question that needed to be answered: How many guns were there?

There could, after all, have been two shooters standing close to one another, although this was not considered a strong possibility by those who had seen the wounds. The pattern of wounds seemed to indicate one gunman, firing in rapid succession at a relatively stationary target.

Krivosta's report was issued a month after the crime. It could be determined that all four of the slugs found by the medical examiner had been fired by the same gun, but the slug found at the scene was too mangled to be compared adequately. In the language of the analyst that fifth slug "failed to display a sufficient quantity of identifying characteristics."

Best guess, however, was that all of the bullets had come from the same gun.

The DNA analysis on the blood and cigarette butts found at the scene showed that all of the blood belonged to Alex. The saliva on the cigarette butts did not belong to Al, but rather to an unidentified male. Because the butts were found outside the rear door of the gym, they could have been put there by any employee or patron of the gym who had stepped outside to smoke, and probably were not related to the crime.

One might think that those who endure cardio and aerobic workouts and those who smoke cigarettes are two mutually exclusive groups, but there are a surprising number of people who belong to both groups.

Should a suspect be developed, it was noted that a DNA sample from that individual might be helpful. Matching the suspect's DNA to the DNA from the cigarette butts would, at the very least, place the suspect at the scene of the crime, although not necessarily at the time of the crime.

The CSI findings were disappointing, to say the least.

Police followed up the CSI with an intense check of Algeri's background. Who would want him dead? His personal and professional life were thoroughly examined. These efforts bore no fruit.

Algeri was an unlikely murder victim. He had been a fun-loving lifelong bachelor who was always smiling. Alex had been a little rough-and-tumble as a youth, but he was no longer known to hang out with persons of questionable character.

Well, except one. And his name was Paul.

The lead detective in charge of the Algeri murder investigation was Detective Robert Anderson, a thirty-four-year veteran of the Suffolk County Police Department (SCPD).

As the lead investigator in many of Long Island's most notorious murders, including those committed by serial killers Joel Rifkin and Robert Shulman, his reputation bordered on legendary.

Not long after being told that his son was dead, Sal Algeri received his first visit from Detective Anderson. Sal was still in the hospital, feeling like his guts had been ripped out by the evening's events, when he looked up and a scholarly man was approaching him. The guy looked like the actor who'd played FDR—Edward Herrmann.

The investigator introduced himself formally as Detective Robert Anderson, of the homicide squad. He didn't look like a cop. Not that he was wimpy, it was just that he looked more than just smart. He looked intellectual.

When Detective Anderson opened his mouth, however, Sal could tell he was a genuine tough guy.

"He came in with a couple of his guys," Sal recalled. "He asked if I had any ideas. The first thing I said was 'Paul.'"

Chapter 4

Riedel

The only person of questionable character in Algeri's life was his business partner, a mountain of a man named Paul John Riedel. Word was he was a bad guy, and the victim had been his business partner.

It got better. Police learned that Riedel and Algeri had recently quarreled. Algeri said Riedel was partying too much, that he didn't want it to affect the business. Riedel told Algeri to go fuck himself. Algeri said he wanted out of the business.

Now Algeri was dead.

Understandably, the investigation focused on Paul Riedel. After all, there was no one else. Cops could find no one else who had an adequate reason to see Algeri dead. Algeri seemingly didn't have an enemy in the world, so they focused on the big guy: Paul Riedel.

Cops asked Algeri's friends and family what they knew. Everybody loved Alex. Alex had a zillion friends.

What did they know? They all knew the same thing. Paul Riedel must have done it. Had to be. Paul Riedel—

for the concrete reason that he had been the victim's business partner and had recently quarreled with the victim, and for the somewhat vague reason that he was a badass dude—became suspect number one. There was no suspect number two.

Investigators soon figured out that Paul Riedel had consciously cultivated his badass reputation. Riedel was an ex-con, having spent six years in prison on drug and armed-robbery charges.

He'd been arrested at age nineteen, in 1988. During the attack for which Riedel served time, either he, as some claimed, or his accomplice had held a shotgun in the face of an undercover cop. The undercover cop was wired and the whole thing was taped. One could hear the cop crying and pleading for his life.

The six-foot-seven, 285-pound Riedel was a former high-school football star. According to Steven Constantino, his matrimonial attorney, Riedel had been so good on the gridiron that he'd been heavily recruited by colleges with major sports programs.

Paul, the lawyer said, had garnered a sports scholarship to the University of Southern California (USC). This was the team O. J. Simpson and many other greats had played for. USC routinely fielded one of the best college football teams in the country. It was the sort of program that routinely sent players to the National Football League (NFL), where there awaited national fame and riches.

But there would be no football fame for Paul Riedel at USC. Before he made it to college, his football career was cut short by a serious shoulder injury. That injury ended football for Paul. Since his stint in prison Riedel had done well for himself. He'd become a successful businessman. He owned a large home in Babylon on the southern shore of Long Island.

Detective Anderson learned he was married, although separated, and had a kid. Maybe the wife knew something.

* * *

Three days after the murder Detective Anderson talked to Lee Ann Riedel, the estranged wife of Paul Riedel. As it turned out, she had been one of the first to hear about the shooting in the fitness club's parking lot.

She told the investigator that on Wednesday night, the night of the shooting, she had been shopping with her grandmother, Rose Jarrett (pseudonym), who lived in Mineola, on Long Island. When they got out of the store, she realized that she had missed a call on her cell phone. Lee Ann called the number back and talked to Marcy Mumphrey (pseudonym), who was an employee at Dolphin Fitness in Amityville. When Lee Ann called back, Marcy put Vincent Sidoti on the phone and he told her that Alex had been shot.

(Sidoti must have been drafted or volunteered to be in charge of notification. He was the same guy who called Sal Algeri to tell him his son had been shot.)

Lee Ann estimated that it was about 7:45 P.M. when she learned the news, only a few minutes after the shooting took place. Lee Ann told Detective Anderson that she immediately started to call her husband Paul to tell him what had happened. But she got no answer. She didn't get in touch with Paul until about ten or ten-thirty that night, three hours after the shooting. She said he seemed shocked. Paul, she said, was at the house of "Rubber" Rob Passantino (pseudonym) in Massapequa when he got the news.

Anderson asked Lee Ann if there were any problems, which she knew of, that Alex or Paul had with other individuals.

"I don't know of any," she said.

"None at all?" Anderson probed.

"Well, during 1999 Paul received some threats."

"From who?"

"I don't know."

"What sort of threats?"

Lee Ann said Paul had received a "rat card" in the mail. Anderson knew that meant someone thought Paul had squealed to the cops. Also, she said, the rear window of one of their vehicles was cracked while in front of their home. Someone sent a dead fish in the mail to the house in Babylon. Also, a glass table on their patio had been broken.

"Anything else you can think of?" Detective Anderson asked.

Lee Ann shook her head no. It was a terrible thing, but she had no other information to furnish.

"OK if I come see you again, you know, if I think of something else that might jog your memory?" Anderson said, being more polite than he needed to be.

"Sure," she said. She could be reached at her grandmother's house in Mineola. Only a few days before Lee Ann had come north, she'd been living with her mom in Florida and came up to visit her grandmother on Long Island.

Three days after Detective Anderson's first interview with Lee Ann Riedel, he went to visit her again at her grandmother's house in Mineola. The date was January 23, 2001. It was still less than a week since Alex had been shot. Lee Ann told the lead investigator that her date of birth was December 29, 1967.

"I want to ask you some more questions about Paul— who he was having problems with and who might want to hurt him," Detective Anderson said.

"Sure," Lee Ann said.

She said that Paul was happy with his investment in the gym in Amityville and that he was thinking of investing in other gyms in Westbury, Farmingdale, and Oakdale, on Long Island, as well as one in Harlem, in New York City. She told the detective that the "money investor" behind the Dolphin franchise was a guy named Murray Wichard.

She said there were some troublemakers, whom she named, who might be after Paul because he had been an informant during the summer of 2000. She didn't know firsthand that Paul had been an informant, but Paul's mother had told her that. Lee Ann said she didn't know any of the details.

She said that there had been a New Year's Eve party at Matteo's Restaurant on Jericho Turnpike, in Huntington, and at the party Paul had had words with a guy she knew only as Sal, whom she'd been told was a captain in the Gambino crime family. She said she didn't know what the argument was about.

There was also a guy, she said, whose nickname was "Bitterman," who said Paul owed him money and had been giving him grief.

With those leads to follow up on, Detective Anderson left. It seemed there was a plethora of people who had a reason to hurt Paul. Did someone try to send a message to Paul by bumping off his friend Alex?

Chapter 5

The "Horror"

At this point in time, just about everyone in the "Western World" had heard of Amityville. It was a great place to live, but that didn't have anything to do with its fame—or infamy, depending on how you looked at it.

Amityville had a population of just less than ten thousand, spread out over 2.1 square miles. The town was a little more than three-quarters white, a middle-class town, and about one out of every five residents was of Italian descent, about the same number as there were Irish and German.

It was 34½ miles from New York City. The nearest big town was Levittown, 7½ away to the north. Out on Long Island, where it was flat and there was plenty of ocean breeze, the temperature normally never got hotter than the pleasant low-80s in the summer.

When news started to get around about the parking-lot hit the night before, the people of Amityville didn't want to hear about another murder, especially not one that was going to bring publicity. Understandably, the residents of Amityville were sick of being synonymous with murders and horrors.

Just when the town thought it had ridden itself of the taint of past crimes that had taken place within its borders, a new book or a new movie would appear and then the unwanted spotlight would be back. Amityville would go from being just a nice town to the people who visited or passed through, to being the town "where *it* happened."

It was the murder of six members of the DeFeo family on November 13, 1974. The murders took place at 112 Ocean Avenue, a three-story Dutch Colonial home in Amityville. (The house still stands, but the street address has been changed. It is only four blocks from the Dolphin gym.) The parents and four of the five DeFeo children (Ronald Senior and Louise, their two young sons, Marc and John, and two daughters, Dawn and Allison) were discovered—shot execution-style.

The lone surviving son was arrested two days later and charged with killing the others. Ronald DeFeo Jr., it was learned, had murdered his parents and his siblings with a high-powered rifle. One by one, he killed them as they slept. None, oddly enough, were awakened by the gunshots preceding their own.

Ronald junior blamed the murders on an evil spirit that was present in the house. He stated that the creature began speaking to him and controlled him while he committed the murders. He pleaded insanity at his trial, but was convicted nonetheless by a jury and sentenced by the judge to 150 years in prison.

Two years after the arrest on December 18, 1975, a young couple bought the old DeFeo house for $80,000. A few weeks later they moved in—the man, a former marine, the woman, and her three children from a previous marriage—but they didn't last long.

Their stay, in fact, lasted for less than a month.

The couple later claimed that they had been driven

out of the house by supernatural activity. Their claims became the basis for the best-selling book *The Amityville Horror* by Jay Anson. In the book George and Kathy Lutz had their lives destroyed by evil spirits.

The family hadn't lived in the house long before they sensed its demonic presence. They heard mysterious noises. Locked windows and doors inexplicably opened and closed. The husband was most troubled by a phantom brass band that would march back and forth through the house.

They called a priest to exorcise the ghost, but an eerie voice told him to "get out." Things got worse after the unsuccessful exorcism attempt. A demon was seen outside the windows at night. After four weeks in the house, the family fled.

In February 1976, a local TV station filmed a séance in the house. Ed and Lorraine Warren, two of America's most famous "demonologists," conducted the ceremony. Following the séance, the Warrens reported that they sensed an "unearthly presence" in the house. Ed claimed to experience heart palpitations, which he blamed on the occult forces.

According to the Warrens, the spirits of Shinnecock Indians, who had once inhabited the area, haunted the house. Those Indians had used that very parcel of land as a place where sick and insane members of the tribe were isolated until they died. They did not bury the dead there, however, because they supposedly believed the land was infested with demons.

That book led to several Hollywood movies, each building on the presumed fact that Amityville is a town overrun by demons, that it is steeped in evil and horror—with one house in particular where all of that supernatural activity is bubbling to the surface.

It was later revealed that the allegations that spirits inhabited the house had been made up, right from the get-go, by Ronald DeFeo Jr. (The true motive for the killings was probably greed. Ron junior figured to inherit quite a fortune, being the lone surviving DeFeo.)

In 1979, William Weber, the lawyer who had represented Ronald DeFeo Jr., confessed to his part in the hoax. Weber not only helped DeFeo with his demon-spirit defense, but he claimed to be the mastermind behind the hoax on the Lutz end as well.

Weber said on a radio talk show that he and George Lutz had concocted the story of the haunting over a few bottles of wine. Weber's motive was to get a new trial for DeFeo, using a "Devil made him do it" defense.

According to Weber, Lutz wanted to get out from under a mortgage that he couldn't afford. His business was in trouble and he needed a scheme to bail him out. And so the "Amityville Horror" had been invented.

But, since the hoax was so much more entertaining than the truth, the truth didn't have a chance. Amityville residents, however, had come to grips with the fact that there were no evil spirits haunting the town.

The house is occupied today, and has been for years, and no one has experienced anything remotely supernatural. Besides, it is on a small lot and neighbors would have noticed if anything such as the Lutzes described actually occurred.

But a predictable portion of the world, the multitudes that are predisposed to accepting a fantastic existence, believed the myth. The book was a best seller. The 1976 movie was campy-scary and could, in the right crowd, be fun in a bad-movie kind of way.

But the 2005 remake, with tons more violence, was too sadistic to be enjoyed by the mainstream. There was certainly nothing there—a made-up story now in a league with Michael Myers, of the *Halloween* movies, Jason Voorhees, of the *Friday the 13th* flicks, and Freddie Krueger, of *Nightmare on Elm Street*—for the Village of

Amityville to be proud of. And the seaside community had way too much going for it to consider mere notoriety a step-up in the world.

By the time Alex Algeri was shot in the parking lot behind the Dolphin gym, the town of Amityville was known globally as the home of horror.

Chapter 6

Algeri's Funeral

Alex's wake was held in two rooms at the Mangano Funeral Home on Deer Park Avenue. People had to line up outside to get in. Traffic was around the block.

"I never saw anything like it," Alex's father, Sal Algeri, would later say. "One guy came up to me and said in high school about five or six kids were beating him up. Alex came along, didn't know him from anything, but stepped in to help him. He had a friend for life. By this time the guy was out of high school fifteen years, and still remembered Alex for what he did."

Police suspected that Paul had killed Alex, but Alex's friends and family didn't *think*, they *knew* that Paul had blown Alex away. They felt it in their bones. So it came as a bit of a shock when Paul Riedel attended his pal Algeri's funeral.

"Someone asked me if Paul could come to the funeral, I said OK," Sal remembered.

If Paul was guilty, there was nothing about his demeanor that betrayed him. Paul seemed deeply distressed by his friend's death.

"While Paul was holding me, he was shaking," Sal recalled. "Although I had my suspicions, if he was involved, I didn't think he did it directly. But I thought he was involved."

Sal saw Lee Ann, Paul's estranged wife, at the wake. "She seemed to be more nervous than sad," Sal recalled. "And her and Alex were good friends. I thought maybe people just don't like to see things like funerals."

Later, Sal would have a different interpretation of Lee Ann's behavior at his son's funeral: "Looking back, her and my son's girlfriend were very close. They talked every day. After the wake, Jean (Alex's girlfriend) never heard from Lee Ann again. Jean wondered why Lee Ann dropped off the face of the earth."

As is true of many homicide cases, police attended the funeral of the victim. They observed how people behaved, saw if anyone seemed to be showing a peculiar lack of grief—or, as sometimes occurred, looked like a phony because they showed too much grief.

Sometimes a cop would sit in a car outside the funeral and photograph those who entered. Later, after the photos were developed, they could determine if anyone unexpected and suspicious had attended the funeral—like a Mob hit man, for example.

As Paul stood over Alex's coffin, the police in attendance felt the vibe in the crowd. They approached Paul, so as to be closer in case there was trouble. According to Paul, the police began to shout questions at him even as he stood over his friend's body.

"A lot of people had a lot of questions," Paul later recalled. "A lot of people kind of pointed the finger toward me. We were partners. I guess it seemed to some people like I had something to gain by killing Alex. I had a past. I had gone away when I was younger, and Alex had no enemies."

Chapter 7

Alex: Rubbing People the Right Way

Alex had been a truly popular guy who had a way of rubbing people the *right* way—but he had not always been an angel, either.

He'd had trouble during his youth, but that was when he was a kid. As an adult, Alex had given little indication that he was the sort of person capable of getting into serious trouble. Alexander Algeri was born on September 18, 1968. He was thirty-two when he died. He was the second of three children. At the time of his death his sister, Christina, was thirty-three and his baby brother, Paul Algeri, was twenty-seven.

Alex's father, Sal, was an exceptionally well-educated man, with a master's degree in mechanical engineering from the Brooklyn Polytechnic Institute.

Sal was born and raised in Brooklyn, but he had moved out to Deer Park, on Long Island, in 1963, five years before Alex was born. The move from the city to the suburbs was common back in those days.

As Sal would say with a shrug: "Moving out to the Island was the thing to do."

Sal used his engineering degree during the remainder of the 1960s to get jobs in the defense industry, first for Korfund Dynamics in vibration elimination in missile silos, then for another company, which was developing pilotless helicopters that could drop torpedoes on targets. When Alex was a baby, less than two years old, his father left the defense industry and went into construction—and that was what he had been doing ever since.

Right from the start Alex was a jock. All of Sal's kids were. Good at sports. Alex loved sports and played soccer, baseball, football, and lacrosse.

"For all but two years of Alex growing up, I was his Little League coach," Sal would later say. "Alex was a very gifted athlete and a good team player."

When Alex was twelve or thirteen, he was confirmed by the Catholic Church, and his father chose that occasion to write a prayer for his son: "I asked that he have love for people, that people care for him, and that he have the desire to be successful. All of my prayers were answered, but he was taken too soon. Alex was a happy, secure guy with a great personality, always a smile on his face, always kibitzing with friends. Alex and I had a great relationship. So did he and his brother and sister."

A promising career as an athlete was knocked off track by illness when Alex was in his teens. During his senior year of high school, Alex contracted mononucleosis and couldn't play sports. He was very disappointed. After that, he began lifting weights, and weight lifting became his passion.

Alex was a smart kid and of course his dad wanted him to go to college. Trouble was, Alex wasn't interested. Unlike his father, Alex had never been an exceptional student. The classroom was about his least favorite place to be.

Without sports, high school would have been without redeeming value, Alex thought. Although he did graduate from Deer Park High School in 1986, Alex refused to participate in higher education.

"I'd rather go to work," the teenage Alex had said.

But it wasn't that easy. He couldn't bag groceries or deliver newspapers for the rest of his life. He took a course and got his asbestos-removal license, but he never took a job in that field. Alex floundered for a couple of years. Eventually Sal came to his aid.

Despite the differences in their educational prowess, Sal and Alex respected one another, and each believed—deep down inside—that they were a lot alike. Sal knew an electrical contractor and got Alex an application for a job. Alex got interviewed, passed, and went into a union apprentice program.

"He loved it," Sal would later say. "He had an outside job in the beginning and I told him to get an inside job. Being outside could be tough, especially in the winter."

Alex's mother and father got divorced in 1992. That was around the same time Alex got in trouble. About Alex's stint in prison, Sal would later say, "Thank God Alex was able to learn from his mistakes. He did something really stupid and paid the price. But he changed things around and looked at that as a great learning lesson."

Many prisoners have trouble assimilating back into society after being away. Being an ex-con carries a stigma, especially when seeking employment. But Alex's reentry into the outside world went more smoothly than most.

After prison Alex got a job back in the union and continued weight training. Around 1996, Alex bought a motorcycle. It was a Harley-Davidson Fat Boy, and it was his pride and joy—his all-time favorite toy.

"I didn't want him to have one because I worried so much, but it was one of his dreams," Sal remembered. "He came to me to help him with a down payment, and I gave it to him."

Alex had a dream job. He worked when he wanted, took time off when he wanted, and then returned to work when he needed money. The freedom in Alex's schedule allowed him a lot of time to ride the open road on his Harley.

The electrical union demanded that employees be paid for the entire year's vacation time in one lump sum in February. Alex liked to coincide his vacations with the big bike rallies, such as those in Daytona Beach, Florida.

He also liked to ride to the Sturgis Motorcycle Rally in Sturgis, South Dakota, which, in the world of motorcycle rallies, was known as the "Granddaddy of them all." His other favorite rallies were in Myrtle Beach, South Carolina, and Laconia, New Hampshire.

Alex, like most bikers, preferred to ride with another biker or in a pack. It was safer. If a bike broke down or there was an incident on the road of some type, there was always someone to go for help. One of Alex's favorite riding partners was a guy he had met while working out in a Gold's Gym, a huge guy named Paul Riedel.

They would throw their bikes in the back of a truck and go to the rally together. They became close, and after a few years of hanging around together, in early 1998, Alex asked Sal for financial help in opening a gym.

At first they leased a large, empty space and converted it into a gym. After a while Sal had some advice: "For what you are paying rent, why not just buy space?"

So that was what they did. Alex, Paul Riedel, and two other guys pooled their funds. They secured a mortgage and placed a down payment, purchasing the building at 88-92 Merrick Road.

While the gym was being built, Alex continued working as an electrician. By this time he was a full-fledged member of Local 25. It had taken him a little longer than most because his five-year apprenticeship was interrupted by his prison sentence.

To raise money to pay for the gym construction, Alex and Paul signed up future members at a lesser fee or discount. Alex did all electrical work in the gym. Dolphin was one of the first gyms on Long Island to be open twenty-four hours.

"Alex was all excited when he got the gym," Sal recalled. "He loved weight lifting and he loved the gym environment. He was very happy. He finally found himself. I was very happy for him."

Alex continued working as an electrician even after the Amityville Dolphin Fitness Club opened. He would visit the club every now and again to see how things were going, but the boss on duty was usually Paul.

"At first," Sal recalled, "Alex and Paul got along great. I couldn't have been happier for both of them."

In 2000, Sal's life changed. After eight years of being single, he married Maria. Alex and brother Paul were both best men, and Maria's two daughters were maids of honor.

According to Sal, the period when Alex and Paul got along all the time didn't last that long. As a business partner, Sal said, Paul left a lot to be desired. Alex told his father that Paul was skimming money from the gym.

Alex liked to think of himself as a guy who could take care of himself. He had an athletic body, now heavily muscled from the weight lifting, and there weren't many people on earth who frightened Alex Algeri. But Paul Riedel was one of them. Paul wasn't just broad—

he was tall, six-five. Alex was about five-eleven. Paul must have outweighed Alex by eighty pounds.

According to friends of Paul Riedel's, speaking under agreement of anonymity, Alex began carrying a knife with him, for the primary reason that he was afraid of Paul Riedel.

"He kept the knife in his boot," one of the friends explained. And there were incidents of violence between Paul and Alex during the time period leading up to the murder. On one occasion Paul threw a chair at Alex, causing a black eye.

Paul had anger management issues, it was true. Paul, during his rare moments of introspection, chalked the anger up to too much partying. It would be an understatement to say that Paul, back in those days, could get edgy. His edge had an edge.

Even though Paul did get mad at Alex, and had abused him physically on occasion, he still considered Alex one of his best buddies. He idolized Alex. When Alex went out and purchased a black 1997 Yukon SUV, Paul soon went out and bought one, too. When Alex put his Dolphin bumper sticker not on his bumper, but on the right rear window, that was where Paul put his sticker, too.

When Lee Ann left Paul, the big guy came to Alex for advice. Paul was concerned that he would lose his son if he divorced Lee Ann. Alex advised him just to go ahead with the divorce. "Just go through with it. Things will work out later" was what Alex said.

Despite the fact that Paul had a good side, the bad side was too scary to deal with. By the winter of 2000, Alex wanted out of the business. But January is usually the best month for a gym, and January 2001 was no exception. January is the best month for gym owners because so many people make New Year's resolutions to lose weight or to get stronger and in better shape. And, for the first month at least, they stick to them.

January was also the month that annual dues came due. So the place was more crowded than usual and there was plenty of money pouring in. Alex kept the knife in his boot and decided to stick with the business at least for a little while longer.

It was a decision that ended up costing him his life.

It was perhaps on Detective Anderson's second visit with Sal Algeri—the first time Anderson came to Sal's home—that Sal told the lead investigator he wanted to get one thing up front. Sal didn't want the cop to think he was being uncooperative in any way, and he knew that they were going to find out about Alex's past sooner or later.

Alex was a good guy, Sal explained, but he'd had to learn some lessons the hard way when he was young. At twenty-two, Alex had been arrested. Armed robbery. He'd done some time.

Detective Anderson looked up the case to get the details on Alex's legal troubles. On July 23, 1991, Alex was arrested for a truck hijacking of more than $200,000 worth of yarn. He yanked the driver from the cabin of the 1985 Mack truck, hit him in the head with a 9mm pistol, and took off in the truck. He was arrested driving the truck on Sunrise Highway.

The driver was cut from the blow to the head with the gun, and later required nine stitches to close the wound. The arresting officer was James Montario, of the "one-oh-five"—the 105th Precinct.

According to the report, the truck was hijacked near 167-16 147th Avenue, which was just outside JFK Airport. The crime sounded like a John Gotti wannabe move. The future head of the Gambino crime family also had been arrested and went to prison as a young man for hijacking a truck, also in the vicinity of JFK Airport. The only difference was, in Gotti's case, the truck contained ladies' dresses.

The charges against Alex were robbery in the first degree, armed felony assault in the second degree, criminal use of a firearm in the first degree, armed felony robbery in the second degree, criminal possession of stolen property in the third degree, and unauthorized use of a vehicle.

Alex was indicted eight days later on all of the counts by the Queens County grand jury. The indictment stated that Alex was not alone in his crime and worked in concert with others.

Alex turned twenty-three in jail, and was tried in December 1991. He was found guilty and sent to prison. He got a two-to-six-year sentence and served his time in a maximum-security prison in upstate New York. He was transferred to the Queensboro Correctional Facility in Queens for the final part of his sentence.

It was not uncommon for prisoners from New York to be transferred to Queensboro when the end of their stint approached. Queensboro was where prisoners from the Big Apple were readied to rejoin society. Being locally incarcerated allowed prisoners to receive more visitors, and thus for them to prepare better for their life after their release.

Chapter 8

A Once Clean-Cut College Graduate Who Had Become a Junkie

After months of looking into Algeri's background, Detective Anderson knew that this was not a case that was going to be solved in a crime lab or using the latest in technological wizardry. This was going to take seemingly endless hours of old-fashioned pavement-pounding detective work.

When all of the theories that had originally pointed at Riedel were discounted, Detective Anderson found himself no closer to a solution.

Alex's family, like the police, was frustrated by the lack of progress in the case.

"For months there were no leads," said Sal. "I would bother cops only to a certain extent. I eventually stopped calling because they wouldn't tell me anything. I would try to get information, but they wouldn't give it out."

Anderson's first break came eleven months after the murder when the New York Police Department (NYPD) busted a subject for grand larceny. The guy's name was Mike Alexander (pseudonym). He was a liar for the most part, but every once in a while, a glimmer of the truth slipped in, maybe by accident. That was what happened here.

While Alexander was being interrogated after his arrest, information was gleaned about the Algeri murder case. Most of the info turned out to be erroneous, but the subject did provide a key clue when he linked the Amityville homicide to a man named Scott Paget, a once clean-cut college graduate who had become a junkie and was living in the Miami area.

Alexander hung out in a strip joint where Paget worked. That was how he knew. Police had it wrong, Alexander said. Paul Riedel might be a sick fuck, but he wasn't the killer. He had been the *target*, not the murderer. Mistaken identity.

Of course, it wasn't the first time it had crossed Detective Anderson's mind. But it was the first evidence directly leading in that direction. The "mistaken-identity theory" moved immediately to the front burner.

It made sense. Riedel's wife did say that Paul had been receiving Mob-type threats, intimidating letters, dead fish, and the like. Algeri and Riedel shared many of the same physical characteristics, a resemblance that would have been even greater in the gym's dimly lit parking lot. In addition, both Algeri and Riedel drove the same make and color of car, a black GMC Yukon. Both men had put the same bumper sticker on the rear window.

Riedel was a bad dude, Anderson knew. He was a hulking, steroid-popping ex-convict with dangerous addictions to drugs and gambling. At the time of Alex "Papa Smurf" Algeri's demise, Paul Riedel was feuding with a rival gym owner. He was saddled with $24,000 in gambling debts. He had recently exchanged less-than-kind words with a Gambino crime family captain.

Riedel had thrown two reputed mobsters out of his gym for harassing a female guest. Some of the lowlifes with whom he smoked crack cocaine thought— perhaps mistakenly—that he was a police informant. (Among those who believed Paul really was working for the cops was his own mother.)

The animosity mentioned to the investigators by Paul's wife weren't the only sources of hostility Paul was enduring. Some of that hostility was coming from Lee Ann herself, along with her friends and relatives.

Although she had been on Long Island at the time of the shooting, paying a visit, Lee Ann had gone south and was living in Boynton Beach, Florida. Plus, even though she had left Paul, she'd apparently gone from one hood to another. She was dating a strip joint bouncer from Miami named Ralph "Rocco" Salierno.

Algeri might not have had any enemies, but Riedel made up for that. Pains in his ass—Paul had a plethora.

Scott Paget, Scott Paget. Investigators had a name to work with now. Through the miracle of today's computerized world with its sophisticated network of law enforcement information, it was only minutes before Detective Anderson learned a great deal about Scott Paget.

Scott Christopher Paget was white, born July 20, 1970, six feet, 230 pounds. Another big guy. Hazel eyes, black hair, born in Connecticut. They had his address in Miami. His most recent occupation was listed as "nightclub manager." Alexander had said Paget was a bouncer in a strip joint. That fit.

Soon police not only possessed Paget's current address, but his residential history as well. A computer popped out a list of every place Paget had lived, dating back to 1990. They knew his Social Security number, the serial number on his Florida driver's license, and the fact that he had failed to feed a parking meter in 1996 and had gotten a ticket. There was also evidence that Paget had at some point used the Social Security number of a deceased Florida death row inmate.

All of this not only indicated a willingness to commit crimes, but a connection to other criminals as well— perhaps a web of criminals.

There was a list of addresses occupied now, or at some point, by individuals who were known to be associates of Scott Paget. There were the current phone numbers of all of Paget's previous addresses. He'd gotten into a car accident in August 1989. He'd gotten a number of speeding tickets over the years, once for zipping too rapidly through a school zone.

Paget's "criminal history" from the Florida Department of Law Enforcement (FDLE) revealed that he had been arrested on November 9, 1994, by sheriff's deputies of the Orange County Sheriff's Office (OCSO). He'd been charged with rioting, battery, resisting arrest, and disturbing the peace. He got six months' probation.

Soon a new item would appear on Paget's arrest record: he was sought by the Metro-Dade County Police Department because he was wanted in New York State for an unspecified felony—that being his alleged participation in Alex Algeri's murder.

Maybe Anderson heard that his suspect was a bouncer in a strip joint, and Lee Ann's new boyfriend was in the same line. Both were in Miami to boot. Even when vice was widespread, it remained a small world.

The investigator looked into Lee Ann's new boyfriend and was intrigued by what he learned: Lee Ann's Florida boyfriend, Ralph "Rocco" Salierno, was like many Floridians in that he was originally from the North. He was born and raised in New York State's Westchester County, which borders New York City to the north.

Guys from Westchester routinely knew guys from Long Island. They went to parties on Long Island, sometimes even worked on Long Island. One bridge across Long Island Sound through the Bronx and you were there.

Another interesting item: Rocco grew up to be a burly bodybuilder. Maybe that was just a sign that Lee Ann liked muscles. Maybe it was a connection of another sort. Certainly something to jot down.

Anderson knew that if a guy used an alias, there was a healthy chance he had something to hide. Salierno had moved to Florida to be near some high-school friends who were already down there. Once he got down South, he decided that he wasn't going to be known as Ralph or Rocco. When in Florida his name would be Randall "Randy" Salierno.

Being intimidatingly large, Salierno was another guy who was gainfully employed as a bouncer at a strip joint, and made extra bucks here and there freelancing as a money collector for loan sharks and bookmakers. He was clearly Lee Ann's type of guy.

Anderson was very interested in learning what Scott Paget might have to say about Ralph Salierno.

Chapter 9

First Confession

As it turned out, Scott Paget wasn't the unadulterated scumbag that Detective Anderson had been expecting. Anderson had seen guys who were rotten to the core and guys who were basically good, but had been defeated by life. Scott Paget appeared to belong to the latter group. Paget was balding and muscular. He took care in his appearance. He had a clean-cut, blue-collar look. Paget looked trustworthy, like an honest contractor or mechanic.

But Anderson gleaned the most information about the character of Scott Paget by looking into his eyes. That was where you could see the rottenness at the core of a man. But there was no rottenness there, Anderson observed. Scott didn't have "perp eyes." In a world of lost causes and the redeemable, Paget gave off an aura of being redeemable.

Paget's drug addiction had caused him to become a small-time dealer. Detective Anderson made regular trips to Florida after that, each time paying a visit to Paget and leaning on him a little bit. He also spent some time asking questions of Paget's friends.

Paget at first said the information Anderson had gotten from the larceny suspect in New York had been nothing but bullshit. Yeah, he knew Salierno, they were gym buddies, met him sometime in the spring of 2000. But, no—there'd been no trip to New York. No fucking way. He said it had been maybe ten years since he'd last been to New York.

The friends were more helpful than Paget was. They confirmed that Paget had been away on the key dates, that he'd made comments that led them to believe that he'd been part of a murder, one that had turned out to be a big mistake.

Anderson eventually amassed enough independent evidence to convince Paget that his best bet was to come clean. Paget agreed. Paget confirmed that the murder of Algeri had been one major fuckup.

The five bullets that had ripped into Algeri's muscular neck and upper torso had been intended for Riedel. The killers, it turned out, may have been hoods that reeked of the Mob, but this was no Mob hit.

Paget and a friend, Ralph "Rocco" Salierno—a thick-necked, and even thicker-trunked weight lifter—were not sent by the Mob, or by a rival gym owner, or by any of the drug dealers the fearsome Riedel was supposed to have betrayed. Mob? *Mob?* The word itself was a forced laugh. Hey, maybe he knew a couple of guys who might be connected slightly or whatever—but Mob? Get the fuck out of here with that Mob shit. The truth was more domestic than all that, Paget said.

Paget and Salierno, Paget told Detective Anderson, had been emissaries of Paul's wife, Lee Ann. Paget told Detective Anderson that he had been paid $3,000 to drive a borrowed minivan from Florida to Amityville.

While there, they were to pay Paul a visit and then return to Florida immediately in the same van.

What kind of a visit? They were paid to liquidate the subject. Paget admitted that he knew the trip to Long Island had been for the expressed purpose of killing Paul Riedel. He also admitted to loading the murder weapon, a .38-caliber revolver, with five bullets.

Although he was knee-deep in the murder, Paget elicited sympathy from Detective Anderson. Both the investigator and the assistant district attorney described Paget as a basically decent fellow whose drug addiction caused him to make terrible personal decisions with tragic consequences.

Anderson arrested him.

Chapter 10

Amityville Creek

There was a key piece of evidence still missing. The gun. Salierno said he wasn't paying any attention. Scott had pulled the car over and had thrown it somewhere. Scott, on the other hand, at least had a bead on the gun's location.

"When I pulled out into the main road, I took a left, and I didn't make any more turns after that. I threw it into a creek or a pond or something right next to the road," Paget told Anderson in a subsequent interview after having been brought north to await his Suffolk County trial.

The location was a little vague. Anderson told Paget they were going for a little ride.

"Show me," the investigator said.

Paget, Anderson, and a group of officers got in a car and drove. They went back to the crime scene and had Paget show them just where the van had parked when the shooting took place. Then they drove east on the main road.

"How far?" Anderson asked.

"I don't know—half mile, maybe," Paget said.

At just about exactly the half-mile mark, the road crossed a body of water. This it? Looks like it. They noted where they were and returned Paget to jail. Anderson learned that the body of water was Amityville Creek.

Anderson was one of the great detectives when it came to finding out whodunit, but he would be the first to admit that he didn't know much about searching bodies of water for missing items. However, he knew who was. The Marine Bureau of the Suffolk County Police Department, under the command of Sergeant Raymond Epps, was called in to search the creek. Epps looked like the guy who should have been on a poster labeled "Good Cop." He was clean-cut, and then some.

Epps's divers started work during the second week of December. A creek flowing under a road in a quaint seaside village might sound remote. Spooky after dark. But the Amityville Creek site was neither remote nor spooky.

The road was very busy, quiet only for a short period during the wee hours of the morning, between bars closing and the morning rush. Otherwise, it was the prime connecting route between the south shore communities of the westernmost section of Suffolk County.

Amityville Creek ran southward toward the Atlantic Ocean. For most of its length it was only twenty or thirty feet wide, but it grew much wider as it approached its mouth. By the time it crossed Montauk Highway, less than a mile from the shore, the creek was eighty-one feet wide.

The site, just south of the main road at Amityville Creek, was overlooked on the west side by the manicured park and its white memorial structure. There were boats docked on the south side, and just inland from them was a two-story office building.

At the time the men in the minivan ditched the gun,

there would have been only a handful of lights still on in that building. But during the day the office building was filled with people, many of whom gathered at the windows facing west to see what the police were up to down there.

The police divers searched a stretch of Amityville Creek as it ran under the Montauk Highway, approximately where Paget said he'd tossed the gun.

Amityville Creek was the body of water that ran behind the DeFeo house, where the Amityville Horror supposedly played out. There was nothing supernatural about this search, though. In fact, a little clairvoyance would have helped.

About a half-dozen attempts were made during December 2002 and during the first week of January 2003. Divers searched the creek from edge to edge, using a grid strategy to make sure that they didn't miss any stops. They were armed with underwater metal detectors.

Several days the divers were out until the grid had been covered and no gun had been found. Maybe start over? Trouble was, as the autumn of 2002 grew old on Long Island, searching for a gun in a creek became increasingly unpleasant.

It was getting damn cold.

The search of the creek by the marine division finally had to be discontinued. Winter set in. The creek froze over. Epps said the chances of finding the gun through a hole in the ice were somewhere between slim and none. Detective Anderson said that they should start again in the spring.

Chapter 11

Ketcham's Creek

There were a lot of things named Ketcham along the south shore of Long Island in the western corner of Suffolk County. The Ketchams were one of the original families in the area. In addition to Ketcham Creek, there is also Ketcham Dock. One of the main streets in town is Ketcham Avenue. Amityville's first fire chief was Milburn Ketcham.

Then there was Zebulon Ketcham who became forever famous in his community when he dined in 1790 with George Washington at his homestead at the corner of Deauville Boulevard and Montauk Highway in Copiague. Today a stone at the location still commemorates the occasion.

That's the area's oldest story. According to *History of Long Island,* "The oldest part of the village lies on the South Country Road and formerly was known as Huntington South. It dates back to about 1780 and had its origin in a gristmill and saw mill erected in that locality. George Washington stopped at Zebulon Ketcham's

Inn at the settlement and begged his host to 'take no trouble with the bill of fare.'"

Legend has it that before Washington left the inn, he gave a gold ring to one of the children. No one knows today what became of the ring, which would be considered a valuable treasure by a collector of historic relics.

The table at which Washington dined is now in the possession of the Huntington Historical Society. In 1927, the Boy Scouts planted an elm tree and placed a memorial stone near the location of Ketcham's Inn, on the north side of Montauk Highway, just east of the Amityville Village limits.

The inn is no longer standing. This is a mere sixty yards, across the road and slightly catty-corner, from the place where Sergeant Epps and his divers renewed the underwater search for the Algeri murder weapon the next spring.

Same divers. Different creek.

Detective Anderson had been driving back and forth along Amityville's main road one day when he noticed that Amityville Creek was not the only creek that passed under the thoroughfare on its way toward the Atlantic. About a mile to the east from the site where divers had searched so thoroughly the previous winter, there was a second creek.

In fact, there were great geographic similarities between the search site and another site a little farther east. To a fellow who had just been part of a murder on a dark January night, the two creeks easily could have passed for one another alongside the road.

Both creeks were approximately the same width. Both had boats docked there. Paget's memories from that dark night were not precise enough to allow him to distinguish between various bodies of water next to the road.

Anderson realized immediately that the chances were good all of that diving had been done in the wrong place. So when the divers did start again during the spring of 2003, Sergeant Epps had moved the operation to Ketcham's Creek.

Ketcham's Creek, or Ketcham Creek, runs through the village of Copiague, in the town of Babylon, just to the east of the Amityville border. A few months after the murder, but not long before the police began looking for a gun there, the site at Route 27A and Ketcham's Creek was bustling with activity. The area had been part of the Town of Babylon's Wetland Restoration Project. Planted along the creeks' restored shoreline were Native American shrubs and trees.

The project was part of the town's ongoing ecological improvement for the area. The volunteers who did the planting also learned about the importance of wetlands and wildlife habitat, finfish resources, and maintaining the water quality of the area. The project restored three hundred feet of disturbed shoreline into vital wetland habitat.

Unlike the Amityville Creek site, in which the shorelines had either been docks or manicured parkland, at the new site the west shore was thick with all sorts of green growth. That section would be searched last.

The west bank had already been combed to a degree by the Town of Babylon's Wetland Restoration Project. As it turned out, the searchers never got to the banks of the creek. In fact, they never got an opportunity to set up a new grid so that Ketcham's Creek could be searched square foot by square foot. No such grid would be necessary.

* * *

When first assessing the new search location at Ketcham Creek, Sergeant Epps sought to narrow the search, to look first where the metallic object was most apt to be. Epps kicked around at the shoulders of the road.

Then he walked off the road a few paces and kicked some more. A couple of times he reached down and picked up something, only to drop it right away with a clucking sound. Several times he picked up rocks, bounced them measuringly in a cupped palm a couple of times, and then discarded them.

Sergeant Epps looked for a rock that was approximately the same weight as a .38 handgun. He wanted to conduct an experiment. Eventually he found one that fit the bill. With rock in hand he sat shotgun in a cop car. Window down.

The driver took the car west a quarter-mile or so and then made a U-turn.

"About thirty-five miles an hour," Epps instructed.

They drove toward the spot where Ketcham's Creek flowed under Montauk Highway. When the car got to the right spot, Epps heaved the rock out the window and into the water. Because of the traffic, one couldn't hear the splash.

The car then stopped and Anderson got out. Others had been stationed to spot the location of the splash. Still, Anderson had to see the spot. He arrived in time to see the ever-growing concentric circles of ripple. The center of those circles was the starting point for the search.

Well, it would turn out to be one of the luckiest tosses in the history of law enforcement. It was reminiscent of the time Vincent Bugliosi and members of the Los Angeles District Attorney's Office found bloody clothes discarded in the woods by members of the Manson gang by using a car driving at the speed limit and a stopwatch.

Epps started searching for the murder weapon in the spot where the rock had landed, and—sure enough—Epps, with an underwater metal detector and a clam rake, soon discovered the gun buried in two feet of mud.

The gun didn't even look like a gun when it was first yanked from its burial spot in the muck of the creek bed. Even after much of the gunk had been wiped away and one could tell what it was, its mechanisms were clogged with mud and there were barnacles growing on the handle.

After sprucing it up, Epps was pleased to see that one could tell the make and the caliber of the weapon as well. It was a five-shot Smith & Wesson revolver and it still had five Winchester Western .38-SPL-caliber cartridge casings in it.

One for each of the bullets fired at Alexander Algeri.

Chapter 12

Proving It's the Same Gun

The next step for the ballistics people at the Suffolk Police Department was to attempt to prove that the gun found by Sergeant Raymond Epps was, in fact, the same gun that had been used to murder Alex Algeri. This was not going to be easy. The gun was in horrible condition.

According to a police report filed on April 1, 2003, the gun was "a revolver encrusted with marine life and sediment."

Under normal circumstances, when bullets in good condition have been discovered at the scene of a shooting, and the murder weapon has been found, test bullets are fired from the gun to see if the marks made on the bullet by the gun matched the marks on the bullets found at that crime scene. That process, in this case, would prove to be problematic.

According to the SPD crime laboratory, the murder weapon was "a Smith & Wesson F.A. Co. .38 SPL caliber revolver, model 60, serial number #R162821." The weapon was found to be inoperative as submitted due to corrosion of internal parts.

In order to generate test-expended bullets for comparison purposes, an attempt was made to place the submitted barrel on a functional laboratory weapon. The barrel was removed from the submitted weapon successfully.

That was as far as the experiment got, however. As the barrel was being mounted on a laboratory weapon, it suffered a catastrophic failure. The gun could no longer be fired. Laboratory test bullets would have to be generated by manually pushing bullets through the barrel.

This was done. It wasn't the best way to go about it, but necessity called. Certainly, if results were good, the evidence would be admissible in a court of law.

In the Suffolk police lab, microscopic examination and comparison of these lab test bullets were made with the bullets found in the body and at the murder scene. The entire homicide squad was disappointed when the lab finally issued its report on the bullet comparison and announced the results "inconclusive." The scientists, to put it simply, were unable to determine if the gun was the murder weapon.

By making a cast of the breech face area of the revolver for comparison purposes, it could be proved that the five casings found with the revolver had been fired from that weapon. No switch had been made.

The fact that the bullets and the casings were of the same caliber and brand was, of course, a persuasive circumstantial argument that the gun found in the creek had been the murder weapon. It wasn't proof, though.

Prosecutors would have to rely on the overwhelming circumstantial evidence and the common sense of the jury to make their case that the found gun had been the murder weapon. The argument had problems.

Some jurors might be impressed by the fact that attempts to prove the discovered gun was the murder weapon had failed. Others might raise a skeptical eyebrow or two at the swift and unusual method with which the gun had been found: the hurling of the properly weighted rock from the moving automobile.

In the end Detective Anderson was convinced that the weapon Epps had found was the murder weapon, and he was pretty sure that a dozen of his peers would feel the same way.

Chapter 13

Lee Ann Meets Paul

Slender and pretty Lee Ann Armanini met man-mountain hulk Paul Riedel in 1998. She was a single mom, raising a twelve-year-old son, working as a bartender at a Suffolk County strip joint. He had a wiseguy reputation and lived on Maynard Drive in Farmingdale.

The place where they met—the "gentleman's club" (wink, wink)—was called The Carousel. It was a popular name for strip joints. This flesh-flashing tavern was in the large Long Island town of Huntington.

Lee Ann and Paul dated. She got pregnant. Paul did the right thing. They married on July 30, 1999. Church wedding. Lee Ann looked beautiful in her gown; Paul's buddy Alex Algeri was the best man. Paul moved in with Lee Ann.

At the time Lee Ann was living in her father's house in Westbury, Long Island. Now Paul lived there, too. He became stepfather to Lee Ann's son, Christopher.

Being a stepfather was hardly the best part of the job as far as Paul was concerned. He wished the kid would take a powder. Just disappear. *Poof.* And the feeling, he could tell, was mutual.

Out of responsibility Paul took Chris with him when he ran errands sometimes, but there was no warmth there. He tried to show him the ropes now and again, but basically Paul thought Chris was a pain in the ass.

According to Chris, when Paul talked to him at all, it was usually to brag. Paul said he had a scam going on. Not one or two. For just about everything. If anyone tried to say "boo" about it, he would just scare the shit out of them—which was easy for him to do with his great height and girth.

Everyone who knew Paul understood unquestioningly that he was not a nine-to-fiver. Actual work wasn't his style. Lifting weights, sure. That kind of work he'd do, but Paul taking orders from some boss. Uh-uh.

The most anyone knew, Paul was some kind of an entrepreneur—and those who didn't know usually didn't ask. Paul had money, though. Everyone knew that.

His family understood some of what was going on. Not much, though. Probably just the outer layer of the onion, they figured.

One of the errands Paul had taken his stepson along to was to his bookie operation. It was a big earner, a sports book that he ran—an illegal gambling operation—that took bets on baseball, pro and college football, boxing, basketball, hockey, etc.

Lee Ann also knew he'd reported a couple of vehicles stolen that weren't really stolen. A Cadillac. A leased truck. Lee Ann figured there were other things cooking, too, but she didn't know what they were.

Ignorance is bliss, Lee Ann would think. She wasn't the first wife in the world to enjoy her husband's money without worrying too much about where it came from. When it came to Paul, the more you knew, the less you wanted to know. Lee Ann' lifestyle had never been so la-di-da, so why rock the boat? Wouldn't be logical.

During the first months of Paul's marriage to Lee Ann, he was busy with the construction of his new Amityville fitness club. He was obsessed with it, and with good reason. For Paul, the new gym represented a major investment. He'd taken a lot of the money he'd made in other enterprises and had sunk it into the new project.

In February 2000, less than seven months after the wedding, they had a child of their own. Lee Ann gave birth to Nicholas. According to Paul, the marriage started out happy, but that didn't last.

"The marriage became turbulent after five or six months," Paul later said.

"Things changed after the baby," Lee Ann recalled.

They moved into a new home, which Paul had built on Little East Neck Road, in Babylon. Fancy, schmancy on Long Island's southern shore. Now Lee Ann was living like a rich lady with oceanfront property. And Paul was close to his mom, who lived in nearby Amityville.

Everybody can come from a broken home, but Lee Ann's broken home came with a twist. Lee Ann's mom had left her dad and resided in Florida with her lover, Liz, who referred to herself as Lee Ann's aunt.

Chapter 14

Splitsville

In the summer of 2000, Lee Ann Riedel left husband Paul. He was not a man of keen foresight and apparently hadn't seen it coming. By all accounts, Paul was ingesting massive quantities of recreational drugs at that time in his life, so it's hard to say what he could and couldn't see.

To everyone else's point of view, there had been a slow buildup to her departure. The major event that led to the split was a row Paul and Lee Ann had on June 5. The fight was over Paul's crack cocaine habit.

When Paul smoked, the crack took over. Crack was king! And a cracked-out brain inside a monstrously muscular body was a very dangerous combination. Preferably, one would keep a locked door between himself and Paul when he got like that. If not, one did one's best to see Paul didn't have access to weapons.

At one point Lee Ann had had to take Paul's shotgun away from him. She was afraid that he would get high one night and decide to hurt somebody with it. It had occurred to her that *that somebody* might be her.

Not that she was a beaten woman. There was a lot more fear than actual violence. But Paul was a master at being scary and there were times when Lee Ann almost got used to the fear. People had to tell her it wasn't a good way to live.

Although Paul and Lee Ann's fights sometimes got physical, he'd never beaten her up. He later claimed he'd never laid a glove on her. Still, he did like to go out and get wired, and when he got like that, he sometimes became insanely angry.

He shouted crazy things, whole lists of people he was going to kill or hurt. Lee Ann wanted to prevent tragedies, so she took the gun to the police station.

Lee Ann's eventual departure, in June, came with an element of surprise. She had not warned Paul, because of the way he was. But her urge to take off had grown, almost from the very beginning of the marriage. It had certainly grown since Nicholas was born.

Lee Ann had spent too long being a cockeyed optimist. She thought she was destined to live happily ever after. She thought that Paul might stop partying, or at least cut back after the baby was born—but this didn't turn out to be the case.

While she did everything with the baby and Christopher and the house, Paul was hanging out with the boys and doing drugs just as much as he had when they met. Her attempts to reform him were in vain.

Lee Ann apparently had seen Paul as a fixer-upper, but she wasn't having much luck fixing him up. She left the Riedel home in Babylon, New York, on Long Island, and took their child and $120,000 of his money and moved to Florida to begin a new life.

"One day I came home and they were gone," Paul would later say. "Obviously, I was very concerned. Nicholas is my only son. It was very important to me to be a part of his life. I couldn't have a normal relationship with my son if he was two thousand miles away."

Lee Ann had wanted to start over when she left for Florida. Paul reacted to her departure with his usual heavy-handedness. He had her mother's phone number down there and called it frequently. There were hostile messages.

Lee Ann's Florida friends and family were appalled at the way Paul acted. Lee Ann might have grown used to the fear, but this was new to the Floridians. By July 3, they had convinced her to get an order of protection.

The "Temporary Injunction for Protection Against Domestic Violence" was issued at the Palm Beach County Courthouse, pending a hearing that was scheduled for July 14. The order said that Paul "shall not commit, or cause any other person to commit, any acts of domestic violence against" Lee Ann. Also, Paul was not to "go to, in, or within 500 feet of" Lee Ann's home. The same restrictions applied to any location that Lee Ann was known to frequent.

The injunction also said that Paul was forbidden to possess a firearm or ammunition. And that, if Paul did possess such items, he should surrender them immediately to the Suffolk County Police Department. It also ordered that Paul had to allow Lee Ann at least one visit to the home they once shared for the purpose of picking up her things.

The order granted Lee Ann custody of their baby, Nicholas Riedel, born February 24 of that year. Neither Lee Ann nor Paul was allowed to move Nicholas outside of the state of Florida. Violation of that order, the injunction said, would constitute a third-degree felony. The typed injunction came with a handwritten addendum. It read: "The respondent shall have no contact with petitioner's child by any means." The injunction was signed by a circuit judge and stamped and signed by a circuit court clerk.

On July 12, a sober Paul, who was nice the way Paul usually was when he was sober, called Lee Ann and told her he had given up crack and was ready to be a good husband and father. Lee Ann bought his story and returned to New York with Nicholas, but the reconciliation only lasted three weeks.

Lee Ann found that Paul might have intended to stay clean, but he wasn't strong when it came to battling his addictions. Soon he was getting high again. By August 7, after only about three weeks on Long Island, Lee Ann was preparing to go back to Florida.

Lee Ann and her mother went to the house in Babylon to pack up some things to take back with them to Florida. Paul showed up while this was going on and there was a big fuss. By the end of the night Lee Ann's mom was swearing out a criminal complaint against Paul.

The complaint said that Paul that day had "intentionally, knowingly, recklessly, with criminal negligence, committed the offense of aggravated harassment." Paul's mother-in-law wrote that Paul "did call me on the telephone while my daughter and myself were removing her belongings from her house and he was very angry and stated 'I am going to kill you, and Christopher, and Lee Ann, and the baby. People are going to start to disappear.'"

As a condition for visitation rights Paul was ordered to attend parenting classes and undergo regular drug tests. Paul didn't think his parenting skills or his partying habits were the point at all. The point was that his wife and child insisted on living two thousand miles away from him, and that was way too far.

Paul sought out some legal advice with the firm of Constantino & Constantino. They advised him as to how to bring Lee Ann and Nicholas home. First order of business, Paul filed for divorce in New York.

Riedel later explained his actions: "Every parent has a God-given right, the law says, that they must live fifty miles within where the other parent lives. So we filed the papers, my lawyer did, Steve Constantino, to bring her back to New York so I could have a normal relationship with my son. She came back, but only because the court told her she either had to come back or they were going to take the child away from her."

Chapter 15

Pat and Liz

When it came to her marriage, Lee Ann's plans for escape were twofold. Not only did she want to get far, far away from Paul Riedel, but she also wanted to be closer to her divorced mother, Pat Armanini, who was living with her lesbian lover, Elizabeth "Liz" Budroni (pseudonym). It was Budroni who first introduced Lee Ann to Ralph "Rocco" Salierno through a contact she'd had at a local Miami-area gym.

Lee Ann and Rocco hit it off. He had kind of changed his name in Florida to Randall. People called him Randy, but his name was Ralph and his nickname was Rocco up north when he was growing up.

They were thrilled to discover they had things in common. Those things were what Lee Ann liked to refer to as "tittie bars." She'd tended bar in a topless joint called Goldfingers. Small world. Rocco had worked as a bouncer there.

By September 2000, the Riedels' marriage looked to be kaput. For one thing, according to Lee Ann's chronology, she "started going out" with Rocco about this time. Up until then, she claimed, their relationship was purely platonic. Rocco got her a waitressing job at a club called Cheetah's. She sometimes went to Pompano Beach with Rocco, where he was building a club.

A couple of months later, as Christmas approached, Lee Ann decided she was going to need information if she hoped to ever get herself and Nicholas free of Paul Riedel. She looked into hiring a private investigator to follow Paul.

She called a friend who was an attorney in Florida and he recommended a guy in Westchester County, but that didn't work out. Rocco told her not to worry about it. He had it covered. He had friends up there that would follow Paul for her—but as far as she knew Rocco was just talking and that never happened.

Chapter 16

Attempted Reconciliation

After Paul Riedel filed for divorce, a court order forced Lee Ann to live within a fifty-mile radius of him. Because of the ordinance, Lee Ann, her mom, and the baby went north. They stayed at Lee Ann's grandmother's house in Mineola. Lee Ann's mom, Pat, stayed only for a brief time—just long enough to get Lee Ann settled—before returning to Florida. Lee Ann and Paul tried to get along, for the sake of Nicholas.

"Obviously, it was very important for me to try to have a normal relationship with my son," Paul later explained. "So we tried to work on reconciling and getting back together; we reconciled for a couple of months after that."

Paul took his classes and tested clean for drugs. Lee Ann returned about three-quarters of the money she'd taken when she split. In compliance with the court orders, the reconciliation attempts continued.

Lee Ann had not let her guard down completely, however. Her attorney told her that she should start docu-

menting things, writing stuff down—like when Paul
stayed out late, and when he came home inebriated in any
way, any verbal abuse he might dish out—information
that might come in handy at a future court proceeding.
Just in case things got nasty again.

On November 9, 2000, Paul received a bill in the
mail from his divorce lawyer. Clearly, this divorce bullshit was costing him on a number of fronts. The bill,
from the firm of Constantino & Constantino, in Copiague on Long Island, was for $3,176.

On September 28, the firm had acquired all of Lee
Ann's medical records. On September 30, the divorce
lawyer had employed Whitehall Associates, Inc., to do
an "activity check on both Lee Ann and her mother."
This task accounted for more than $3,000 of the bill.
And, on October 19, 2000, the firm had filed on Paul's
behalf a "Notice of Pendency" with the Suffolk County
Clerk's Office.

Despite all of the legal activity, Paul and Lee Ann
moved in together one more time during December
2000, until the required time limit elapsed at which
time Lee Ann left again for Florida, taking the kids
with her, and filed for divorce herself.

According to Lee Ann, one of those most eager to get
Lee Ann and Nicholas away from Paul was Paul's own
mom, Lucy Miller. Lucy had nothing nice to say about
her son. It was Lucy who told Lee Ann that Paul had
been getting Mob-like death threats—a dead fish that
arrived at the gym in the mail, a card that said "You rat."

Then came the night Alex Algeri was shot in the
gym's rear parking lot and died. Everyone was very
upset. Both Paul and Lee Ann Riedel, in separate statements, called Alexander Algeri their "best friend."

Another reconciliation between Paul and Lee Ann

commenced immediately following the shooting. This time Lee Ann was more enthusiastic about getting back together with Paul. In the wake of the Amityville tragedy, the Riedels thought as a team.

Cops had already talked to both of them. Paul felt hunted and Lee Ann was one of the few people in the world who didn't suspect him of shooting Alex. Lee Ann suggested and Paul agreed that they should get away from things for a while—go someplace where there wasn't so much heat.

Paul knew those bullets were meant for him, so he took Lee Ann up to Vermont for a skiing vacation.

After a relaxing stay among the New England mountain slopes, they returned to the real world on Long Island, and lived as husband and wife in their seaside home in Babylon. As usual, the tranquillity was temporary.

Before long, Lee Ann convinced Paul to move down to Florida with her. Paul should face it. He had enemies. By being with his wife and baby all the time, he was putting their lives in danger. Paul sadly admitted that he could see her point.

At the beginning of February 2001, she took Nicholas and went to the South, renting a town house when she got there. The plan was for Lee Ann and Nicholas to live in Florida permanently while Paul, because of business, commuted back and forth.

He went along, blissfully ignorant of Florida law. Paul did not know that if Lee Ann could maintain a residency in Florida for six months, she could legally have the jurisdiction of the divorce case moved to Florida.

Even years later, Paul would be under the impression that it had been his idea to move to Florida. After Lee Ann no doubt repeatedly pointed it out to him, Paul thought that it wasn't safe around Long Island with bullets flying and all, and he told Lee Ann she should go back to Florida and take the kids with her.

"You'll be safer in Florida," he said, glad he'd thought of it.

Lee Ann pretty much stayed in Florida all the time after that. Paul went back and forth. There was business to take care of up there. Mostly the gym. Business was doing OK. The shooting hadn't hurt much.

Still, Paul wasn't a trustful man, and he didn't like the idea of going too long before showing up at the gym in person and making sure everything was running smoothly. He believed regular appearances created the feeling that he could show up at any moment. That tended to promote employee honesty.

Lee Ann never gave up Rocco during all of this. According to Lee Ann, it was on March 26, 2001, that she conceived her third child, and the father was Rocco. Less than a week after Rocco got Lee Ann pregnant, she caught him in bed with another woman. As a result she stopped talking to Rocco and once again began sleeping with Paul. Later, she spoke with Paul and Rocco and told each that he was the new baby's father.

Only days after the six months were up, and Lee Ann had established herself legally as a resident of Florida, she filed for divorce. This time it was Paul who was served with the papers.

Detective Anderson was still calling Sal Algeri regularly, asking questions. At first the questions had mostly to do with Paul Riedel, but now the intention changed. They were more interested in Paul's estranged wife.

"They kept asking questions about Lee Ann, so obviously they had designs on her," Sal recalled. "They asked a lot about fidelity, but I didn't really know anything. For a long time I didn't think they would catch anybody."

Chapter 17

Lee Ann's Story

A year passed. Lee Ann gave birth to her third son, Zachary, on Christmas Eve, 2001. Things were relatively cool for a time, but during the spring of 2002, the heat returned.

On April 10, 2002, Detectives Anderson and Eugene Walsh, along with Detective Sergeant Edward Fandrey, interviewed Lee Ann in Boynton Beach for a third time. The first two interviews had taken place in the days following the murder. Now, fifteen months later, they were back.

Prior to the interview Lee Ann was advised of her constitutional rights. As it was explained to her that anything she said could and would be used against her in a court of law, Lee Ann realized, perhaps for the first time, that she was considered by the police as something more than just a witness in the case.

If this realization troubled her, she didn't let on. She told the investigators that she understood her rights and waived them. She was willing to cooperate. She would tell them whatever they wanted to know.

She explained again about her relationship with her husband, Paul. Did she know someone named Ralph Salierno? She said she did, and admitted that she had had a relationship—and subsequently a child—with Salierno. Yes, he was also known as Rocco. Sometimes as Randy.

They asked her point-blank if she had any knowledge that would help them with their investigation of Alex Algeri's murder. She said she did not. They asked her if she had ever attended a meeting at which the murder of her husband was discussed. She said no, she had not.

At this point Lee Ann must have realized that the police knew something. She didn't know what, and she didn't know how much. Someone, she must have suspected, had let something slip. She did not know who.

She was asked if it had ever crossed her mind that the murder of Alex had been a case of mistaken identity, and that her husband had been the actual target. She said sure, it had occurred to her. After all, Paul knew some bad people and he wasn't shy about pissing them off.

Police asked Lee Ann what her current marital status was. She said that she and Paul were separated and that she was living in Boynton Beach, Florida, with her sons and her mother.

If Lee Ann had been confused initially about who had told the police about the meetings at which hurting Paul were discussed, the mystery did not last long.

"According to your mother . . . ," the next question began. Police told Lee Ann that Pat Armanini had described a meeting that took place in her house in Delray Beach. Pat said that attending the meeting were herself, her live-in friend, Liz, her daughter, Lee Ann, and two guys named Richie and Randy.

According to Pat Armanini, Lee Ann had told Richie and Randy at the meeting that she wanted Paul to be beaten up. Oh yeah, Lee Ann said, come to think of it, she did remember something like that.

Was there any reason why she remembered it now, but she had not remembered it when she was asked a few minutes before? Nope, no reason, Lee Ann said. Her recollection had been refreshed, that's all.

"Was there talk of having Paul killed at that meeting?"

"Yes, but I said I didn't want him killed, I didn't want him hurt, just beat up," Lee Ann said.

She told the police that the major problem between her and Paul had been her teenage son, Christopher. Christopher, she said, was not Paul's kid, and Paul and Christopher did not get along.

She verified that the Randy who was at the meeting was Ralph Salierno, the guy who called himself Rocco sometimes and Randy at others.

"When did you first meet Salierno?" they asked.

"July 2000," she answered. "We got along because we found out we had mutual friends in the *tittie bar* business."

"Would you be willing to put what you just told us in writing?"

"Sure," she replied.

Lee Ann was taken by police car to a nearby real estate office, where the services of a notary public could be used. She was again advised of her rights, this time in writing. She was handed a piece of paper with her rights printed on it. She initialed her deposition "LR" to signify that she understood that she was waiving the right to write her statement without being in the presence of an attorney.

The deposition form made it clear that she was under oath, and any lies in her statement would be considered perjury. She said she was thirty-four years old, born December 29, 1967, in Mineola, New York. She gave her current address in Boynton Beach, Florida, and listed her phone number. She said she lived with her mother, Pat, her sixteen-year-old son, Christopher, her two-year-old, Nicholas, and her three-month-old baby, Zachary.

"I am separated from and in the process of divorcing my husband of two-and-a-half years, Paul Riedel," she wrote. She noted that Paul owned the Dolphin gym on Merrick Road in Amityville, the one outside of which Alex Algeri was murdered. Lee Ann acknowledged that she had known Alex for about two years before he was killed.

She said that she and Paul had been having marital difficulties dating back to the summer of 2000. She recalled leaving her marital home in Babylon and going to stay with her grandmother in Mineola. She later went to live with her mom and mom's friend Liz in Florida. She didn't remember exactly how long she stayed there.

"After I got back to NY, I eventually moved back in with Paul at our house in Babylon. We had more difficulties and on Halloween 2000 I had Paul arrested for some domestic violence issues that had occurred two weeks before," she wrote.

She moved out again and then split her time between her grandmother on Long Island and her mom in Florida. Her son Chris stayed down in Florida full-time so she would make periodic trips down South to visit him.

Lee Ann then began to discuss the new man in her life. She said she'd been introduced to a man who went by both the names Randy and Rocco Salierno by her mom's girlfriend, Liz. Liz knew Randy from a gym in Delray Beach, Florida.

Liz and her mother had explained to her that Randy was the kind of fellow who could "help me get over Paul." She met Randy in the summer of 2000. Liz and her mom wanted Lee Ann to stay in Florida permanently, start a new life.

The first time Randy came over, he had a friend named Richie with him, and Lee Ann, her mom, Liz, Richie, and Randy all talked in the living room. Lee Ann's marital woes became a primary topic of conversation.

Liz said, "Someone should kick his fucking ass. Someone should break his legs."

Richie replied, "We can do that. We can whack him, if you want."

Lee Ann wrote, "I said that I didn't want Paul killed, that he was the father of my kids. Liz is always going off like that, saying that someone should kick Paul's ass, kill him. That's just Liz.

"That same summer I was with Randy one day and he said that he had to go see Larry. Larry is a guy from the gym that Liz always talks about. He's a bodybuilder and Liz says that he has a production company that makes movies. I met him with Randy that one time. He was at his job somewhere in Boynton. He's a white guy in his late thirties."

She hung around Randy all that summer before returning to New York on September 11, 2000, exactly a year before the terrorist attacks in New York, Washington, DC, and Pennsylvania. At that time Randy was getting Lee Ann a divorce lawyer and a job. He was also, she noted, "driving a Lexus."

She recalled one occasion, although she did not remember the specific date, when Randy came over with a friend named Mike. He was a white male, about twenty-seven years old, from New York. He'd grown up near Randy, he said.

Lee Ann wasn't sure, but she thought Mike might have been staying at Randy's apartment in The Fountains in Delray Beach. Mike wanted Liz to get him a job at Dillard's. Mike talked to her son Chris about fishing. As far as she could remember, nobody said anything about anybody doing anything to her husband, Paul.

"I got pregnant by Randy in March 2001. On December 24, 2001, Zachary was born. It is Randy's baby. Randy has asked me several times when my divorce is going to be final. I don't know why he asks me that because we don't have a relationship, other than he is the father of Zachary."

Lee Ann and Ralph had had a falling-out only days after she got pregnant. She caught him cheating on her. Ralph was arrested four months later in Westchester on a gun violation. He wasn't supposed to leave New York State because of his recent gun arrest, but he did.

When her written statement was complete, Lee Ann was asked when was the last time she had seen Ralph Salierno. She said that she did not remember the exact date, but that it had been a couple of weeks.

They wanted to know what, if anything, Salierno had said, and Lee Ann said he had told her that the police in New York might be looking for him. The police took Lee Ann back home. They would not return for eleven months, but when they did, they'd be carrying an arrest warrant.

Chapter 18

Paget Arrested

On April 11, 2002, the day after Lee Ann's deposition, the trap was set for Scott Paget. Realizing that Paget was apt to make a run for it if informed he was a suspect in a murder, Detective Anderson sought out the cooperation of local Florida law enforcement, the Cutler Ridge, Miami, Police Department.

The Cutler Ridge cops would call Paget and say that police in West Palm Beach needed to talk to him about an incident at the Wild Side bar, the strip joint where he worked. The call was made and the Cutler Ridge police got ahold of Scott's mom.

They gave her the message, and Scott got it. He wondered which incident they were talking about. He worked security at the joint and there were "incidents" every night. It was called the Wild Side, as in "Walk on the Wild Side," the classic Lou Reed song.

When Paget showed up at the police station, his first question was "Which incident at the Wild Side are you interested in?"

They didn't bother to answer.

Paget was taken to Detective Anderson, of the Suffolk County Police Department. The second he saw Anderson he knew that this had nothing to do with a fight in a Florida "gentleman's club." This had to do with the murder of Alex Algeri. He was in big trouble.

Paget was arrested and told police that Salierno pulled the trigger and he was just along to drive the car. Prosecutors quickly cut a deal with Paget—his truthful testimony against Ralph Salierno and Lee Ann Riedel in exchange for a comparatively lenient sentence.

Chapter 19

The Interrogation of Ralph Salierno

By the spring of 2002, Ralph "Rocco" Salierno was no longer Lee Ann's boyfriend. In fact, he didn't even live in Florida anymore. He'd returned up North to where he'd grown up. He was picked up by police in Eastchester, New York, during the early afternoon of April 13, 2002. He was arrested and placed in the back of a cop car.

Detective Anderson, along with Detectives Pasquall Albergo and Eugene Walsh, accompanied him. They pulled away into the road and headed for police headquarters in Yaphank, Long Island. Anderson didn't wait until they reached their destination. He began the preliminary interrogation right there in the car.

Anderson confirmed that the arrested man was Ralph Salierno. He asked Rocco his date of birth and was told June 21, 1967. He was two months shy of his thirty-fifth birthday. Anderson asked his address. Rocco said he lived with his father, his father's wife, and his brother. He specified a street address in Eastchester.

Rocco then told the cops about his job and, briefly, about his work history. He said he was currently employed at Deco Contracting in Yorktown, New York, working construction.

"How come you arrested me?" Rocco asked at one point.

"One of your friends had a few things to say about you," Anderson replied.

"I don't have any friends," Rocco replied dejectedly.

Detective Anderson told Rocco that he was going to have an ample opportunity to tell his story when they arrived at police headquarters. Upon arrival at the station, Salierno was taken immediately to a drab interview room, where he was informed of and waived his Miranda rights. The interrogation continued. Anderson asked the questions; Albergo took the notes.

Rocco told the police that he had been born and raised in Westchester County and had lived in Westchester until January 1998 when he'd gone down to live in Florida. At first he lived with his mother and worked at a concession stand in Daytona Beach.

After a time he got his own place in Fort Lauderdale, then another place in the town of Delray Beach. He lived in an apartment by himself from the early part of 2000 until August 2001. He got a job working as a doorman/bouncer at a strip club called Aphrodite's. He said he had worked in the phone business and in another strip club called Cheetah III in Pompano Beach.

"You have a girlfriend, Salierno?" Anderson asked.

"Sure. Different women every week," Rocco replied.

"What are their names?"

Rocco gave the police a list of names. On the list was the name Lee Ann Armanini. Anderson zoomed in on that name right away.

"Lee Ann Armanini is your girlfriend?"

"No."

"Not now?"

"Not ever," Rocco said. "I was never really going out with her."

They asked if he knew where Armanini lived and he gave them a street address in Boynton Beach. Rocco also volunteered his knowledge that Lee Ann lived with her mom, Pat Armanini, and Pat's girlfriend, Liz.

Rocco said that, yeah, Lee Ann was married. Her husband's name, he knew, was Paul Riedel. They had three kids. The third kid might not belong to Riedel, however.

"She says the youngest kid is mine," Rocco said.

"Did you know that Paul Riedel lived on Long Island?" Anderson asked.

"Yeah."

"Did you know that he operated a gym called the Dolphin?"

"Yeah."

With these admissions on the record, Anderson shifted the focus for a moment: "How did you meet Lee Ann?"

"I met her through Pat, Lee Ann's mother, at the World Gym on Military Trail in Delray Beach. Pat's girlfriend, Liz, worked out there, too. Her mom told me Lee Ann was looking for a job. I got her one as a waitress at Cheetah three."

"How long did Lee Ann work at the club?"

"She only worked one day. Then she quit."

"And you never went out with her?" Anderson asked.

"No, I just visited her once in a while. Just for sex."

Again Anderson changed directions.

"Do you know a man named Michael Alexander?"

"Yeah, but I wish I didn't. I met him in a bar in Eastchester," Rocco said. "I let him stay with me in

Florida and the son of a bitch stole shit out of my home."

"What did he steal?"

"Jewelry and a gun," Rocco said.

Anderson asked when this had taken place and Rocco estimated that it had been sometime during July 2001. Rocco said that he hadn't known when he invited Alexander to live with him that Alexander was a junkie.

"I treated him nice, too. I even did him a favor by getting him a trip to Venezuela to help promote a gym opening," Rocco said. "It was in Venezuela that I found out Alexander was a drug addict. I was doing the right thing, working for the gym. Alexander partied with women and drugs. He refused to leave the country. When we went to the airport, he freaked out and refused to go through security. He said he had drugs on him."

"What did you do?"

"I left him in the airport and came home," Rocco said with a shrug. "When I got back to Florida, I got a call from an embassy in Venezuela. Alexander got busted for drugs. I was holding two thousand dollars of Alexander's money, so I wired some of it to him to help him out."

When Alexander got back to the United States, Rocco said, he began to pester him with harassing phone calls. "He said I owed him money."

Rocco summed up his tale with a shake of the head: "After all I did for that bastard, he ends up robbing me."

Anderson dropped the subject of Alexander and moved on.

"What sort of car did you drive while in Florida?"

"I drove a Grand Am that belonged to one of my girlfriends. Her name was Kim Buckley (pseudonym). I also leased a white Ford Expedition and a red Lexus."

"How did you afford all of that on your income, Salierno?"

"My mom gave me money."

"You make any money doing collections for loan sharks?"

Rocco shook his head.

"That's not what Michael Alexander told us."

"He's a liar."

"The info is good. We checked it with other people."

"A lot of people think I'm a mobster. It's bullshit."

Anderson, armed with phone records, made Rocco admit that he owned three different cell phones with four different numbers. He was shown the numbers and recognized them as his own.

"I'm collecting money from some people who are owed money. That's all. They're not loan sharks."

"You get paid for collecting for these people who are owed money?"

"Sometimes. Sometimes not. Sometimes I just get bought lunch or something."

"Did Alexander ever go along with you when you went out to collect money?"

"Sometimes. Not much. He wasn't in Florida that long."

"These phone numbers, are they yours alone?"

"They belong to me and another guy," Rocco admitted. Anderson asked if the guy's name was Richard Pollack, and Rocco reluctantly admitted that it was.

"Why did you guys get the phone numbers?"

"Pollack wanted to start a bookmaking business, but it never got off the ground. Most of his deals never got going."

Anderson asked when Salierno had last seen Pollack, and Rocco said it had been more than a year.

"I don't want to have anything to do with that asshole. He's another Alexander," Rocco said. Anderson asked what he meant by that and Rocco said, "Pills and weed."

"When was the last time you heard from Pollack?"

"I heard he got arrested in Georgia."

"What about your latest arrest, Salierno?" Anderson asked.

"It's done," Rocco replied. "I got probation last February. It was bullshit. I got jumped by a bunch of guys, so I pulled a gun and got popped."

"Did your probation limit your travel?"

"Yeah. It said I couldn't go to Florida."

"How did that affect your relationship with Lee Ann?"

"I couldn't see her no more. Just phone calls. Now and again."

"When was the last time you were in Florida?"

"February 2002, just before I went on probation."

"I heard you were down there in March. Tell me about that."

"Oh yeah," he said, admitting to violating his probation. "I borrowed a car from my friend Mike Scauzillo."

Anderson asked how long he had stayed in Florida on that occasion and Rocco told him it had been five days. He visited Lee Ann at her house during that visit and remembered seeing a Palm Beach sheriff. He said the only reason for the trip was that he "needed to get away."

"When was the last time you spoke to Lee Ann?"

"About a week ago. Monday or Tuesday last week."

Anderson again shifted subjects, now zeroing in on the crux of the matter.

"When was the last time you were on Long Island, Salierno?"

"Longer than two years ago," Rocco said with a shrug. "I used to go to Jones Beach."

"When was this?"

"Starting around 1993. I went to a club named Metro seven hundred."

Anderson asked Rocco to reiterate that he met Lee Ann because her mom said she needed a job, and Rocco said that was the case. Then Anderson told him that he had sworn statements from Pat, Liz, and Lee Ann, stating what the real reason for that meeting was.

"Oh yeah, well, that meeting wasn't my idea," Rocco said. "I went with Rich Pollack to that meeting. Lee Ann, Pat, and Liz were also there. I think this was sometime during the summer of 2000. Pollack had the number of Liz and Pat. He told me the daughter had a husband problem."

A couple of weeks after Pollack told Rocco this, the two men went to the women's house in Delray Beach. Rocco and Rich talked to Liz and Pat about what a prick Lee Ann's husband was, and what could be done to take care of him.

"They wanted the husband scared, or set up with drugs," Rocco said.

"They asked you to hurt the husband?" Anderson asked.

"I don't remember anything about hurting him. Pollack was in more contact with the women than I was. Pollack thought the women had money. A guy named Larry Ortolano (pseudonym) told him that."

"So you lied about getting Lee Ann a job?"

"No. That happened later. She was a waitress at Cheetah three for one night. That happened in the fall of 2000."

"When did you start having sex with Lee Ann?"

"After that. After I got her the job," Rocco said.

"You would pick Lee Ann up at her house?"

"Yeah."

"And you'd see Liz and Pat on those occasions?"

"Sure."

"Did Mike Alexander ever come with you when you visited Lee Ann at her house?"

"I don't remember."

"Did Alexander know Lee Ann?" Detective Anderson asked.

"Oh sure."

Anderson now zoomed in for the kill. "Tell me about your involvement in the murder of Alex Algeri, Salierno," the lead investigator said. "You know, we got the other guy's side of the story."

"What other guy?" Rocco asked, a note of concern in his voice. "I don't know what you're talking about. I didn't kill the guy. All I know is what Lee Ann told me—that her husband's partner got murdered at the gym they owned. She said maybe her husband did it, or maybe it was meant for her husband."

"Mike Alexander says you killed Alex Algeri," Anderson said.

"Mike Alexander is a piece-of-shit liar," Rocco replied.

"There were some clubs you forgot to mention when you were telling us where you worked," Anderson said. "You forgot to tell us about Diamonds and Wild Side. You forgot to tell us about all the people you know from those clubs."

Rocco sagged in his seat a bit as Anderson said this. "Who am I supposed to know from those clubs?"

Anderson promptly pulled out a picture of Scott Paget. A bit of the color drained from Rocco's face.

"Know this guy?"

"Maybe."

"What's his name?"

"Not sure. Might be Scott."

"Scott what?"

"Dunno."

"Where do you know Scott from?" Anderson asked.

"From Wild Side. He works there," Salierno replied.

"You ever go out collecting money with Scott?"

"No," Rocco said, shaking his head vigorously. Rocco also denied ever seeing Scott outside the Wild Side club, and that he had ever exchanged phone calls with Scott.

As huge as he was, Rocco still managed to appear as if he were shrinking when Detective Anderson again pulled out phone records, these documenting the many phone calls that had been placed by Rocco to Scott Paget.

"Scott confessed, Salierno. He told us about Long Island," Anderson said. The lead investigator demonstrated his point by showing Salierno the first and last page of Paget's written confession. Rocco was not given an opportunity to read those pages, however.

Salierno was then shown a phone message from Paget's attorney, dated April 12, 2002—the previous day.

"Paget's already been arrested," Anderson then revealed. "He's looking for a deal to testify against you."

Rocco threw his head into his hands. "Stop talking and give me some time to think," Salierno said.

"Sure thing, Salierno. You hungry?"

Rocco said he was and he was brought a sandwich and a container of orange juice.

After twenty minutes to collect his thoughts, Rocco said, "Look, I don't want to take all the weight myself. I can see I'm getting fucked here, so I'll tell you what happened. Paget is a liar. Richie Pollack got Pat Armanini's phone number through a guy named Larry Ortolano at the gym. Pollack was a bullshitter and a scammer and he thought he could make some money scamming the women."

According to Salierno, Pollack told him the women wanted a guy "taken care of" and asked Salierno to go with him to the meeting. Salierno went and first met Pat and Liz. Later, Lee Ann joined them.

Asked what type of meeting it was, Rocco said sarcastically, "It was a tea party." Rocco said that the women and Pollack sat around and shot the breeze about people they knew in common. Then they got around to business.

The women wanted Lee Ann's husband Paul "taken

care of." At first they discussed beating him up. Then they discussed the pros and cons of setting him up with drugs. Pollack told the women that he would make a few phone calls and see what he could do.

"Did Lee Ann ever say that she wanted her husband hurt?" Anderson asked.

"I don't remember her saying that. No. Liz talked about living in Little Italy in New York, and how she used to live on Mulberry Street, across the street from Neil Dellacroce."

"Who's he?" the detective asked.

"Some mobster. Died a long time ago." (Aniello "Neil" Dellacroce was an underboss of Don Carlo Gambino, and an early father figure to the young John Gotti. According to authors Jerry Capeci and Gene Mustain, Dellacroce "was Carlo's bad cop. He was fierce, violent, foul-mouthed and clever, and Carlo relied on him when a mix of treachery and trickery was needed to settle some contentious matter.")

"What happened then?" the lead investigator inquired.

"Pollack and I left the meeting," Rocco replied with feigned nonchalance.

"Did you and Pollack have any conversation after the meeting?"

"Yeah, I told him that I wanted in on the scam," Rocco said.

"Tell me about the killing, Salierno," Anderson said, exuding calmness.

"It was Paget's idea," Rocco said sharply, his forehead creased.

"Tell me again how you met Paget," Detective Anderson said.

"I met him in the club where he worked."

"How did Paget know about Lee Ann's husband problem?"

"I introduced Paget to Richie Pollack and Pollack told him about the women wanting Lee Ann's husband taken care of. Pollack told Paget that Lee Ann figured to come into a lot of money if her husband was out of the way. She would get a house, a lot of cash, and the gym. Paget told me he wanted to get in the collection business. He wanted to come with me when I went on collections."

"Did Paget go with you on collections?"

"Yeah, but we usually never did nothing. We sat in the car out in front of the house of the guy who owed money. Usually we never even saw the guy who owed money. While we were doing that, Paget kept on me, saying we could make a lot of money if we took care of Lee Ann's husband."

Rocco said that Lee Ann's mom also was pushing the issue, and Paget eventually came up with the idea of renting a van and going to Long Island to take care of Paul Riedel.

"At the time it was just supposed to be a beating," Rocco said.

"Did you make arrangements to get a gun for the trip to Long Island?"

"Yeah, I called Mike Alexander about that. I figured I might need a gun for backup. At that time I didn't know that Paget already had a gun."

Anderson asked if Salierno and Paget had taken the borrowed minivan to the Bronx, the northernmost borough of New York City, and Rocco replied that they had.

Anderson inquired if the trip had been to pick up a gun, and Rocco said no, the trip had been to put New York State license plates on the vehicle. It was after putting the new plates on the van that he and Paget had driven out to Amityville.

"We got lost twice," Rocco said. "Once on the way out to the gym and once on the way back." Rocco said that when they got to the gym, they saw what they thought was Paul Riedel's truck in the parking lot. They pulled into the lot and parked.

"What happened then?"

"Paget got out of the van. Then I heard gunshots. I was sitting in the driver's seat when I heard the shots. I slid over into the passenger seat so that when Paget got back in, he could drive."

"Paget says that the plan was always to kill Lee Ann's husband."

Rocco was silent.

"No one's going to believe this bullshit story you're telling us," Anderson said.

"What the fuck. I'm probably going to get forty years anyway. We went up there to kill him," Rocco admitted. "I was getting annoyed, listening to Lee Ann complain about her husband all the time."

That, combined with the fact that Paget was constantly pestering him about taking care of Paul Riedel as a way to make money, finally tipped him over the edge. He agreed to go along with the killing. He reiterated that it had been Paget's idea, but he admitted that both he and Paget planned to make money on the deal.

Rocco told the detective that it had been Paget who picked up the minivan. "Then he picked me up," Rocco said. Anderson asked him to describe the van. Salierno told him it was a white passenger van with Florida plates.

"We left Florida in the afternoon and drove straight through. We got to New York five in the afternoon the next day," Rocco said. They went to a chop shop in the Hunts Point section of the Bronx. The chop shop was owned by a friend named Tony.

It was there that they acquired the New York State license plates for the van. Several times during the trip, Rocco called Mike Alexander looking for the gun, which Alexander failed to provide.

"I wanted the gun for backup, but Paget told me not to worry about the gun. He said we should just drive straight out to Long Island. He already had a gun, he said, so I shouldn't worry about it."

Salierno and Paget weren't sure how to get to the Dolphin gym in Amityville, so Rocco called information and got the gym's phone number. He then called the gym and asked for directions. Using the directions, they had little trouble finding the place.

Anderson noted that the scenarios told by Salierno and Paget agreed for the most part. They simply disagreed on who had gotten out of the van in order to ventilate Alex Algeri. Not that that was a minor detail, but the fact that they agreed on so much was a good indication that those portions of the story were true and accurate.

"I drove past the front of the gym and then turned right. I drove past the rear parking lot, where we saw the black Yukon truck in the back of the building, so I made a U-turn and parked next to the building," Salierno said.

"What time was it?" Detective Anderson asked.

"About seven-thirty, eight o'clock at night," Rocco replied. "There were people coming and going from the rear parking lot. Then I saw a guy come out of the back door of the gym. Then I saw the interior light on the Yukon go on. That was when Paget got out of the car and ran over to the truck. Then I heard shots."

"How many shots did you hear?"

"Three or four."

"What did you do then?"

"Like I told you, I slid over into the passenger seat so Scott could drive. We got out of there."

"What did you do with the gun?"

"After driving for a while, Scott chucked it. I don't know where we were."

"Where did you go then?"

"I don't know. We got lost and drove around for a while. We found the George Washington Bridge, and from there we were able to drive back to Florida. We got back to Florida the next day. Paul dropped me off and returned the van."

"Would you be willing to put what you just told me in writing?" Detective Anderson asked. Rocco said that he was. It was now 5:30 P.M. Rocco had been in custody for about four hours.

Rocco was handed a pen and a deposition form and went to work, with Detective Anderson's guidance. On the top of the first page of the form was a repeat of Salierno's Miranda rights, which he had been informed of and had waived verbally before his interrogation began.

Now he initialed "RS" in the blanks next to each of his rights:

You have the right to remain silent. ———
Anything you say can and will be used against you in a court of law. ———
You have the right to talk to a lawyer, right now, and have him present with you while you are being questioned. ———

Then, by putting yes or no in the appropriate blanks, and by initialing each response, Rocco stated that he understood his rights, that he did not wish to contact a lawyer, and that he was willing to prepare his written statement without a lawyer present. He then signed and dated the first page of the deposition form, and Detective Albergo signed in the blank for "witness."

Using the statements Salierno had already made,

and some additional questioning, a written statement was prepared. The statement eventually filled six pages in a neat and steady handwriting. This was the confession that Salierno's defense counsel would later claim was coerced, that "Rocco the Bouncer" had been beaten until he confessed.

In Salierno's written statement, dated April 13, 2002, he stated that he was thirty-four years old, that his birthday was June 21, 1967, and that he'd been born in the upstate New York town of Mount Vernon. He wrote that he worked in the construction business, and was currently employed by Deco Contracting in Yorktown, New York. He grew up in Westchester County, but he moved to Florida in the winter of 1998.

He lived in three places during his years in Florida: Daytona Beach, Fort Lauderdale, and Delray Beach. In Delray Beach he lived in an apartment building known as the Fountains. He lived in that apartment during the early months of 2000. While living at the Fountains, he wrote, he belonged to a health club on a road called Military Trail in Delray Beach. It was a World Gym. During his time in Florida, he noted, he was very popular and social, and had many "friends and associates." One of his friends was a guy named Richie Pollack. They met in a nightclub in Boynton Beach called Aphrodite's.

"Richie contacted me in the Summer of 2000 and said he had the phone number of two women who have a daughter that has a problem with her husband and they wanted to meet me and Richie," Salierno wrote.

Richie, Salierno claimed, had gotten the women's phone number from another friend of theirs named Larry Ortolano. Larry produced movies at Worldview Pictures (pseudonym) in Boynton Beach. Richie was in Larry's office at Larry's studio when he got the phone number.

According to Salierno, a couple of weeks passed before he and Richie went to the Delray Beach home of Pat Armanini and Liz Budroni. After a while they were joined by Pat's daughter, Lee Ann Armanini, who was married to a guy named Paul Riedel.

"Pat and Liz discussed with me and Richie about keeping Paul away from Lee Ann. They wanted to set him up to be arrested or scared. They wanted us to go talk to him," Salierno wrote. Larry had told Richie that the women had money, Salierno noted, so they had every reason to believe that they would be well compensated for any favor they might do for these women. He didn't recall, however, any specific mention of money at that first meeting. They talked about the situation and then he and Richie left.

Salierno wrote that the women got in touch with Richie after that, and during one of those contacts, one of the women asked Richie if Salierno, being a man of contacts, could get Lee Ann a job. He did get Lee Ann employment as a waitress in a nightclub called Cheetah's III in Pompano Beach. She only worked one night before she quit. It was after that he started dating Lee Ann. He wasn't clear on the date. "In the fall of 2000, maybe October," Salierno wrote.

Not long after that, according to Salierno's written statement, a guy named Mike Alexander, a friend from back in Eastchester, came down to Florida and moved in with him. Mike was with Salierno once when he went over to Pat and Liz's home when Lee Ann was there.

According to Salierno, Pat was always griping about Paul Riedel. She called him an "abusing bastard." She bitched about Paul making big-time bucks with the gym, but not "doing the right thing" with the money.

Mike had gone out on "collections" with Salierno and knew a business opportunity when he saw one. He was impressed by Pat's tale of woe and brought it up in later conversations with Salierno. Mike wasn't around much longer after that, however. He soon returned to New York.

Salierno then switched topics and began to discuss another friend he had met at the World Gym, a guy named Scott Paget. Salierno introduced Paget to Richie Pollack. They became friends and partied together. Salierno wrote: "Richie had a scheme to start a bookmaking business. I told him to get the cell phones. He got three different phones with four different numbers. They were [phone numbers deleted]. The bookmaking thing never worked out so I kept the phones and used them."

After that, Salierno wrote, Scott Paget became his collections buddy, accompanying him when he talked to people who owed loan money regarding the wisdom of prompt payback. During those jobs he and Paget would discuss Lee Ann's problem and the money that might be made taking care of it for her.

At one point Salierno and Paget sat in a car for a week together trying to collect money from someone, so they had a lot of opportunity to chat. Besides, Salierno was seeing a lot of Lee Ann and her family, and was getting sick of hearing Pat Armanini complain about Paul.

"Scott and me decided to take a trip up to New York on Long Island where the Dolphin Gym is located," Salierno wrote. He then admitted in his written statement that he and Scott Paget had driven up to New York to kill Paul Riedel, but he claimed that it was Paget who had done the actual shooting. Salierno wrote that there was no money up front for the job, but that he and Paget figured that there would be money in it for them later if they took care of it for the women. He and Paget rode up North during January 2001. He wasn't sure of the exact date, but he thought it might have been near the middle of the month.

"I'm not good with remembering numbers and dates,"

Salierno added. Before leaving for the trip, Salierno wrote, he saw photos Lee Ann had of Paul Riedel and his black GMC Yukon. Salierno noted that he had not been given a license plate number for Riedel's vehicle.

According to Salierno, it was Scott Paget who rented the van for the job. He didn't know from whom Paget rented it, only that Paget came to pick him up with the van. They talked first on the phone, Scott picked him up, and they began their trip up North sometime in the middle of the afternoon.

Salierno wrote that the vehicle was a "passenger van, color white, full-size with seats in the back and windows. It had a Florida plate on it." They drove straight through to New York, only stopping to take a leak.

They arrived in New York late in the afternoon on the following day, about five o'clock. They went to the Hunts Point section of the Bronx, where they purchased a New York State license plate to be attached over the Florida plate. He knew a guy named Tony who provided this license plate service. After the job was done, they would remove the second plate, and eyewitnesses couldn't connect the vehicle to the crime scene.

Salierno wrote that he also called Mike Alexander a couple of times, the guy who had lived with him briefly in Florida before moving back to New York. Salierno hoped Alexander might be able to provide him with a gun. Alexander told Salierno that he was unable to provide a gun, but, Salierno claimed, it was Paget who said, "Don't worry about it, let's go out to Long Island."

They stopped in Mount Vernon and used a pay phone. Salierno wrote that it was he who called information and got the phone number for the gym. He then called the gym and got directions from someone at the desk on how to get there. According to Salierno, it was he who then drove the van out to Long Island and to the crime scene, while Scott Paget sat shotgun. He wrote that he drove past the front of the gym and made a right just after he had passed the building. He drove past the rear parking lot, saw that there was a black Yukon parked there, with its front end almost flush against the rear of the gym only a few feet away from the building's rear entrance.

He made a U-turn on the dark street, which he remembered was lined with houses. He parked on the street where they could have a clear view of the gym's back door. By this time, he wrote, it was seven-thirty or eight at night.

Salierno reiterated that it was he in the driver's seat and Paget in the front passenger seat as they waited. Some time passed, but not a lot of time, when they saw a man exit the rear door of the gym.

"We saw the interior light go on in the Yukon and at that time Scott got out and rushed over to the Yukon. I heard about three or four shots and Scott returned to the van. I slid over into the passenger seat while Scott jumped into the driver's seat. We took off making a left on the main street," Salierno wrote.

According to Salierno, Scott threw the gun away somewhere down the road, but he didn't remember where. They got lost a couple of times and spent some time not knowing where they were. After a lot of driving around, they finally located the George Washington Bridge (which connects upper Manhattan with New Jersey) and from there it was easy getting back to Florida. It was a simple matter of getting on the New Jersey Turnpike.

They didn't stop until they got to the Jersey Turnpike. At that point they pulled over at a rest stop and bought cigarettes for Paget and beer for Salierno. Paget drove and Salierno drank the beer. Eventually, Salierno wrote, he fell asleep. When he woke up, he took over the driving chores. They switched back and forth all the way down to Florida. There wasn't much talk. "We spoke very little about the murder," Salierno wrote.

When they got back to South Florida the day after the murder, Scott dropped Salierno off at the World Gym in Delray Beach and then returned the van. Where Paget returned the van, Salierno didn't know.

A couple of days later, Paget and Salierno had a number of conversations back and forth. They went to Salierno's apartment on Lantana Road, where he lived with Al Zisk (pseudonym). Paget showed Saliemo an Internet copy of a newspaper article on the murder. It was at that time that they learned they had killed the wrong guy.

"We killed his partner by mistake," Salierno wrote. "His name was Alex. I was upset that we got the wrong guy. I felt like a real asshole."

About a week or a week-and-a-half after the murder, Lee Ann called Salierno when she returned from a short vacation with Paul Riedel. She told Salierno that Paul's partner at the gym named Alex got murdered and she was wondering if Paul had something to do with it.

According to Salierno, she said a lot of people thought it was meant for Paul and that was why they had gone away for a week.

That concluded Salierno's written statement. At the bottom he added, "I am giving this statement to Detective Anderson at Police Headquarters in Yaphank and have read it and sworn it is the truth."

Rocco signed and dated each page of his statement. It was then notarized by Anderson, who was a New York State notary public in addition to being a cop. Because it was a legal deposition, if anything in Rocco's statement turned out to be untrue, he would have been guilty of perjury.

Rocco then signed a separate document that read: "I, Ralph Salierno, of [address deleted], have given a statement concerning the murder of Alex Algeri to Det. Anderson and Albergo and have been given the oppor-

tunity to make my statement on videotape. I do not wish
to give a video statement." Signing the statement as
witnesses were Detectives Anderson and Albergo.

Next step, Salierno was charged with first-degree
murder and conspiracy. The day after Rocco's arrest—
barely, at 1:33 A.M.—Detective Anderson used something that looked like a long Q-tip to take a sample of
Salierno's saliva. Rocco signed a form stating that he was
aware that he had the right to refuse the taking of samples and that he was waiving that right.

Rocco was then taken to the jail in Riverhead, which
would be his home until the conclusion of his murder
trial. If Salierno had done any thinking on the matter
and had to choose where he would like to get busted for
first-degree murder, the chances are good that he would
not have chosen Suffolk County, on Long Island.

Not only were the cops good at drawing out confessions, and the prosecution good at persuading juries to
see things their way, but the jails in Suffolk County
were in miserable shape.

Chapter 20

Rocco's Jailhouse

Alan Croce, the chair of the State Commission of Correction, had said that because of jail conditions—the condition of the Riverhead Jail in particular—he would pull all of Suffolk County's variances and force the county to build a new jail.

The most recent portion of the Riverhead Jail was built in 1988, and housed "the most serious, or higher security, inmates, as well as those prisoners who are in protective custody."

The Riverhead Jail was built in thirteen "pods," each with two tiers of cells circling a common area. In addition to the thirteen pods is a special section for extra-high-security inmates and those with discipline problems.

The maximum-security cells in the special section of the Riverhead Jail, used for inmates who had demonstrated severe disciplinary problems, had Plexiglas covering the bars. The Plexiglas was used to prevent inmates from throwing feces at the guards.

The county's other jail, in Yaphank, is for the lower-security cases. It is built in a dormitory style and generally houses those who are considered little risk to others or themselves. Because of the difference in levels of security, Riverhead was at one time used to house the county's female inmates and those with mental difficulties.

The Yaphank and Riverhead Jails each had their problems. The Riverhead Jail was in better condition, but the prisoners there created their own hell on earth. The Yaphank Jail was falling apart. Things rained rust and leaked with an ominous, echoing drip.

The Riverhead Jail suffered from what Suffolk County undersheriff Donald Sullivan called "operational inefficiency." The pod layout only allowed guards to look directly into a couple of cells at a time. Modern designs, Sullivan said, offer guards a simultaneous view of many more cells.

Sullivan also said that any future jail should have more single-occupancy cells and fewer doubles. Doubles seemed like less trouble because they minimized the amount of space needed per prisoner, but from a social viewpoint it was a nightmare for correctional officers. Authorities had to put two inmates in together who at least had a chance of getting along. Two prisoners who were constantly trying to kill one another took up more than their share of the guards' time.

If a prisoner couldn't get along with a cellmate, and there was no single cell available, the antisocial prisoner would be kept alone in a double cell, with one bunk going to waste. Better to have more single cells because antisocial behavior was not uncommon among prisoners.

When Ralph Salierno got to jail, he was going to find that a significant portion of the inmates were gang members. Though he was only in his thirties, he would feel ancient compared to the boys who filled the cells.

Sullivan has said, "Over the past twenty years the nature of Suffolk County's inmate population has changed substantially. The most dramatic change is the increased number of violent street gang members being held in our facility."

Out of more than fifteen hundred prisoners at the Riverhead Jail, more than two hundred were identified gang members. But only thirty-six were charged with first-degree murder, as Ralph Salierno had been.

"We have also seen a substantial increase in the number of people afflicted with some type of mental illness. We also have alternatives-to-incarceration programs in place, so far fewer people are in jail for lower classes of offenses."

The Riverhead Jail experienced about nine inmate-on-inmate assaults per week. There was about one inmate-on-guard assault every two weeks, on average. Handmade weapons confiscated from inmates by guards included sharpened toilet bowl cleaners, modified can lids, and sharpened steak bones.

The jail was overcrowded. One of the ways they hoped to lessen the future population of the jail was by providing the kids in local schools and community groups with free tours of the jail. This way they could get an idea of what was in store for them if they were caught breaking the law.

According to the "Police Blotter" column of the *Amityville Record*, April 24, 2002, police had announced that both men, Salierno and Paget, were arrested on April 14. The paper reported, "The Police investigation revealed that Algeri was not the intended victim of the murder. Instead, it was his co-owner, Paul Riedel, who was the target. Riedel and his wife Lee Ann were having marital difficulties and she was having a relationship with Salierno. Police said Page claimed Salierno paid him $3,000 for his role in the killing. Both defendants claim the other did the actual shooting."

Amityville Village mayor Peter T. Imbert reacted

quickly to the news of the arrests. The mayor said, "While this incident resulted in the death of a man who was described by many as a nice person, we are at least relieved to hear that those responsible have been arrested and that the incident was not related in any way to the village."

Not long after Salierno signed his confession, Detective Anderson gave Sal Algeri a call. Sal hadn't talked to Anderson in a while and was pleased to hear from the case's lead investigator.

"After so much time Detective Anderson called me at two o'clock on a Sunday morning," Sal said. "I heard his voice and knew they had something. He said they had Salierno and that there would be an indictment on Monday morning. He told me about Lee Ann and Lee Ann's mother. I said, 'God bless you, Mr. Anderson.'"

Chapter 21

The Private Eye

Lee Ann, by this time, knew she was in trouble. By the spring of 2002, Lee Ann had hired a lawyer—Bruce Barket—and Barket's private investigator was working the case. His name was Jay Salpeter and he was sort of the Paul Drake to Barket's Perry Mason.

Jay Salpeter was fifty-one years old. He joined the NYPD as a trainee in 1969 and was appointed a patrolman in 1971. He was raised in a Jewish household in Whitestone, Queens, the son of a longtime cabdriver who went eventually into the check-cashing business. Salpeter was the one and only cop to ever come from his family. He distinguished himself early on in the police department. When he was a young patrolman, he was partnered with a young black officer. They made so many arrests, they were put into plainclothes anticrime teams.

"Me and Bennie (pseudonym) were a crazy salt-and-pepper team," said Salpeter. "But Bennie had a drinking problem. He really knew the streets, which I didn't.

He grew up in Bed-Stuy and his mother was mugged. The word was, when he got his hands on the guy who mugged his mother, Bennie dished out the worst beating he'd ever administered.

"Unfortunately, Bennie had lots of personal demons and no common sense or direction. He also went out with the ugliest women in the world. Women were his weakness and he died of AIDS in the 1990s. But in the '70s, we had a good run. We complemented each other."

Salpeter chose to chase the gold shield of a detective, aspiring to be appointed to that rank by the police commissioner, while Bennie opted to take civil service promotional exams and eventually became a sergeant and lieutenant. They parted ways.

As a decoy cop in the Street Crime Unit, Salpeter made himself as muggable as possible by dressing up as, among other things, Hasidic Jews and drunken businessmen. Dozens of arrests later, he received his coveted detective's shield.

After much success there, he was transferred to the 69 Detective Squad in Flatbush, Brooklyn, in the early 1980s. Within a month he recovered a Torah that had been stolen from a local Yeshiva. Being a Jewish detective assigned to such a high-profile case, he was embraced by the area's waning Jewish community, which was clinging precariously to the vestiges of its glorious middle-class past.

"Recovering the Torah was big news as far away as Israel, so when I got invited to a dinner by the rabbi, I figured I was the guest of honor," deadpanned Salpeter, who has a self-deprecating sense of humor not uncommon among police investigators. "But the guest of honor was the Torah. I had had a few drinks and was asked to carry it to the dais. It was a balancing act because the thing was huge."

Salpeter followed up that case with the quick arrest

of several white youths that had chased down and beaten a group of black kids on Flatlands Avenue. "They really beat the shit out of these kids, for no other reason than them being black," he said. "I had Al Sharpton at the station house, but managed to arrest the perps within a few days. That calmed things down right away.

"I brought one guy into the station house half-naked," he continued. Earlier, knowing that he had his guy trapped inside his building, he had a uniformed cop ticket the guy's car. When he came running out, dressed as he was, Salpeter popped him.

Within a year-and-a-half Salpeter became a hostage negotiator and was promoted to detective second grade. His early success as a cop, he believed, was due to his intuition, his ability to stay calm amid bedlam, and his respect for people of all races and ethnicities.

"I can easily walk both sides of the line," he said. "Wherever I worked, all sides trusted me: blacks, Jews, Italians, even street mutts. I was good at making friends with the public, which greatly enhanced my career."

Petty politics, he said, got him transferred to the 104 Detective Squad in Ridgewood, Queens, a once predominantly German bastion that was becoming more and more Hispanic by the day back then.

There comes a case in many cops' careers that breaks their emotional back. That occurred not long after he was transferred to Ridgewood. To his horror, Salpeter solved a case in which young parents were awakened after drinking by the crying of their one-week-old child, who needed a diaper change. As Jason, the father, changed the diaper, the boy peed in his face. Jason instinctively threw the kid against the wall. The baby's skull was fractured. The dad panicked. He didn't know what to do with the body, so he started feeding it to the dog, whose name was Apollo.

"It took me nine hours to get Jason to confess, but he

would never tell me where he dumped the remainder of the body. And the fucking wife? She's watching Dad feed her little baby to the dog and doing nothing about it.

"It was the first time I ever cried on the job. I retired within a few weeks. That case took everything out of me emotionally."

Now it was years later and he was in business for himself doing private investigations. The defense attorney Bruce Barket was one of his top clients. Barket and Salpeter were also working together in the infamous Marty Tankleff case, in which they represented a man who was in prison for the brutal murder of his parents, murders Barket and Salpeter believed he did not commit.

Salpeter gave Lee Ann a call, and some familiar advice. Write things down, he said. Make lists. Everything she could remember. The phone numbers of everyone she ever knew. On April 29, 2002, Lee Ann sent Jay Salpeter a fax to help him with his investigation.

Salpeter was planning a trip to Florida to talk to the principals down there and Lee Ann offered some travel suggestions. For one thing, she said, he should talk to her dad before he made any plans. He knew how to get the best deals when it came to transportation and accommodations.

The rest of the fax consisted mostly of contact information. She told Salpeter how to get in touch with Paul's mother, who, Lee Ann was certain, would be more eager to slam her son than to defend him. Lee Ann gave the woman's phone number at her home in Amityville and the street she lived on. She didn't remember the house number.

She gave four phone numbers for Rocco, whom she referred to as Ralph. One number was his home number, two were cell phone numbers, and the fourth was either a home or a cell number, she wasn't sure.

She told the private detective that Salierno lived in an apartment building called The Fountains, which was on "Military Trail in Delray Beach." She gave a phone number for Richie Pollack, although she didn't use his last name, and she finished her message by saying she thought "Scott" worked at a club called Diamonds in West Palm Beach and that he worked out at a gym called Planet Fitness in Lantana.

Salpeter approved. The fax was fact-filled. Lee Ann had done a good job. Salpeter then sought out other sources that might have some dirt on Paul. He contacted people Paul ran with, both now and in the old days. Some were in jail. A couple of old girlfriends were contacted.

Salpeter needed to find out what the police knew, and how they had acquired the information. One of his first interviews was with Lee Ann's mom. On May 7, 2002, Salpeter went to Pat Armanini's home and interviewed her.

The interview was taped and later transcribed. Salpeter's questions were short and firm. Pat spoke in a steady and well-enunciated voice, with just a touch of Long Island in her accent. Pat told him that she was fifty-five years old and was eleven days shy of her fifty-sixth birthday. She said she had spoken to Detectives Anderson and Fandrey, from the Suffolk County homicide squad, about two weeks before.

The detectives had picked her up at her home and had taken her to the police station on Forest Hill at West Palm Beach, where they had interviewed her. The subject had been the murder of Alex Algeri.

Specifically, they were interested in finding out how she had met a person named Ralph Salierno. Pat had told them that sometime during the summer of 2000, her daughter, Lee Ann, had left her husband and had come down to Florida to live with her.

Her husband, whose name was Paul Riedel, had been doing drugs—smoking crack—and acting scary. When Paul wanted to be scary, he could be very scary. So the daughter had gotten an order of protection against him.

"She was staying at my home in Delray Beach. At that time Elizabeth Budroni, who I was living with, had been a member of the World Gym in Delray Beach," Pat said. Liz had met a guy whose name was Larry. Pat didn't know Larry's last name. "Liz was complaining to him that Lee Ann was being harassed by her husband and that she was concerned about her. And Larry had said to her, 'Well, I have a couple of guys that I know that can scare him and maybe he will stay away from her and leave her alone.' And he gave her a phone number."

Salpeter asked if Pat had known the name of the person Liz was told to contact. She said she didn't know full names. She just knew they were a couple of guys named Rocco and Richie. Pat pointed out that she now knew that Rocco was Ralph Salierno, but she didn't find that out until much later.

Rocco and Richie came over to Pat's house for a meeting, she said. Present were Pat, her friend Liz, and Lee Ann. Pat said, "And we proceeded to have a conversation. It consisted of what did we want from them.

"Liz's kind of New York expression was, we need somebody to scare him. He needs his head busted or his legs busted. Something very New York that she said which was what she said all the time. And they said OK.

"And my daughter, Lee Ann, immediately said, 'Wait a minute, I don't want him hurt.' And Liz turned around to Lee Ann and said, 'Well, if someone beats him up, he's gonna get hurt.' And Lee Ann said, 'You know what? Forget it. I can't do this. He's Nicholas's father and I don't want him hurt.'

"Richie turned around and said, 'Well, we could dump him in the Everglades'—or something to that effect, 'or just make him disappear.' My daughter put her hands up and said, 'Don't even go there. I don't want to discuss this. I don't want to have anything to do with this. This is not happening. There's no way.'

"That was the end of that conversation. It lasted maybe three or four minutes. After that, I said to them, something to the effect of, 'You know, he's working with the police in New York, on Long Island. He's so protected. He does drugs. Why can't they find this guy with drugs? Everybody gets caught doing it. He never gets caught doing anything. Can you find out if he's working with the police?'

"Richie said, because Ralph at this point said nothing this whole entire conversation, Richie said, 'Let me make a phone call. I know some people. Maybe they can find out if he's working with the cops.'

"They went outside. They were outside a couple of minutes. They came back inside and said, 'You know what, we will let you know. Right now we can't find out anything. We will let you know if these guys can tell us about what Paul is up to.'

"And that was it. We proceeded talking about where we were from and the Dolphin gym and what's this all about? We gave him a little mini-history that he [Paul] owned the Dolphin gym.

"They said, 'We know people in Westchester that own the Dolphin gym.' The conversation became very friendly and very informal. We were talking about mutual friends that Lee Ann had worked at the same club at Goldfingers, pretty much at the same time that Rocco worked there, but they had never met each other, and who knew this one, and who knew that one and it became a we're-all-from-Long-Island conversation.

"That was it. They got ready to leave and they said,

'Look, Lee Ann, if you ever need any help, give us a call. Let us know. Here is my number.' Richie said, 'We're opening a club. We'll give you a job. Come down here. Stay with your mother. You'll be safe and we'll get you a job. You will be fine.'

"That's how it was left. They left. Richie came back one other time to tell me they couldn't find out anything about Paul. They didn't know anything about any connection with the police. Whoever their connection was had nothing to tell them, and that was the end of that.

"And I think he called her a couple more times after that and said, 'Come on, Lee Ann. Come to Florida.' He had called me to ask how she was. I said, 'I'm worried about her. She's in New York.' Blah-blah-blah.

"And he said, 'Maybe I'll call her and tell her we got a job for her and to come back.' That was it. We didn't see them again until July seventh because my daughter had a miscarriage that morning and did not see Rocco again until sometime in September when he took Lee Ann for an interview at Cheetah's and got her a job, which she kept for like a day. One night. That was it. After that, they became friends. He started showing up once in a while and took her to meet a lawyer. He became her friend. They became closer and that was where the relationship started."

Now Salpeter knew the story Pat had told the police about the first meeting with Rocco and Richie and its aftermath. The investigator wanted to know what Pat had told the cops about a meeting with Rocco and his friend Mike "Big Balls" Fiaccabrino (pseudonym).

Big Balls was a guy who had worked for his dad. Some scam involving selling pay phones that was rendered obsolete by cell phones. Later he sold sprinklers, and after that he went into the "entertainment business." The business was called Show World Unlimited Inc. Again, Mike was in it with the old man, Frank Fiaccabrino.

Pat said, "The officers showed me a statement that Mike wrote regarding that visit, which I think they said was in October or November 2000, that Mike stated there was a conversation about killing Paul. It never happened. I told the officers it never happened.

"The conversation was based on a phone call that Ralph made to me and to Liz asking if she can get a job for Mike in Dillard's. Liz worked in Dillard's in the Boynton Beach Mall. He said he needed to get this kind of job. He needed to work.

"And Liz said, 'Well, come on over, we can talk about it. We'll see what he knows.' They did come to the house, Rocco and Mike. The entire conversation was regarding employment: what he had to do, who he had to talk to in the interview, that he had to get a suit and he had to take a class. It was either the next day or the day after that, that Liz had Rocco bring him over to Dillard's so he could buy a suit so he could go on an interview. They went to Dillard's, Ralph bought him a suit. During that week Mike went to the class. Liz referred him and he interviewed with the manager. I don't remember the guy's name."

"Did you give the detectives the fella's name?" Salpeter asked.

"No, I did not. I didn't remember at that time."

"If I gave you the name, would you recall the name? Mar—"

"Marty Zikes. Exactly. Marty Zikes interviewed Mike. Hired him. Mike went to the class, never showed up again. When Liz went to work, Marty said to her, 'Whatever happened to that guy?' Liz was totally mortified. Mike never showed up again and that was the end of Mike. Never saw him again.

"There was never any conversation with Rocco and Mike about Paul at all. Nothing ever—other than the fact that Lee Ann would talk to Ralph about what was happening with the divorce and separation.

"Nothing was ever discussed with regard to doing anything to anybody ever. The police wanted to know from me if in fact Ralph told me that he had anything to do with this [Alex's murder]. My answer was always 'Absolutely not.' Ralph never indicated for one minute that he had anything to do with it."

"So what you are saying is that Ralph never told you that he was involved in this murder."

"Never. He never told me anything like that at all," Pat emphasized.

"And about how many times did the police ask you the same question?"

"Oh, my God. They had to ask me in every conceivable way a hundred times. And I kept telling them that there was no way that I could tell them that I knew anything, because I did not."

"Did they ask you if you had any conversations with Ralph on the phone?"

"Yes."

"And can you tell me about that?"

"I had numerous conversations with Ralph on the phone. It's been over a year-and-a-half. He called to ask about my daughter. He called for my daughter. I spoke with him on the phone. He had dinner in my house. I thought he was a nice guy. I trusted him. I liked him. I never thought for one minute that he was anything other than a nice person.

"He took (Lee Ann's oldest son) Christopher fishing. He was a genuinely nice guy. The officers asked me about the phone conversations. I told them that I used to leave my cell phone with Lee Ann on occasion, so she always felt she had a connection when she would be with the baby, when she was by herself. And, yes, he called my cell phone. Did she use my cell phone when she was out? Absolutely. She had no reason not to."

Salpeter then moved the subject to Alex's murder and its immediate aftermath.

"Did your daughter call you to tell you about this?" the private investigator inquired.

"My daughter called me hysterical," Pat said. "Al was Nicholas's godfather."

"When she called you," Salpeter asked, "did you then try to contact Ralph?"

"I tried to contact him, because I was frightened for my daughter. Paul had been the target from what I was told by the racket squad and by his mother. He had been a target for a hit previously. A while, way before this."

"OK. So before the murder of his partner, you knew that Paul Riedel was a target of a hit?"

"Yes."

"And how do you know that?"

"His mother told me and the racket squad talked to me. Detective Grant. Paul's probation officer from when he was in prison. After he got out of prison, I spoke to them in Florida," Pat said.

More disturbing was the info that came from Paul's mother. "I spoke to Paul's mother when I was in New York with my daughter. She kept telling me to get my daughter out of New York, that her son was dangerous, that he was evil, that he was better off dead, that my daughter should be in Florida, where I could keep her safe. She cried. She told me stories about her son that I wish I'd never heard—things he had done and what kind of person he was and that I should save my daughter and save our grandson from him. [She told me to] take Lee Ann and Nicholas and bring them safely to Florida.

"The police, when I got her to Florida, told me the same thing. Detective Grant got me on the phone and said to me, 'Keep your daughter in Florida. It's dangerous for her in New York. Paul is a bad guy.'"

"And this was all prior to the murder?" Salpeter asked.

"All prior to the murder. Absolutely. So when Al was killed, my immediate thought and response was, 'Oh, my God, they are after Paul again. I have to get my daughter out of there and bring her here.'

"I told Lee Ann [the news about Al's death]. She was staying at my mother's [in Mineola, on Long Island]. She was hysterical. My ex-husband was hysterical. The entire family was terrified for her and for Nicholas. All I kept thinking was if they come after Paul, and Lee Ann's on the street and she's standing next to him, it's not going to matter."

"After the murder, did the detectives ask you what you thought?"

"Yes. That was my exact thought, that they were after Paul—and everybody seemed to think the same thing."

"After the murder, did you have a conversation with Rocco?"

"Yes. A couple of days later. I'm not sure if I got him on the phone or if he returned a phone call. One way or another we talked. I told him that Al was killed and that I was very upset and my daughter was frightened to death, and what should I do? And for him to help me.

"His response was, 'Oh God, I guess they got the wrong guy.' Which was what everybody said. So I really didn't think anything of it. He said, 'Look, just get Lee Ann to Florida. She can come and stay at my apartment. Don't worry about anything. If Paul comes after her, I'll take care of it. It's not a big deal. It will be fine. He won't know where to find her. She can hide out at my apartment.'"

"So what Rocco wanted was for Lee Ann to move in with him at this time?"

"Yeah."

"And did you ever have to answer questions? Did it ever cross your mind if Ralph did it?"

"Yes. I had spoken to Detective Anderson. He had called me from New York and had questioned me about what I thought and about Paul in a very casual conversation. It did cross my mind. Not that he did it—but that maybe he knew somebody up North that may have owed him a favor, something. I still don't believe that he could have possibly done something like that."

Salpeter asked if Pat remembered any of the questions she answered for police. She said that the questioning became repetitive, and that they were looking for a quote, some sort of admission from Ralph Salierno's mouth.

"They said to me over and over again, did he say things to me like 'I finally did it' or 'I got the wrong guy.' They asked me in a million ways. The only thing they wanted to know was if I could validate the fact that he did this. And I could not. No matter how they said it. There was no way I could answer that because I never had any knowledge of that ever," Pat said.

They also wanted to know if she had ever said anything to Salierno that was pertinent to the crime. "They asked me over and over again if I said to him, 'Get rid of this guy,' 'Do this for me,' or 'Can you do this?' They asked me if money was exchanged. The answers to all of those questions were totally negative. Absolutely no."

"Prior to giving your statement, did they read you your rights?"

She said they did, but not until they were well into the conversation. She said the conversation with the officers had lasted about eight hours, and that her rights were read to her at about the six-hour mark.

At the end of the conversation, she said, Detective Anderson handwrote a statement.

"When he was writing this statement, he was reading it back to me. I kept saying to him, 'That's not what I said.' And he said to me, 'Well, I'm just paraphrasing what you're saying. It doesn't matter. It's just so you recall it when you're in court.' And my answer was 'But I didn't say it like that and you are making it sound different.' I was very uncomfortable about that, but I was telling the truth."

"When Anderson was taking this statement, was anyone else in the room?"

"Yes, the other officer, Pat. I don't remember his last name, but his first name was Pat."

"And is there anything else that you recall?" the private investigator asked.

"Before they took this statement, they told me that either two people were going to be arrested or five people were going to be arrested. They told me that my daughter, Liz, and I were suspects—that we were suspected of conspiracy to commit murder." As she said this, baby Zachary could be heard crying and fussing in the background.

Pat said that she already had spoken to the officers for a few hours before she was told that she, her daughter, and her girlfriend were suspects. It was after she was told that she was a suspect that she was read her rights, and after that Detective Anderson began making the written statement.

Salpeter wanted to make absolutely sure that he had the order of events correct.

"You spoke to them for a couple of hours before they took a statement and before they gave you your rights?" he asked.

"Yeah," Pat replied. "They had me in the car in front of the house for at least an hour, an hour-and-a-half of sitting there talking and threatening me with the fact that I was suspected of this crime and told me that they knew in fact that he had committed the murder. They told me he did it with somebody that I never met called Scott. They showed me pictures and phone records."

"Do you recall whose phone records they showed you?"

"They showed me mine."

"Home phone?"

"Home phone, cell phone, every phone number I've ever had. My daughter's. Apparently, phone records that were Ralph's. I think my son's. My son Dave. My mother's. There was a huge binder filled with phone numbers. They were letting me know in certain terms that this was the way it was and they knew exactly what had happened."

"And what was that?"

"According to them, that we had asked them to kill Paul—which was a total lie. They said they knew that this was the way it was and that we had knowledge that he did it. Which we don't. Never did. But this is what they were trying to get from us."

"And before Mike came over to your house for help finding a job, had you ever met Mike before?"

"No."

"Could you describe him to me?"

"Medium height, medium build, dark hair. He was kind of a scruffy-looking guy," Pat said.

Salpeter asked if Pat remembered anything else about her long interview with the police and she said no.

"That's pretty much it. There may be odds and ends in there," she added. "They wanted to know what I knew. That wanted me to confirm that, in fact, Ralph committed the murder."

"And they also wanted to confirm that he called you after the murder, is that correct?"

"Right. And there was conversation. There was absolutely conversation afterward. There was no reason not to tell them that. That was the truth," Pat said.

Then she remembered something: "Oh, there is something else. Ralph visited after Zachary was born, and they wanted to know about that. They wanted to know what was said during those visits. They wanted to know if Ralph said anything to the effect of, 'If the police talk to you, don't say anything.' That conversation never happened."

Pat did recall that there was one incident that might have seemed suspicious on the face of it, but in truth meant something different.

"We have a friend named Brian that's with the sheriff's department," she said. "One time Brian, in his uniform, had dropped by to give Lee Ann an application, and the cop car was in the driveway when Ralph came to visit the baby. Ralph had his friend Mike with him. Ralph and Brian were introduced, but Ralph didn't seem happy. He was very abrupt with Brian. Brian only stayed for a couple of minutes and then left. With Brian gone, Lee Ann asked why Ralph had to be so rude, and he said he didn't like cops. Lee Ann said to him, 'But you didn't have to be like that.' I said, 'What's the matter with you?' Ralph said, 'Well, I walked in the door and I figured they were here to get me. I figured, what the hell? Come and get me.' We knew that Ralph was on probation and wasn't supposed to leave New York, so he was breaking probation each time he came to visit the baby."

Police knew Pat wasn't making it up about Ralph being on probation. He'd already discussed with them how he'd gotten popped on weapons charges. It was all bullshit, he'd said, a bunch of guys jumped him and he pulled a gun.

"We figured that was the reason he felt uncomfortable with a cop in the house," Pat continued. "Later, when the police talked to me, they tried to make it sound like Ralph was saying, 'Come and get me for the murder.'"

"The police knew about this already?"

"They knew that Ralph had been here, but they didn't know about this conversation. I still believe that Ralph was talking about breaking probation. The police were trying to use that conversation to mean that Ralph was telling me don't talk to anybody because of what happened in New York.

"Ralph had also said, 'Some guy up North is talking about me to the police.' And I told him, 'You need to go back to New York and not get yourself in trouble.' That was the end of the conversation. But the police were trying to make me think—or say, or believe—that the conversation was regarding Al's murder."

Pat told the private investigator that she had mentioned the meeting between Brian and Ralph, and its aftermath, both before Detective Anderson wrote her statement and while he was writing it. "I told them that the conversation happened and that, as far as I was concerned, it was regarding his breaking parole—that he was in Florida and needed to be in New York, and that was it."

"When you reviewed your written statement, did they put it down truthfully that you thought it was about parole?"

"I believe they did."

"Besides writing a statement, did they record your statement?"

"Not to my knowledge."

Salpeter informed Lee Ann's mother that he had no further questions and that ended the interview.

Chapter 22

Custody and Visitation Battle

In a deposition dated May 28, 2002, Paul Riedel used the murder of Alex Algeri and his wife's alleged involvement as a reason to improve his custody and visitation situation with his son, Nicholas.

With the help of his lawyer, Steven Constantino, Paul sought to have custody of the infant transferred to him, and an order restraining "the child's removal from the State of New York." The order would have to supercede the November 16, 2001, order of a Broward County, Florida, court that gave custody of Nicholas to Lee Ann while allowing Paul visitation rights.

In the section subtitled "Background of the Action," the statement said that Paul and Lee Ann were married on July 30, 1999. Nicholas was the only child born of that marriage, on February 24, 2000, at Good Samaritan Hospital, in West Islip, New York.

During mid-June 2000, Lee Ann "fled" New York State, the deposition stated, taking Nicholas with her, and went to live in Florida with her mother. Paul responded on August 25, 2000, with a simultaneous court order directing Lee Ann to return to New York and a divorce action.

On September 21, 2000, a New York judge determined that New York was Nicholas's home state and he could not be taken out of state without his father's consent. Lee Ann and Nicholas were represented by Donna England, a court-appointed law guardian.

The outcome of that hearing, according to the deposition, was that Nicholas had to live in New York State, and Paul had a right to visit his son regularly as long as he attended a Smart Parenting Program, which was monitored by the court. Lee Ann complied with the court order and moved to New York in early October 2000.

A section of Paul Riedel's deposition was entitled "The Conspiracy." It stated that, unbeknownst to him, in mid-July of 2000, prior to the respondent's return to New York for the evidentiary hearing conducted by Judge Kent, she, her mother, Patricia Armanini, and her mother's life partner, Elizabeth Budroni, had selected one Ralph Salierno and a third party whose name he didn't know to murder him.

The deposition stated that it was "apparent" that Elizabeth Budroni had met Salierno while working out at a gym in Florida and had arranged a meeting with Salierno, Lee Ann, Pat, and this unknown third party to plan Paul's murder.

Paul noted in his statement that he had been partners with the murder victim in a health club on Montauk Highway, in Amityville. He stated that Alex Algeri had been his best friend. He had been the best man at Paul and Lee Ann's wedding. He was the godfather of baby Nicholas. Paul noted that he and Al drove identical black Yukon sport utility vehicles. Both vehicles had identical stickers on their rear windows. Paul, however, worked the night shift, from 5:00 P.M. until 12:00 A.M. every night except Wednesday.

The only time Al worked the night shift was Wednesday nights, which was Paul's normal day off. Since they never worked a shift together, each parked his vehicle in the exact same spot—the parking space immediately behind their "headquarters" rear door.

Paul stated that the murder had taken place at approximately 7:30 P.M. on a Wednesday in January. There had been an aerobics class going on. There were always classes going on in the gym during the evening. Apparently, at the request of one of the patrons, Al exited the rear door of the gym to retrieve certain CDs from his vehicle to play over the gym's sound system during the aerobics session.

"Unbeknownst to Al, at the time he exited the gym to retrieve those CDs, the above-referenced Ralph Salierno and Scott Paget (who also resides in Florida) were waiting in the parking lot in a rented van they had driven from Florida to conduct the murder of me that had been planned by the respondent, her mother, and Elizabeth Budroni, for nearly one and a half years," Paul wrote. Al retrieved the CDs and turned to reenter the gym. Salierno and Paget exited the rented van, and shot him three times in the head and back. Alex, mortally wounded, had stumbled to the rear entrance of the gym, collapsed on the floor, and died shortly thereafter. That concluded Paul's description of his friend's murder.

The next section of Paul's deposition was called, "Respondent Returns to the State of Florida with My Consent." Paul wrote that, following the murder of Alex, he had allowed Lee Ann and Nicholas to return to Florida. Lee Ann had consulted with a Suffolk County detective, who had advised her that he believed there was a contract out for Paul's life. Paul wrote that Lee Ann had gotten herself into a hysterical state.

Lee Ann had told Paul again and again that she felt the murder had been a mistake. She felt the murderers were contract killers whose target actually had been Paul. She convinced Paul that the situation was not only dangerous to Paul, but to her and Nicholas as well. That was why she and the baby had to leave New York.

Lee Ann eventually had convinced Paul that those bullets were meant for him, so he agreed to go away with her. Paul wrote that he'd been completely unaware of her participation in the conspiracy to murder him. Paul wrote that he consented to her request to return to Florida with Nicholas, and even went so far as to accompany them on their journey and assist them in setting up house. Lee Ann, Paul wrote, established a formal residence in Florida in February 2001.

In the following section of the deposition, entitled "The Florida Action," Paul pointed out that Lee Ann was very quick to see a lawyer once she got out of New York State. The timing had been suspiciously perfect. As soon as she established the Florida residency requirement, she served Paul with divorce papers. It was then that Paul retained Steven Constantino as his divorce lawyer, and a custody order was issued in Florida that allowed Paul to have visitation rights. Paul got "extensive overnight visitation with Nicholas in New York for at least one full week of each month and four weeks over the summer."

The affidavit then commented on what a great father Paul was. He noted that his home was equipped with all of the facilities and toys a small boy would need. He wrote that he and his son had a fabulous relationship: "During our visits I bathe him, feed him, attend to his needs, and spend quality time with him. I am intimately familiar with Nicholas' needs, his schedule, and all items necessary to properly care for him." Paul noted that although he worked full-time managing two fitness centers, both of those facilities contained "certified child care nurseries." Each facility, he noted, was staffed by licensed child-care professionals. While Paul was working, it was always assured that Nicholas would get the care he needed.

The next section of Paul's statement was called "Murder Case Broken." Paul wrote that the Suffolk County Police Department homicide squad had conducted a long yet eventually successful investigation into the murder of his friend Alex. Paget and Salierno had been arrested on April 13, 2002—Paget in Florida and Salierno in Scarsdale, New York. The pair were charged with the murder of Alex Algeri. During their interrogations by law enforcement, both men had admitted to being present at the scene behind the gym at the time of the shooting, but each side maintained that the other had pulled the trigger.

At the time of Paul's statement, Paul noted, both Salierno and Paget had been indicted by a Suffolk County grand jury. Salierno was arraigned before Judge Louis Ohlig on April 23, 2002, and Paget was awaiting extradition proceedings in Dade County, Florida. That was outrageous enough, Paul wrote. But that wasn't the worst of it. Lee Ann had also continued to cuckold him. The affair between Lee Ann and Salierno proceeded until they bore a child together in January 2002.

The next section was called "Respondent's Involvement in the Murder Conspiracy." Paul noted that he had been told that Lee Ann, her mom, and Liz Budroni had all made sworn statements to police in which they admitted to recruiting Salierno and a third party (who had not yet been arrested). According to Paul's understanding, Salierno and his accomplice's job had been to travel from Florida to New York to commit a crime against him.

The unknown accomplice Paul mentioned would have been Richie Pollack, who backed out of the deal and, as it turned out, would never be arrested in connection with Alex's murder. Paul noted that because of confidentiality agreements over which he had no control, Paul actually had not read the sworn statements by Lee Ann, her mom, or Liz.

However, the statements had been described to Paul and it was Paul's belief that, in Lee Ann's sworn statement, she had said that she admitted to asking Salierno and his friend to come up North to commit a crime against him, but that she denied that the object of the exercise was to murder him.

Paul stated that it was clear that Lee Ann had committed acts following the solicitation of Salierno and his friend, that, according to New York law, made her guilty of conspiracy to commit murder and murder in the second degree. He noted that as he was writing, Lee Ann remained a free woman.

Paul insisted that he could prove that Lee Ann was involved in the murder. Neither her mother and Liz, nor Salierno and Paget, could have arranged the hit without Lee Ann's cooperation, Paul insisted.

There were several reasons for this. None of the others had ever been to the Amityville gym. In fact, they'd never been to Amityville. They had no idea how the building was laid out. They didn't know that there was a rear parking lot, that Paul drove a black Yukon SUV, or where he usually parked it when he was working. Only Lee Ann had that information.

Based on the fact that Lee Ann had talked him into allowing her to go to Florida under false pretenses, she had planned to have him killed, and only a quirk of fate had led to the tragedy of a wrong man being killed.

Despite the fact that Lee Ann hadn't yet been arrested by Suffolk County police, he wrote, it was Paul's understanding of the situation that both Lee Ann and her mother, Pat, were to be arrested.

When the day of his wife's and mother-in-law's arrest came, Paul noted, Nicholas was going to need a new full-time caretaker and he was the obvious choice. Other than her mother, Paul noted, Lee Ann had no other relatives in Florida. "Based upon the foregoing," Paul's statement said, "I am begging this Court to invoke the emergency provisions of the Uniform Child Custody Jurisdiction Act."

Paul wrote that if it weren't for the blunders of his assassins, he would be dead today and Nicholas would have had to grow up without a father. Instead, he would have been raised with Ralph Salierno as his father—Ralph Salierno, a murderer.

That fact alone, Paul explained, should be enough to win him custody of his son. The mother was a murderer, and the father isn't. As a custody issue, it was a simple matter of black and white.

The statement was signed by Paul Riedel, then stamped and signed by a Suffolk County notary public. Constantino, Paul's lawyer, simultaneously made his own deposition, which reiterated the facts and theories in Paul's statement, and was meant to reinforce Paul's allegation that an emergency existed and he should be granted custody of Nicholas immediately.

If the Suffolk County prosecutors were looking for a strategy by which they could use the testimony of Pat Armanini and Elizabeth Burdroni against Lee Ann—prosecuting neither two nor five for the murder, but rather three—Paul's divorce lawyer had just laid it out for them.

As a brief regarding how to prosecute a murder case, the statement had value. According to Judge Marion T. McNulty, of the Supreme Court of the State of New York, Suffolk County, it had considerably less value as a custody argument. Judge McNulty refused to sign the order that would have transferred custody of Nicholas to Paul Riedel based on the "emergency circumstances." In a handwritten addendum Judge McNulty said he refused to sign because Paul had failed to show that an emergency existed and therefore his court lacked jurisdiction over the matter.

Chapter 23

Ortolano's Written Statement

On June 26, 2002, Detective Anderson questioned Larry Ortolano at the World Gym in Delray Beach. He was the guy people said was Liz's first contact when the woman first sought help for Lee Ann's domestic woes.

Ortolano said he was forty-four years old, born September 7, 1957, in Manhasset, New York, on Long Island. He gave his current address in Lake Worth, Florida. He said he was self-employed and owned a business in Boynton Beach called Twins Consultants.

For a while he'd been a movie producer and his Worldview Pictures made a handful of movies. Nothing you ever heard of. He was a fairly well-to-do entrepreneur. Not only did he have a boat, like a lot of people in Florida, but he also kept it docked at the Palm Beach Yacht Club, which was pretty exclusive.

Ortolano said he'd known Randy Salierno since he was a kid, maybe sixteen years old, in Eastchester, New York, where they grew up. He relocated to Florida 3½ years before. Randy was already living in Florida. They worked out at the same gym, the World Gym in Delray.

Randy used to call him and hang out at his office. At one point Ortolano loaned $5,000 apiece to Randy and his friend Richie Pollack so they could start an after-hours club. Both signed notes acknowledging the loan.

A copy of the loan contract between the men revealed that for Ralph "Rocco" Salierno, the name Randy might have been more than an alternative nickname. It was an alias. The loan from Ortolano was made out to "Randall Salierno," and Ralph signed his name "Randy." There wasn't the slightest hint on the loan that the man's name was Ralph Salierno, who was on parole in New York State and wasn't even supposed to be in Florida.

The notes also revealed that the loan was made on July 7, 2000. Its terms were that "Mr. Salierno and Mr. Pollack agree to reimburse Mr. Ortolano in full 90 days from the date of original loan. Loan due in full 10/5/00."

Ortolano said Richie's father paid him back. Randy still owed him the money. Then the statement got down to business. He knew which events and conversations Detective Anderson was interested in.

"Just about two years ago," Ortolano said, "a woman I know from the gym named Liz Budroni approached me. She asked me to help her out with a problem. She said her niece was trying to get out of her marriage because her husband was abusive and a drug addict."

Liz told him that Paul was a tough guy and a lot of trouble—and he owned a gym on Long Island. Liz wanted to know if Larry could "have a talk with him or scare him." If not, did he know someone who could?

Liz gave Ortolano her phone number and asked him to give it to someone who could help. Ortolano said he'd give the number to a "guy named Randy," who would give her a call. And that's what he did. Sometime later, Randy and Richie were in his office and Randy mentioned that he had called Liz and they'd had their meeting.

Ortolano said that he knew that Randy subsequently began to go out with the niece, who was Lee Ann. He met Lee Ann once when she came over to his office with Randy. When Lee Ann wasn't around, Randy told him that Lee Ann had money, something about a house in Babylon.

"Around the end of March or early April," Ortolano wrote, "during the week, Randy showed up in the parking lot of the World Gym in Delray. He had been back in NY for some time. He was waiting in the parking lot for me and approached me quite abruptly. He asked me if anyone talked to me. I asked him what he was talking about. He kept asking me over and over until I became annoyed and asked him who is coming to talk to me. He said the Feds. I asked him why and he didn't say. He said that he was driving back to New York that night and that he had borrowed a friend's car to come down. That was the last time I saw him."

It was only a couple of weeks later that a friend from Eastchester called Ortolano and told him that Randy had been arrested for murder.

Chapter 24

"A Lot of Money When Paul's Dead"

On February 7, 2003, Michael Fiaccabrino gave a sworn written statement to the Suffolk County police. He began by stating his name, Michael Fiaccabrino, his age, thirty-three years, his birthday, June 7, 1969, in the Bronx, New York. He gave his current address and phone number in Loxahatchee, Florida.

Fiaccabrino wrote that he had known Ralph Salierno since the ninth grade. They went to school together in Eastchester, New York. Salierno, Fiaccabrino noted, was known both as Randy and Rocco.

Fiaccabrino said that he'd moved to Florida about thirteen years before. Randy moved down South about five years ago or so after that. He'd been hanging around with Randy for about 3½ years. Mostly they knew each other from the gym, the World Gym in Delray Beach, where they worked out together.

In the summer or fall of 2000, Randy met a New York

woman named Lee Ann Riedel. She frequently visited Florida because that was where her mother lived. Randy met Lee Ann via an introduction made by Larry Ortolano, a guy both Fiaccabrino and Salierno knew from the gym. Fiaccabrino wasn't sure who first approached Ortolano in the matter, but he did know that it was about putting a major beating on someone's husband, who he later found out was Lee Ann's husband, Paul Riedel.

Salierno and Fiaccabrino spoke at least five out of seven days a week. Those conversations took place either at the gym or going out socially. Salierno told Fiaccabrino that Ortolano made the introduction and that he (Salierno) and Richie Pollack met with Lee Ann and her mother, Pat Armanini, in Delray Beach.

"Randy said that Lee Ann would come into a lot of money when Paul's dead. He mentioned a number to me of $750,000 and that he and Lee Ann were going to buy a big house together in Florida and live together," Fiaccabrino stated. "Pat was also going to benefit from the money. I know that because I was present at the house on occasions when all three of them spoke of it. Once I heard Pat mention about getting money as a result of Paul's murder. Randy would tell her to shut the fuck up and call her a fucking leech."

Fiaccabrino had heard Lee Ann and Pat say to Salierno, "When are you going to New York?" He knew from the numerous prior conversations he'd been present for that they meant to kill Paul. He'd heard Lee Ann say she "couldn't live like this anymore" so that Salierno would go ahead with the murder.

In December 2000, Salierno asked Fiaccabrino to go to New York with him to kill Paul. Salierno offered Fiaccabrino $3,000 just to drive. Salierno assured Fiaccabrino that he wouldn't have to do anything violent. Salierno had said that he would take care of Paul.

Salierno wanted Fiaccabrino to rent a van for the trip up and put it on Fiaccabrino's credit card. Fiaccabrino claimed to have said, "Are you fucking crazy? I don't want any part of that."

Salierno then asked if he would be willing to just rent the van, and again Fiaccabrino said no. Salierno asked Fiaccabrino if he knew anyone who would be willing to rent the van and put the rental on that person's credit card. Salierno wanted it known that if Fiaccabrino did know of someone who was willing to provide this service, there would be an extra $500 in it for that individual. Again, Fiaccabrino said thank, but no thanks.

Then Salierno asked Fiaccabrino if he knew anyone from whom he could get a gun. Fiaccabrino said he didn't. Salierno eventually told Fiaccabrino that Mike Scauzillo, a friend from Westchester County, was going to hook him up with some New York Albanians, who were involved in crime. He'd be able to get a piece okay.

Fiaccabrino wrote that, in the middle of January, Salierno told him that he was able to get a van for the trip up to New York by someone in Larry Ortolano's company, or Larry. Fiaccabrino didn't recall the guy's name, only that it was an associate of Ortolano's.

Fiaccabrino had last worked out with Salierno at the gym early in that mid-January week. It was on that occasion that Salierno told him that he and Scott Paget were going to be the ones driving up to New York. Fiaccabrino noted that he knew Paget, also from working out together at the gym. He didn't recall the exact date that Salierno and Paget planned to make their trip up North—maybe it was in the middle of the week—but he was certain of the purpose of the job. The men were taking the van to New York to "take care of" Paul Riedel. The next contact Fiaccabrino had with Salierno was when he was driving back down to Florida from New

York. Salierno called Fiaccabrino's cell phone and said he was on his way back to Florida.

Fiaccabrino asked Salierno how everything went. Salierno said it went good. He started laughing and told Fiaccabrino about how Scott Paget was so nervous that he was a riot. Paget had been shaking and smoked four packs of cigarettes. Salierno and Fiaccabrino made arrangements to meet at the World Gym and work out together the following day.

"Before Randy got back I got a telephone call from Mike Scauzillo telling me to go to the Internet and look up a news article about the Dolphin Gym. I went to my father's house after Randy got back and retrieved a newspaper article about the murder. Randy was there with me and I handed it to him. When he read it he said holy shit and was freaking out over having killed the wrong person," Fiaccabrino stated.

According to Fiaccabrino, Salierno then told him the details of how the murder of Paul Riedel had gone down. Salierno had said that Paget drove and parked the van somewhere near the back entrance of Riedel's gym. Both Salierno and Paget were wearing zip-up hooded sweat-shirts. Salierno said that Paget stayed in the van and Salierno got out. Salierno said he walked up to the guy's vehicle to the passenger side as the guy was going into the glove box and called out "Paul." When the guy turned around, Salierno said he shot him three to five times.

Salierno said, "I think I hit him in the neck and chest— all in the upper body." Salierno said that the guy made noises like he was gasping for air. When Salierno and Paget were making their getaway, according to Salierno, they made a left onto the major thoroughfare with Paget still driving. Salierno said that the murder weapon had been a .38 caliber, and that Paget had thrown it into a body of water not far from the murder site.

Fiaccabrino stated that there came a time, after the

murder, when he was at Lee Ann's house with Lee Ann and Salierno, who were arguing. During the argument Lee Ann had said to Randy, "You stupid bastard, you killed the wrong guy." According to Fiaccabrino, Salierno had said, "I told you that you should have given me a better picture."

He also heard Lee Ann say that it was killing her that she had to go to the funeral of Alex and look his girl-friend, who was her friend, in the eye, knowing that she was responsible for Alex being dead.

Mike "Big Balls" Fiaccabrino said that Salierno had told him following the murder that he was worried. Salierno was afraid that Lee Ann was going to break down and spill the beans. That completed Fiaccabrino's statement. The homicide squad was thrilled. Here was testimony that Lee Ann wanted her husband dead and was willing to pay for it. Detective Anderson felt he was ready to make his third arrest.

Chapter 25

The Arrest of Lee Ann Riedel

Maybe Lee Ann had convinced herself that she wasn't *really* guilty of anything in this case. Maybe she said to herself that she had wanted to have Paul killed and Paul was alive. Alex had been killed, but that was an accident.

Maybe the fact that the outcome of her scheme had infuriated her, and eliminated from the earth a good friend, made her feel even less guilty. Surely, she had paid a big enough price already. She—like everyone else, if you got right down to it—had lost Alex.

But, to the rest of the world, it didn't matter how she felt about the victim. On March 17, 2003, uniformed officers knocked on Lee Ann's door. She refused to open the door. Subsequently Detective Anderson came to the door and Lee Ann let him in.

"How come you didn't open the door for the officers?" Anderson asked.

"I was afraid," she replied.

"I need to speak to you alone," the lead investigator said.

Lee Ann was given a few minutes to throw together a bag of essentials and then was taken by police car to the Boynton Beach police headquarters. She was charged with conspiracy to commit first-degree murder.

Lee Ann's primary concern seemed to be her children. Detective Anderson reassured her. "Don't worry, they will be taken care of," he said.

Lee Ann, by this time on a first-name basis with the lead investigator of Alex Algeri's murder, said, "Bob, even with everything that's gone on, I'm still a good mother."

Because police believed that Lee Ann had been a conspirator in a crime that had crossed state lines, an FBI file was opened for her. On March 20, 2003, she was assigned FBI No. 386551AC6. The file listed her as a white female born 12/29/1967. Her height was five-four, and her weight as 110. Brown eyes, brown hair. Her occupation was listed as "Laborer."

Her Social Security number was there, and the address of her mom's place in Boynton Beach where she'd been living. The "Arrest Agency" was listed as the Boynton Beach Police Department. It then listed her three charges, Murder 1st, Murder 2nd, and Conspiracy. The report concluded: "This is a multi-state offender record." A copy of her fingerprints was attached.

Lee Ann was taken up North and deposited in the Riverhead Jail. That meant she was considered a maximum-security case. She would have been transferred to Riverhead as her trial approached anyway. The location would give Lee Ann proximity to her trial.

The Riverhead law-and-order complex—formally known as the Alfred M. Cromarty Complex—was a grouping of connected buildings. Lee Ann could go from her jail cell to the courtroom and back again without having to go outside.

Chapter 26

The Second Pat Armanini Interview

On March 29, 2003, private investigator Jay Salpeter—working for Bruce Barket, legal counsel for Lee Ann Riedel—interviewed Pat Armanini, Lee Ann's mother, for the second time. The first interview had occurred May 7, 2002, only weeks after Pat had spoken to the SCPD for the first time. The 2003 interview, like the previous one, was recorded and transcribed.

In the first interview Salpeter had tried to learn all he could about what Pat had said to the police when they interviewed her, and the circumstances surrounding the statements she had provided law enforcement.

This time the subject was going to be Liz Budroni. Liz was a prosecution witness who was going to hurt Lee Ann, and Salpeter wanted to dig out any ulterior motives the woman might have for saying bad things about her ex-lover's daughter, the woman she used to refer to as her niece.

Salpeter would want to know: Was Liz a liar? Was she a braggart? Was she vindictive? Did she cheat? Were the stories about her being Mobbed-up true? Anything that might sully her words when she spoke in court—*that* was what Salpeter was after.

In the first interview Pat had been strong and steady when speaking to the private eye. This time she seemed far less sure of herself. She spoke, at first at least, in a low, perhaps tired, voice. As the interview progressed, her self-assurance seemed to improve, as did the volume of her speech.

Another difference between the two interviews was the location. The first interview had been conducted in Pat's home in Florida. This time Lee Ann's mother was sitting in Salpeter's office in Great Neck, Long Island.

Salpeter gave the date. He noted that he was in his office on a major thoroughfare through the town of Great Neck. They were just out past the Queens border in the northernmost section of Nassau County.

He introduced himself and said he was a licensed private investigator in the state of New York. For identification purposes he had her state her name and her date of her birth. She said, "Patricia Armanini, 5/18/46."

Salpeter told her that they were there to discuss her knowledge of Elizabeth Budroni. He wanted to know where and when they met. "I met Elizabeth Budroni at a bowling alley in New York. That was in"—she had to think for a second—"in 1992, approximately."

Salpeter asked her to be more specific about where in New York they had met. Pat said, "In Long Island." She said that when they met, Liz was living in Medford, New York, in Suffolk County. She gave the specific street address.

At that time, Pat told the detective, "Liz lived with her two children Louis and Edie, and her girlfriend. Louis was twenty-one at the time, and Edie was twenty-five or twenty-six."

Liz had another daughter, Phyllis, who also lived nearby.

Today, Pat said, Edie was married with a kid, but she couldn't remember Edie's married name. Salpeter said that he was going to write down all of the things she couldn't remember, and then she could get back to him when she recalled that information.

Pat said that she was living in Mineola, New York, with her mother at the time she met Liz. Salpeter wanted to know how Pat and Liz's relationship grew.

Pat said, "Elizabeth and I both belong to the same bowling league. She invited me to dinner. We started seeing each other and it developed into a relationship, where six months later I moved in with her."

When Pat moved in with Liz, the other woman in Liz's house moved out. She estimated that she moved in with Liz during January 1992—approximately. She was more certain of the month than the year.

Pat recalled that Liz worked as a bakery manager at a Waldbaum's when they met. She couldn't be sure what town it was in, but she remembered that it was on Sunrise Highway. Pat told Salpeter that Liz grew up in Little Italy, on Mulberry Street.

He asked her if Liz had ever lived in Queens. Pat said she didn't know. The investigator wanted to know if it was true she lived next door to Gotti. Pat said it was across the street from Gotti, but, yeah, it was true.

"What did Liz Budroni's father do for a living?" Salpeter asked.

"She told me her father ran numbers. Her brother ran numbers also," she said.

The brother, Pat recalled, had died. It was a heart attack or a stroke. He was so young. When she and Liz were together, he was fortyish. Pat remembered the name of Liz's brother, her husband, and her mother, but couldn't come up with the name of Liz's father. That was because he'd been dead for a while, dead long before she met Liz.

At the time she and Liz got together, Pat said, "I was working at Empire Blue Cross and Blue Shield."

Salpeter shifted gears and asked if Budroni had any bad habits that made her hard to live with. "Mega habits," he called them.

Pat said, "No drinking. No drugs. She was stable. Paid her bills. Had kids. Owned her own home." She gave the investigator Liz's birth date: 5/29/40. Salpeter wanted to know if she remembered Liz's Social Security number and Pat said no. "But I can find it," she added.

Salpeter asked what Liz's husband did for a living. "Not much," Pat replied. "According to Liz, he didn't really work." She'd met him and he'd seemed like a nice enough guy. He'd since remarried. Had a son. Living in Manhattan. She didn't know his phone number. Salpeter asked if the husband was a *schlep* (Yiddish for a lazy person). She said not when he was younger. It was only when he got older that he turned into a *schlep*, according to Liz.

"He didn't work, so I'm sure he did whatever they do," Pat said.

"Are you saying you think Liz's husband was connected?" Salpeter asked. She said yes and he asked, why? She answered, "He didn't do anything else. And somebody was making money somewhere. And because they all hung out on the streets."

Every once in a while the husband went into Manhattan and did whatever he did. Came back with money. Always paid the bills. Absolutely connected. Maybe he was a runner. Pat didn't know for sure.

Pat said Liz was married to the guy for twenty-five, twenty-six years and she didn't know why they got divorced. Maybe they didn't socialize enough with each other, Pat guessed.

Getting back to Liz, Pat said she had a "good heart. Good person. Good intentions. But she had a big mouth."

"What do you mean by that?"

"She stretches the truth big-time," Pat said. "And she is a tremendous braggart. She was always, like, ready to be tough."

Pat said it was difficult to get Liz to tell the truth—not just because she was a good liar, but because she came to believe what she said. Salpeter asked if Liz was "into the Mob." Pat said she thought it was "the coolest thing ever."

Pat said that knowing Gotti was Liz's claim to fame. She added, "That she met Gotti and she used to hang out in the clubs. Her husband and she used to go to the . . . I want to say the Copa. And they used to go into the back room through the kitchen. Just like in the movies. Her favorite movie was *The Godfather*."

Salpeter asked who owned the house in Medford. Pat said that it had been a gift to Liz from her father, so she kept the house after she divorced her husband. The investigator wanted to know how long after Liz's husband moved out did the new girlfriend move in.

"There were two lesbians that lived next door to her, which is where she discovered her sexuality. And she was having an affair with both of them, while her husband was still living there. Um . . . there were two other people and two other women in her life after her husband left."

"All women?"

"Yeah, four women."

Not long after Liz and Pat got together, they decided to head to the South. Pat recalled, "We decided to move to Florida because the snowstorms were really bad and we'd really had it. We had this one big happy family life. My four kids, her three kids. Grandchildren. Everybody lived in the area. At Christmas there was twenty-five people at the house. It was normal. It got to where Liz fell a couple of times on the ice and we got tired. So we said let's go to Florida on vacation. We decided to move to Florida."

The house had been mostly paid for, although there might have been a second mortgage, and it was in Liz's name. So, when she sold the house, Liz got to keep all the money.

"I don't remember what we got for the house. I remember that she had something like thirty-five thousand that we had to put into a house in Florida, so she wouldn't have to pay taxes on it. So, it was like thirty cash there," Pat said.

Pat and Liz moved to West Palm Beach. At first they rented a place. They stayed in West Palm for maybe a year. Then they bought a house in Delray Beach. Salpeter asked and was given the address of their new home.

The investigator asked what kind of work the women got when they first arrived in Florida. Pat said it took her a while but she got a job as a recruiter for an employment agency, working for commission.

Liz got work more quickly, a job at Publix grocery store, in the bakery. She didn't have that job long, though. No benefits. She got another job as a salesclerk at a little smoke shop in the mall called Smoker's Gallery. She stayed there for six years. There she got benefits.

By the time Liz finished up there, she had been promoted to store manager. Salpeter was familiar with that mall, and they agreed that it was a horrible mall. Given a choice, they both would rather shop just about anyplace else.

Despite the horror of the mall, Pat also got a job there, working part-time there and part-time at Barneys.

About that time they moved from West Palm to Delray Beach. They split the house.

"She paid for half of it," Pat remembered. "I got a settlement; I had worked for [an electronics store]. I had gotten a settlement from them for sexual harassment. And then they fired me. And I paid her back for my half of the house, which was fifteen thousand."

Salpeter wanted to know how Liz and Pat were getting along these days and Pat said fine. She said Liz was the same as ever, same personality.

"Did you ever meet any friends down there?" the investigator asked.

"Actually, when we started out down in Florida, we knew all guys. We joined a bowling league. A gay bowling league. And we met a lot of guys. And they were really cool. They were a lot younger than us. But they were really fun and that was our circle of friends.

"It was mostly guys. The women in that bowling league were young and tough with the key chains hanging. And we were just not like that. We didn't really hang out with the women. We hung out with these guys."

Liz worked out at the Globe on Atlantic Avenue, in Delray Beach. It was around this time, Pat said, there began to be stress on her relationship with Liz. That was because one of Liz's daughters had just suffered a failed relationship and moved in with them.

That addition of Liz's daughter into the household created a stressful situation—one that involved Liz more than Pat. It wasn't long before there was trouble between Liz and Pat. But what could you do? The daughter, who was a grown woman, needed a place to stay.

Pat discussed Liz's relationship with her children: "She has a tremendous amount of control over her children. She's a control freak. And she had a tremendous amount of control over their behavior and the fact that they are totally engrossed in her happiness. Her oldest daughter is married. Had a child. Lives in New York. But it's almost like they would stand on their heads for this woman."

She continued: "I would say to her: Why are they so engrossed in your future? Your happiness? Why do you act so helpless around them? As though you need to be taken care of. You're a sixty-year-old woman. What's your problem?

"So I, on the other hand, would say to my kids, 'I'm fine. Go do your thing. Whatever makes you happy.' She would have input. You know this isn't the right thing. You know your boyfriend is a bum to Edie. She was with some guy that she really cared about. But he really wasn't that great. And he was Armenian. And Edie is the type of person, whoever she's with, that's who she turns into. So when she's with someone who smokes, she smokes. If they don't smoke, she doesn't smoke. If they do yoga, she does yoga. She dates a vegetarian, she becomes a vegetarian. She's a little bit meek. So she becomes her environment.

"And Liz would say to her, 'Why do you put up with that stuff?' And, 'I'm going to tell him what I think.' And she would say something to her kids and they would just do exactly what their mother said.

"She also felt as though her space was being invaded. Because it was. Living there with Christopher—who was a teenager," Pat said, referring to Lee Ann's oldest son, the one she had had when she was a teenager.

About her grandsons, Pat said, "Christopher was a nightmare. Nicholas was an infant. Liz loved Nicholas. But Christopher really drove her crazy. So she used to get mad at Lee Ann because of the crowded house."

Too many people crammed into one home wasn't the only reason that the orderliness of Liz's world had been disrupted, apparently. Pat said, "Lee Ann is not the neatest person in the world. And baby stuff was everywhere. And Christopher was disrespectful to his mother. And Lee Ann wouldn't really discipline him. Liz thought he should be disciplined. So that's where it started. With Christopher's disrespect. And blah-blah-blah."

According to Pat, Liz became more upset when Lee Ann left Paul and also came down to Florida to live with them, bringing Nicholas with her. That was June 2000, about four months after Nicholas was born. About seven months before the murder.

There weren't enough bedrooms in the first place and one of the bedrooms now held a crib and had been converted into a nursery. Liz felt that the house was getting crowded, and that she didn't have any privacy anymore.

Pat said that Liz and Lee Ann never had words. *Never, never.* But the mess got to Liz. Liz was a neat freak, and because the place was overcrowded, there was always a mess. Noise. Chaos. Liz enjoyed a little quiet every now and again, and she wasn't getting any in her own home.

So that was part of the problem, but the rest was Edie and Leo who came to live with them. Edie was Liz's daughter, and Leo was her new son-in-law. Luckily, they never all lived there at once. By the time Lee Ann showed up with the baby, Edie and Leo had already found an apartment.

Pat remembered that it was in August 2000 that Lee Ann was served with court papers from Paul. A judge was ordering her to return to New York.

Pat said, "She had to be back to New York, September twelfth, fourteenth, whatever it was, with the baby. In the meantime, before this happened, this is when Paul was calling and threatening her: 'I'm coming down there. I'm taking the baby.' Paul is calling my house. He's harassing everybody. Liz, me, Lee Ann. Threatening us by taking the baby.

"When she left New York, that's where this whole box-of-money thing comes up," Pat said, referring to the money Lee Ann took from Paul when they initially separated.

"The box of money was in Florida?" Salpeter asked.

"She took the box," Pat said. "But she never opened it. Nothing."

"Was the box in the house?" Salpeter asked.

"Yes, it was," Pat admitted.

Pat said that Paul always screamed about the baby, but it wasn't really the baby he wanted.

"He wanted his money," she said. "He was threatening everybody. He was a lunatic. OK. And she goes back to New York. But in this time frame here is when Liz was at the gym, and I remember his name. It's Larry. Oh, my God. She meets this guy Larry at the gym and she used to refer to Lee Ann as her niece. She tells me, 'I'm telling Larry about Lee Ann, and I'm saying this guy is threatening to come down here and he's going to take the baby.' And if you're really bad, she's really upset and it turns out now that in this little period of time, Lee Ann is pregnant."

"With Rocco's child?"

"This is not Rocco's child. This is Paul's child. She didn't even know Rocco."

"She was going to lose—"

"She lost that baby, the day she met Richie and Rocco."

"Which was July."

"Right. July. This works in my head. OK. She meets Larry and she is complaining how bad she feels about Lee Ann's problems. And she said, you know, we don't know anybody.

"And Larry, according to her, said, 'You know, if he comes down here and threatens you guys, I have a couple of friends. They're big guys and at least you won't feel like she's alone, and if you need to call somebody for help, if he really gets abusive and he comes down because he's threatening to come down here and kill everybody, then at least they will be there for her.'

"OK. Nothing about anything at all except, here is a phone number to Liz. You want to call this guy Rich. It happens to be Rich's phone number. We didn't know anything about these guys, OK.

"So Liz comes home and goes, 'I got a phone number here. Larry said, you know if he really is threatening you, and Paul comes down here, and you know Paul's down here. You call these guys; in fact, call these . . . we can call these guys and meet them just so they know what's going on. And God forbid you need them.'

"Days went by. Paul is threatening with the telephone and Liz says call these guys and let's just meet them just in case, God forbid anything. You know. He's threatening to come in the middle of the night. Break the windows. Take the baby. OK. We call this guy Richie."

"Who is we?"

"I don't know who made the initial phone call. It was a cell number. Probably me. Because Lee Ann never made phone calls. We left a message on the machine."

"Lee Ann never called?"

"Lee Ann never called. Never called. It was either Liz or I. I couldn't swear to it one way or the other. I called. He called back, 'This is Richie.' OK. Um . . . I think it was Liz that talked to him on the phone.

"Richie says, 'We'll come over and meet you. You can tell us what's going on. We don't want to talk about stuff on the telephone.' You know, whatever these guys are like. PS, they show up on the day. They made an appointment to come in a couple of days, whatever it was, and they show up on the day."

"The day Lee Ann has a miscarriage?"

"In the morning she has the miscarriage. In the afternoon they show up. Like, hours later, in walks Richie and Rocco."

"She would have been home the same day?" the investigator inquired.

"She didn't go to the hospital," Pat replied.

"She miscarried in the house?"

"She miscarried at home."

"Did she see a doctor?"

"She saw Dr. Briggs," Pat answered.

"Was she on medication that day?"

It was an important question. If Lee Ann had been sedated at the time of the initial meeting, at which hurting Paul was discussed, her words might have diminished meaning in the minds of a jury.

"I can't remember. I'll get her records from Dr. Briggs. She was very weak. She was very white. She had just lost a baby. She was bleeding. I don't remember exactly how that scenario went.

"We were sitting at the table and they said to her, 'Are you OK?'

"And she said, 'Well, actually, I just had a miscarriage this morning.'

"And that's why the date is sticking in my brain," Pat said. "Because I would have not remembered otherwise."

"July fourth?"

"Right. Now that you mention it, yes. The doctor had told her it was because of stress. And that's when she was arguing with Paul."

"So the guys come over the house now."

"The guys come over the house and we sit down and they're like, 'OK, what can we do to help you?' Liz did most of the talking. Liz was saying like: 'Her husband. He's a dirtbag and he's really abusive and he's threatening to come and take the baby.'

"The guy said, 'What do you want us to do?'

"And Liz's mouth—because she's Mulberry Street, and everything, she says to 'bust them up' and 'break their legs'—she said, 'Well, can't you break his legs?'

"And Lee Ann went, 'Wait a minute. I don't want him hurt.'"

Pat confirmed that it was Larry who gave his number when Liz was asking at the gym if anyone knew anything about taking care of certain kinds of problems. Today, Pat said, Lee Ann hadn't seen Larry in years. And Pat never met Larry. Larry gave the number, but it was Richie and Rocco who showed up at the house.

"Richie and Rocco sat down, and if I tell you that Rocco said one sentence the whole time he was there, that was all that he ever said. Richie did all the talking. Then Liz said. 'Well, you know, if he comes here, you can break his legs.'

"Lee Ann said, 'I don't want him hurt. I can't live with that kind of guilt. He's Nicholas's father. I just don't want him to take my son. I feel like I need a friend in Florida because we're all alone here.'

"This whole entire conversation might have been five minutes. That's all it was. Lee Ann said, 'Well, he owns the Dolphin gyms up in New York. Now these guys (Richie and Rocco) are from New York. Richie did all the talking. Rocco said nothing.

"So Richie said, 'I know some guys.' And he turned around and said, 'You know we can just make him disappear.'

"My daughter and I looked at each other, looked at them, and I went, 'Wait a minute. I don't even want to hear that stuff in my house. Do not even say these words to me. This is Nicholas's father. Regardless of what kind of a dirtbag he is, I could never do that. Not because I care about Paul.'"

Salpeter informed Lee Ann's mother that he considered Richie a very important witness. He wanted to get in touch with Richie. Pat didn't know how to get in touch, but she'd see what she could do.

Salpeter asked if she knew if police had contacted

Richie. Pat didn't know. She knew about Rocco, but she didn't know regarding Richie. Salpeter again told Pat that Richie was a "valuable witness." He later called him a "critical" witness.

Pat said, "I heard from Rocco that Richie kind of disappeared. He went off wherever he went. They had a falling-out and Richie took off." Then she told the investigator, "You need to find Richie."

Salpeter returned to the relationship between Pat and Liz. Bruce Barket's theory—that the lies about Lee Ann started soon after Liz and Pat broke up—was never far from the surface of Salpeter's mind.

Salpeter asked Pat to return to the summer of 2000. Lee Ann and the baby had moved in and there was friction with Liz, who felt that the orderliness of her universe had been disturbed and that she wasn't getting enough privacy.

After a deep sigh Pat said, "Lee Ann and the baby returned to New York in September. Christopher stayed with me."

Because of Christopher, the relationship between Liz and Pat remained strained. He'd been thirteen at the time and, like many adolescents, Chris was hellish to have around.

"I had to get him to the bus stop at six in the morning," Pat explained. "It was very difficult. And it interfered with two older women living by themselves, and now all of a sudden, you have a teenager. It was very hard.

"Now my son Jamie had moved to Florida. He was living in Florida—on his own, not with us—and he had been living in Florida through most of this. He was helping with Chris."

Infidelity was not a factor. Pat wanted to make that clear. With Pat and Liz it was never a who's-doing-who problem. Pat reiterated that it was Liz's problems with Pat's family that caused the stress in their relationship.

Salpeter asked point-blank if Liz had been seeing another woman. Pat said, "No." Despite the fact that they were sexually faithful to one another, however, Pat said that her relationship with Liz deteriorated even more after Al was murdered.

Salpeter asked if Pat had gone into business with Liz. Pat said yes, they owned and operated a nail salon together. The business, Pat offered, "put a lot between us."

The salon, Pat explained, was called Nail Spa Plus and was located on Northlake Boulevard, in Pine Ridge Gardens. Pat said she didn't remember the date that they opened their business. She would have to look up the "corporate papers." But she did remember one thing: the salon only remained open for six months before, as Pat put it, "we had to dump it."

Pat and Liz had invested everything they had, about $20,000 that they had built up through playing the stock market. It was tough being lovers and business partners, especially when things went wrong.

"We lost everything and Liz blamed me," Pat said. "It was my dream—it was my dream to have a nail salon business, because I was a nail tech. And it was our money."

This had all occurred long before Al's murder, long before Lee Ann moved in with the baby. "Liz is the kind of person, so you know, that resents something and holds on to it until she goes to her grave," Pat added.

Salpeter wanted to know why the salon had gone out of business so rapidly and Pat began to kvetch about the overhead. The other nail salons all employed Asian girls, who worked "twenty-four hours a day for zero."

Not everyone wanted a Chinese girl working on their nails, Pat had noticed. There was a lot of prejudice. Pat's idea was to have a salon with white girls working for snooty women who would rather have a white girl than an Asian girl work on them.

"You could charge more money," Salpeter said.

"Hello," Pat responded.

Trouble was, the white girls who did nails wanted an arm and a leg, and they didn't want to work too hard, either.

"These girls wanted fifteen minutes in between appointments so they can do their things. They were prima donnas," Pat said, summing it up. "And right after we went into the contract, the landlord raised the rent five hundred a month immediately. So the whole thing was a nightmare."

All the money was gone. They were in debt. Pat and Liz had to file for bankruptcy.

"When did you and Liz finally break up?" the investigator inquired.

"January 2002. Last year. It's been a year she's gone. She left me."

"Why did she leave you?"

"I don't know. We were fighting a lot." Pat tried to nail down the circumstances of their separations, but she found the details hazy. "She actually left and I don't know what the date was. Lee Ann was with me. No. Lee Ann was living at the Yacht Club and she left me before Christmas. Then she came back. Her daughter Phyllis was visiting and . . ." Pat's energy fizzled midsentence.

"What were the fights about?"

"Everything. Garbage. Nothing specific."

"You both turned each other off?"

"Turned totally off," Pat said. "Cold. What started the fighting was that during this time that Liz left, Paul . . . This was when Alex was killed. OK. Paul sent Lee Ann down to Florida because he thought the Mob was after him and he was afraid. In complete contrast to the story that he says Lee Ann wanted to go to Florida. He sent Lee

Ann to Florida. He started visiting; every other weekend he would fly down. He moved down his Jet Ski. He wanted to buy a house. They looked at houses."

"But why did you and Liz break up?" Salpeter asked, trying to get back to what he believed was the crux of the matter.

"Because Leo, this is very complicated . . . Leo is seeing Edie, and on Easter Sunday, Leo and Edie, Lee Ann, the kids, and Paul came to my house for dinner. Leo met Paul. Leo is a bragger, Paul is a bragger. They had an immediate connection. I have money. You have money. And Paul is telling me in the back, 'This guy is full of shit.' And Leo is telling me, 'This guy is full of shit.' But they were full of shit to each other. So Leo takes Paul and takes him to his office. 'I'm going to show you my office. You come down here and you live. I'll introduce you.' Bolognese (pseudonym) is Leo's last name."

"Leo Bolognese?"

"Yes. And his family. Very wealthy. Bolognese Realty are his relatives. But his family is Bolognese Construction in Canada."

Salpeter made sure he was spelling the name right. Pat spelled it for him without having to think very hard.

"So Edie married rich?"

"'Boo-coo' bucks. Millions. You can't count the millions. But he's got less class than anyone I ever met. Anyway, so Leo takes Paul and they go for a ride and they're doing their thing."

"Leo's really not bullshitting. Leo's—"

"Leo's loaded, but he's a jerk," Pat said. "Good businessman, not a nice guy. So he takes Paul off and they disappear for an hour or two and then they come back and he's got all kind of stuff with real estate in it. And going into business in Florida 'cause Paul is telling him, 'I'm moving to Florida with my wife and my kids.' And they're going to buy a house. During this period of time Edie and Paul came over. Edie and Leo came over for dinner after that Easter Sunday and Leo was talking to me like, 'What's the matter?' He said, 'What's up with . . . is your daughter seeing somebody?' She's not seeing anybody. She's got friends. One of the guys brought her to see a lawyer in the beginning. And she knows this guy Rocco and they tried to get her a job and help her out, and whatever.

"Leo calls Paul. And says to Paul, 'You know, if I were you, I would kind of watch it. Your wife has this friend Rocco.' And that's when all the private investigating bullshit started," Pat said.

According to Pat, Paul thought that Rocco was Lee Ann's boyfriend even before anything romantic actually happened between Lee Ann and Rocco. They were still just friends when Leo started trouble.

"Paul's already jealous and in fact at that time all Rocco did was get Lee Ann a job. She worked one day at this club. Then Rocco took Lee Ann to see a lawyer. And at that time they were just friends. Leo is the one who started all this stuff. This stupid Leo, what is he saying this to Paul for? And why is he getting him all wilded up. They're just friends and now he's starting this whole bunch of crap.

"So Liz and I are fighting. Leo's on the phone saying, 'I didn't say anything to him.' Paul's on the other line. We got conference calls going. Back and forth and fighting and Paul is saying, 'He said this and . . . go ask Leo.'"

"Did Paul hire a private investigator?"

"Yes."

"He had her watched?"

"Yes. And all he had was a picture of her getting into Rocco's car. That's it. So he knew who Rocco was."

Shifting gears back to his favorite subject, the private investigator queried, "Why would Liz want to hurt you?"

This was in reference to Liz's statements that Lee Ann was the one who paid to have her husband killed.

"I don't know that she would look to hurt me. She's dumb. And she doesn't think before she speaks. And she says things—"

"When the police came down, were you both together?"

"No. Oh no. They nailed her by herself."

"How did they nail her? Who gave the first statement when the police came down about this meeting? They wanted to talk to Lee Ann. I mean Lee Ann would be the first person."

"Well, they showed up at Lee Ann's house. I was not actually living there. OK. I had moved out. She moved into my house after all this crap. And moved in after Liz left. And she bought Liz out after they settled on a house. She bought Liz out and then there was resentment on Lee Ann's part, because she didn't really want the house and Liz really convinced her that this is what she needed to do. So she moved in with me into the house and I couldn't take the pressure with Christopher and the fighting. And all that bullshit.

"So I moved and rented a room from a friend of a friend. I was on my way to work. I was working at Starbucks. I pulled into the driveway. It was like a movie. Six cars came around me. (Detective) Bob Anderson—who I didn't know then, I only spoke to him on the phone—comes out.

"They're flashing badges and I'm sitting there in my uniform, saying what's happening here. They wanted to question me. I said, 'Where's my daughter?' I went into the house and there's my daughter in her pajamas at twelve o'clock. Babies running around."

Pat said that when the detectives came, they spoke to Lee Ann privately for hours.

"Well, the first thing they said to her, according to her, was whose baby was it? She didn't know why they were asking that. There was nothing to hide. If she had something to hide, she wouldn't have had her baby, for God's sake.

"Anyway, they take me. They want to question me. You know when you have nothing to hide. You don't say, 'I don't want to talk to you.' So I went with them. Eight hours."

Pat said that she and Liz also gave statements, and that all three statements were consistent with one another.

"But how did the police find Liz?" Salpeter asked. "Did you or maybe Lee Ann give the police Liz's address?"

"Nobody gave nothing to nobody," Pat said. "The police already knew Liz's address."

Salpeter pressed the matter: "But how did they know about Liz? If they didn't have a statement already. They came to Florida specifically because of Lee Ann's association with Paul."

"I guess" was all she would say.

They established that Rocco was already under arrest when the police came down to Florida to question the women. Pat remembered looking at a statement Rocco had made, so it must have been after his arrest.

"Scott wasn't at the initial meeting?" Salpeter asked, referring to Paget.

"I never met Scott, ever," Lee Ann's mom reminded the investigator.

Salpeter then returned to how the police knew about Liz when they called on Pat and Lee Ann following Rocco's arrest. Pat said that the police knew about Liz long before that. They knew about her when they called the first time, not long after Al was shot.

"Did the police know about the meeting when they called after Al was shot?"

"No."

"They didn't know about the meeting until after Rocco was arrested?"

"I suppose."

"Or they knew about the meeting from Lee Ann."

"Possibly."

Salpeter went over the order in which the women had been interviewed by the police following Rocco's arrest. Pat said that Lee Ann had been interviewed first, then Pat, then Liz. Pat did not call Liz ahead of time to warn that the cops were coming. She allowed it to be a surprise.

"The police knew where she lived. They knew who she was living with. And they went and got her."

"She was with someone else now?"

"Yeah."

"Is she still with that person?"

"Yes."

Salpeter wanted to know how long after Liz left Pat did she move in with her new girlfriend. Pat said that it wasn't very long at all, something like two months. Pat admitted that Liz knew her new girlfriend before she and Liz had broken up. She knew because they had both known her.

"So maybe they were doing something while you were together," the private investigator suggested.

Pat said, "I don't believe so, because everyone saw the initial interaction between the two of them and it was very obvious. Liz left me and then she came back for a month. Couldn't go back. We separated pretty amicably. She moved in with someone else. Then she rented a room and she was alone. I used to run into her." Only then did she get together with the new girlfriend, Pat suggested.

Salpeter wanted to know if Pat had ever discussed with Liz her statement to the police. Pat said that they had, and they had said basically the same thing, which was basically the same thing that Lee Ann had said as well.

"The truth is the truth is the truth," Pat said.

Salpeter wanted to talk to Liz, find out why she had changed her statement, why she had turned on Lee Ann. Salpeter said he'd be speaking to Liz.

About her former lover, Pat said, "The woman is honest and I know her heart. I know she feels bad. She knows Lee Ann. She knows her personality. She knows about Paul."

Pat said that although she had seen Liz the previous Sunday, they didn't really talk to each other much anymore, hardly ever calling each other on the phone. Salpeter urged Pat to call Liz and talk on behalf of Lee Ann, tell her that the investigator wanted a piece of her time. Pat said she may not call her, but she might take a walk down to the Starbucks where Liz worked and give her a heads-up in person. Salpeter said he would appreciate that. The object was to get a new statement out of Liz that Lee Ann was "incapable" of doing something like conspiring to murder another human being.

Chapter 27

Barket

Lee Ann's lawyer, whom she'd hired months before her arrest, was Bruce Barket, a prominent Long Island defense attorney whose offices were on the sixth floor of an office building in the upper-middle-class suburban village of Garden City.

Not far from Mineola, site of Nassau County's main courthouse, Garden City was a town where the streets were lined with trees, and traffic along the main drag was separated by a well-manicured grassy mall.

Lee Ann's case had taken a turn for the worse, and he was going to have to reschedule some things. After months of investigation, police had finally arrested her. With Lee Ann behind bars, Barket had his work cut out for him.

Based on his interviews with his client and the information supplied to him by his private investigator, Jay Salpeter, Barket believed that Lee Ann was completely innocent.

The case against her wasn't that strong, he felt. It was

based, he believed, almost entirely on the statements of liars. His job would be to prove they were liars, so juries wouldn't believe their testimony.

Barket was well-known on Long Island. For a time he had been Amy Fisher's lawyer. She was the "Long Island Lolita" who dated Joey Buttafuoco and shot Joey's wife in the face.

Barket represented Amy during the time after she got out of prison. She was living with her mom in Long Beach, Long Island, and was marketing a hardcover book based on her experiences.

Barket was born and raised in Connecticut, right across from Long Island. He attended Central Connecticut State University, in New Britain, earning an undergraduate degree in political science and speech communications, with an emphasis on persuasion.

He must have done his homework, because as a professional, he was known for the clearness of his communication, as well as his skills of persuasion. Truth was, Bruce Barket was known as a *very* persuasive man.

During the mid-1980s, he attended the University of Connecticut Law School in Hartford. After graduation and passing the bar exam, both for Connecticut and New York State, he moved to Long Island to work as a prosecutor for the Nassau County District Attorney's (DA) Office from 1986 to 1991. He worked his way up to the felony trial bureau.

He left the DA's office in 1991 to attend Jesuits Navidad Society of Jesus for New York Province, in Syracuse. "I was on track to be a priest," he later said. "I was nine years away from ordination."

He eventually returned to law, this time as a defense attorney. Having worked on the other side, prosecuting cases, gave Barket a depth of perception and strategy when it came to defending clients. He understood the "tricks" that the other side might use, and he knew how to diminish the effectiveness of those techniques.

Even with a secular job, Barket remained a devout Catholic who was known for sticking to his guns. He fought for his client's freedom as if he were fighting for his own. He was a devout pro-lifer, who once had defended James Kopp, an abortion-doctor killer.

From a professional standpoint, Bruce Barket had the type of personality people either loved or loathed. One Long Island reporter who covered several of his trials said he was "a big baby who always accuses prosecutors of vast conspiracies, calls everyone liars, and then whines if he doesn't get his way."

He particularly noted the Martin "Marty" Tankleff case. That reporter had covered the Tankleff case for quite some time, and had no doubt that—despite Barket's public statements to the contrary—young Martin did in fact kill both of his parents.

While the merits of Barket's courtroom tactics might be disagreeable to some, he had his faithful fans as well. One former client can't say enough good things about his well-known lawyer.

Vincent McCrudden, a graduate of the University of Rhode Island, had done very well as a Wall Street investment adviser for close to twenty years. Several years ago, however, he was federally charged with fifteen counts of mail fraud by the Eastern District of New York. Then in his early forties, McCrudden was accused of misrepresenting the Net Asset Value (NAV) of a fund he was managing in a letter to fifteen clients. The total disparity amounted to about $1.5 million.

McCrudden, who had a hard-earned and well-deserved reputation for integrity in the financial community, initially interviewed about twenty to thirty New York City defense attorneys. He was determined to be fully vindicated, whether it was through the Feds dropping the charges or trial by jury.

The case against him involved his becoming, at the request of Scotland Yard, the lead plaintiff in a lawsuit against the Japan-based Sumitomo Bank and several other well-known corporate entities for their involvement in a mammoth scheme involving the fluctuating price of copper. The price of copper, they knew, had tremendous ramifications on the worldwide financial market.

McCrudden was singled out by an attorney for some of those financial entities, as well as the plaintiffs in the suit against McCrudden, who felt they were treated "disrespectfully" and vowed to put him in his place. That attorney who singled out McCrudden had tremendous power that reached far beyond Wall Street and well into the tentacles of the enforcement arms of the federal government.

"I was innocent of the charges," McCrudden insists to this day. "I couldn't do that to myself or my family. In my business you live and die by your reputation. It is not something I take lightly."

Although McCrudden insisted that he represented the NAV to the best of his ability, most of the attorneys he spoke with strongly suggested he take a plea bargain of eighteen months in federal prison, followed by six months of home confinement. The Feds didn't charge people in cases they couldn't win, they said.

When these attorneys told him of the Feds' 98 percent conviction rate (either through trials or plea bargains), McCrudden, a former standout college soccer player with immense competitive zeal, felt like he was David fighting Goliath.

If he rolled the dice and lost at trial, mandatory sentencing guidelines would guarantee that he spend at least three years in prison. With a beloved wife and two children at home, he was living a nightmare.

Then McCrudden learned of Bruce Barket. Barket, he was told, was quickly establishing a reputation as a courtroom superstar. Upon meeting him, he immediately liked Barket and was disappointed when told that he wasn't all that experienced in white-collar crimes. Barket suggested that McCrudden retain a better-known, more established "superstar."

McCrudden retained that attorney, who had an avuncular personality, for $75,000. After two weeks and one court appearance, he wound up telling McCrudden that he had gotten him a great deal: in exchange for a plea of guilty to all charges, McCrudden would do a mere eighteen months in prison. Not surprisingly, McCrudden was devastated.

"That lawyer told me I had been carrying the ball too long; to let him put the ball on his shoulder and carry it for me," said McCrudden. "Then all he could do was get me the same deal that had already been offered. I thought I found an attorney to take me to the promised land, and it was disastrous. I can't tell you the depths of despair I was in."

Trusting his instincts, McCrudden went back to Barket. He was impressed by what he perceived to be Barket's sense of morality and integrity. McCrudden was steadfast in his commitment to not plead guilty to a crime he did not commit. He asked Barket to fight the case to the end with him. Barket agreed.

"I admit I was a little concerned with Bruce's lack of knowledge of the securities industry," said McCrudden. "With a lot of the other lawyers I spoke to, I had to explain things over and over. Bruce's ability to retain information is amazing. I never met anyone who understands such complicated concepts so quickly and clearly."

Barket also proved to be a bit of a courtroom

chameleon. While he fought like a battle-hardened guerrilla in Lee Ann's case, McCrudden was surprised how unassuming and downright likable he was during his own trial.

"Bruce made the jurors understand this wasn't a securities case with some hotshot, fast-talking crook," said McCrudden. "This was the case of an everyman who was being targeted by corporate bulldogs who stood to gain leverage by getting me out of the picture. Bruce led several of the witnesses down a path of their own self-destruction, but he was always respectful of them."

McCrudden's defense was that he had incorporated the potential recovery of a class action lawsuit into the financial picture he presented to his clients. Using general accounting principles, McCrudden refused to even concede that he erred in his judgment. The whole case, he said, was about one-upmanship in a business that was known for deception and fraud, even among colleagues and contemporaries.

After a 2½-week trial that took place in the Long Island Federal Courthouse, Central Islip, in September 2003, McCrudden was acquitted of all charges in one hour.

"I literally put my life into Bruce's hands," said McCrudden, who was forty-four years old in 2005. "I always felt that he wanted to win as much as I needed to win. Compared to what all these other lawyers wanted to charge me, he took a minimal amount of money. He worked so hard on the case. He knew what was at stake. I would have been taken from my family and then barred from the securities industry, which was my life. I can never thank Bruce enough for how he represented me. I am so indebted to him. He gave me my life back, when every other attorney I spoke with just wanted to pick my pocket."

Not only was McCrudden vindicated of all charges against him, the case in which he was the lead plaintiff settled for $125 million, the largest settlement ever by the Commodities Futures Trading Commission (CFTC).

Long before his client went to trial, Barket was making statements to help Lee Ann in the court of public opinion. About Alex's murder, Barket told the press, "It's going to be an odd case, to say the least, but I predict that my client will eventually be exonerated."

He noted that the lack of eyewitnesses and physical evidence against Lee Ann would mean that prosecutors had their work cut out for them.

"Prosecutors have alleged that the killing was the result of a contract hit gone awry, but they aren't seeking the death penalty for anyone. I believe my client and Salierno were charged with first-degree murder for another reason," Barket said. "By pursuing a case of murder in furtherance of a conspiracy, prosecutors apparently intend to try to introduce at trial a hearsay statement by Paget that Salierno told him that Lee Ann Riedel wanted her estranged husband dead."

Barket referred to Salierno as "nothing more than a leg-breaker, an enforcer, and a murderer." He acknowledged that Lee and Paul were having marital difficulties, but that these did not constitute a "motive for murder."

According to Barket, the very fact that Algeri was the victim showed that Lee Ann had not been involved. "If Lee Ann had been a part of this, the wrong man would not have been shot," Barket claimed.

Barket was a tenacious attorney who would provide Lee Ann a spirited defense. He would concede both in and out of court that Lee Ann was an adulteress with a propensity for bad men. But he would insist that she was no murderer.

* * *

Although Barket was keeping reporters' pencils busy with his pretrial statements, the other side was mum. John Collins, the prosecutor in charge of the Suffolk County District Attorney's Office homicide bureau, refused to discuss prosecution strategy with the press.

All Collins did say was "Salierno made a statement admitting his involvement."

Chapter 28

Muraskin

Ralph Salierno's attorney was Seth Muraskin, a former Suffolk County prosecutor. He was a short guy with glasses, resembling more an eccentric filmmaker than a defense attorney.

The prosecution's short public statement about Salierno admitting his involvement rankled Muraskin. His defense strategy was implied by his countering statement to the press, which was, "If Salierno did make statements against his interests, they were not voluntary and will be challenged during pretrial hearings."

The injustice here, Muraskin said, wasn't specific to his client, either. It was systemic across the board. Salierno was hardly the first suspect to confess in Suffolk County against his will.

Muraskin noted that the Suffolk County police had come under criticism in the past for the rate of confessions obtained in murder cases. That rate had been as high as 95 percent.

"That means that out of every twenty persons

arrested for murder, nineteen confessed," Muraskin said. Muraskin suspected that the time was right for a police-brutality defense in a first-degree murder case in Suffolk County. It was the sort of place where people routinely questioned the validity of confessions.

Some of those confessions had already been subjected to scrutiny, such as in the notorious Marty Tankleff case. Because of this, Muraskin was going to be happy with nothing less than complete vindication for Salierno.

"Mr. Salierno has no intention of taking any disposition and intends to prove himself completely innocent at trial," said Muraskin. He called the indictments against Rocco and Lee Ann a "squeeze play."

Like many places in America, Muraskin figured, Suffolk County was a place where rumors of police brutality and coercion might affect a prosecution's chances of selling its case to a local jury.

Sure, Salierno's "confession" was in writing and he had signed it, but there was no way to corroborate the validity of the statement. No recording, audio or video, had been made.

Illinois had been the most recent state to require police in that state to record their interrogations of homicide suspects. It was already required in Minnesota and Alaska. Six other states were considering such a rule.

Those in favor of the must-record rule when it came to interviewing murder suspects said that detectives who were getting their confessions fair and square had nothing to fear from the recording equipment.

Those who were against the rule, which included just about every detective, said that the presence of a tape recorder or a video camera in an interrogation room changed the chemistry of the room and affected the results. And not in the favor of justice.

Those detectives argued that, psychologically, interrogations were conducted in small rooms without windows, to emphasize the absolute privacy of the space. It was a place where the suspect should feel open to baring his soul.

The addition of recording equipment was, in essence, changing the interrogation room from a private space to a public space. The suspect, instead of focusing on just one interrogator, or perhaps one interrogator and his partner, now had to think about what this would look and sound like to the countless number of people in the future who might listen to the audiotape or watch the videotape on television.

For many years police in America had conducted long interviews with homicide suspects and had taken minimal notes. Re-creations of those interviews came in the form of condensed synopses written after the fact by the interrogator.

In many cases the police report included only the responses to questions that the suspect gave, but edited out the questions. The result was a chain of statements by the suspect, each admitting to something.

Police did not have to worry about how questions were worded, because there was no way the wording of the questions would be remembered. They would either be eliminated altogether or altered to be politically correct.

With the new method, the questions themselves would be subject to scrutiny by any future defense attorney, the prosecution, and by a judge. It would be essential for interrogators to be self-conscious. This adjustment would be toughest for the most experienced interrogators. They may be the most set in their ways.

Detectives would have to be extra careful to avoid crude remarks that might have been effective in the shadowy privacy of an interrogation room, but would look bad in the bright sunshine of a public hearing.

Detectives who used empathy—no matter what the subject matter of the case—would now have to reconsider the tactic on a case-by-case basis. In the past empathy had been effective in gaining confessions, but on tape it could put the interrogating officer in an awful light.

For example, an interrogator could no longer lie and say, "I understand the child molester's pain. I know how you feel."

Detectives would have to be especially aware of tactics that might be construed as bullying because that got to the crux of the complaint, that the cops were using brute force to get suspects to confess against their will.

The biggest adjustment would be to the loss of spontaneity. If taped, detectives who were used to spitting out the first question that popped into their head would have to consider each word before speaking.

Judges and juries might not be kind to even the smallest error by a police officer. Interrogations might be thrown out because of a single flubbed word when reading the suspect's Miranda rights.

On the other side, of course, was the argument that all of these inconveniences and effects on the interrogation process were worth it because they would rid the police forever of the suspicion of impropriety during interrogations. That would be one less weapon that defense attorneys would have to throw at law enforcement during murder trials.

And detectives would adjust. Many were already masterful at the tactics that would need to be used anyway. Instead of badgering the witness, if that was their style to begin with, they would frame their questions so that they exposed the suspect's lies.

* * *

Despite the claims of the Suffolk County police to the contrary, Muraskin told the press that his client had been nowhere near the gym on the night of Alex Algeri's murder.

"We put in a notice of alibi. He was literally on a date," Muraskin concluded. The lawyer added that his client had been in Westchester County at the time of the crime, on a date.

"They had a nice night," Muraskin said of Salierno and his mystery date.

Muraskin was asked about the fact that the defendants were pointing fingers at each other, and that informants who were persons with long criminal records would supply much of the testimony against them.

"There are a lot of crazy characters in this thing," Muraskin conceded. "A lot of mud is going to be slung everywhere."

As the trial approached, even Paul Riedel spoke to the press. He said yes, he expected to be called as a witness. He said that he was spending much of his time taking care of Nicholas, his son with Lee Ann, who was only one week away from his fourth birthday. He also said that he still missed Alex Algeri very much, pointing out that Alex had been his son's godfather and had been the best man at his and Lee Ann's wedding.

Asked for a comment on the case against his wife and her boyfriend, Paul said, "I want to move forward and hope for as much of a normal life as I can with my son."

Chapter 29

Paul's World, According to Chris

Among Bruce Barket's first goals when he took on Lee Ann's case was to build a file on Paul. He wanted to know every illegal or antisocial act ever committed by the big guy. He wanted to know the details of every time Paul Riedel ever looked at anyone funny.

Among those he asked for help was Chris Armanini, Lee Ann's oldest son. About a week before the trial started, Chris faxed Barket an eight-page document, seven of those pages consisting of a single-spaced essay involving all of Chris's recollections of Paul.

Chris said he'd grown up in a town in Long Island called Carle Place. In 1997, he was eleven years old and lived with his twenty-nine-year-old mother, Lee Ann, and his twenty-five-year-old uncle, Jamie, who rented out their basement apartment.

The house was stable. Everyone got along. Lee Ann had a steady job working as a bartender at a Huntington,

Long Island, club called The Carousel. Chris was in the fifth grade, where he played soccer and football, and considered himself an average kid.

Christopher had never met his father, Craig. Craig, who now lived in California, and Lee Ann had separated before Chris was born.

"He never made an effort to try to have a relationship with me," Chris said.

Chris spent the summer between fifth and sixth grades at his grandfather's house in Mount Pocono, Pennsylvania. He got back to Long Island on Labor Day weekend and it was then that he met Paul Riedel for the first time.

The boy had had an inkling that there was a new man in his mother's life even before he got home to Long Island, because he had overheard bits and pieces of conversation to that effect. Chris later learned that his mother's "manager" had introduced Paul to her.

Chris wasn't happy that his mom had a new boyfriend, although at first Paul was well-behaved. "He just needed some time to get some control," Chris said, regarding Paul's at-first harmless behavior.

Chris was impressed with Paul's size—"three hundred pounds and very muscular"—and noted that the new boyfriend had "black hair and squinty eyes." Some of the neighbors thought Paul looked like a movie star, but Chris characterized him more as "a typical Guido."

The first trouble between Paul Riedel and Chris Armanini came two weeks later during a trip to Six Flags Great Adventure in New Jersey. Chris was only eleven and didn't want to go on the rides alone, and Paul became increasingly hostile each time the boy asked him to accompany him.

Paul worked himself into a temper tantrum over not wanting to ride the rides. He called Chris an "unappreciative motherfucker," and insisted that they leave the amusement park immediately.

On the way home Paul drove in a reckless manner and yelled at Lee Ann, saying things like, "I should have known what I was getting into. I am not going to deal with this shit."

On the way back to New York, they stopped at a gas station, and Paul continued to scream as they got gas, which proved to be quite an embarrassment to Chris and his mother.

To this day, Chris wonders why his mother didn't end her relationship with Paul right then and there at that gas station. Would it ever be any clearer that the man was an unadulterated asshole?

Later on, Chris said, he met some of the people that Paul referred to as friends. Chris didn't think these people were friends at all. He saw them as leeches who had attached themselves to Paul because of his wealth and power.

Chris started to catch on to the "type of lifestyle" Paul lived. He was impressed by the fact that though Paul never went to work, he still griped all the time about how he had to bust his balls to put food on the table.

Chris used to go along with Paul sometimes and visit a place where there were a lot of phones and operators taking bets. Team names. Point spreads. Dollar amounts. Mostly football, the boy thought, but that was the season. One of Paul's jobs was running an illegal sports book.

One of the guys Paul had working for him answering phones was also a postal employee and used to take packages out of the mail for Paul sometimes. Chris got some CDs in a Columbia House box that way once. Paul said he was going to teach Chris "the game."

Around Thanksgiving, 1997, Paul moved in with Chris and his mom. Sometime between Thanksgiving and

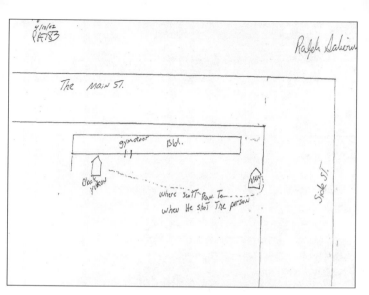

Diagram drawn by Ralph "Rocco" Salierno during his "confession." Figure shows Salierno's version of the murder, in which it was his partner Scott Paget who crossed the gym's rear parking lot and shot Alexander Algeri. *(Photo by Tekla Benson)*

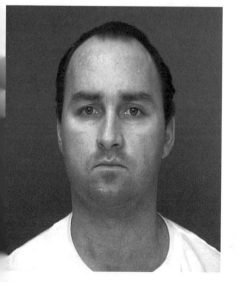

Scott Paget, according to some members of law enforcement, didn't have "perp eyes." Still, he drove the murder car, fully knowing that the sole purpose of his trek was to snuff out a life. His cut of the deal: $3,000. *(Photo courtesy of the Suffolk County Police Department)*

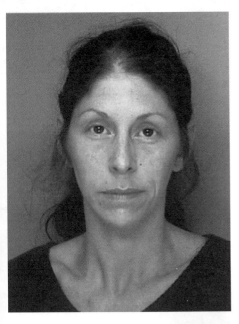

Not looking her best upon the occasion of her arrest for murder, Lee Ann Riedel denied that she offered Rocco Salierno big bucks in exchange for her husband's death. *(Photo courtesy of the Suffolk County Police Department)*

Ralph "Rocco" Salierno was the man's real name. In Florida he was known as Randall "Randy" Salierno. He thought he'd killed Lee Ann's badass husband until he realized his blunder. Yet he still impregnated Lee Ann, who bore his child. He said he did it for money. She said it must have been love. He says she never really was his girlfriend. *(Photo courtesy of the Suffolk County Police Department)*

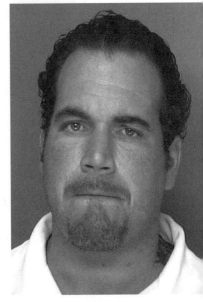

The front of Dolphin Fitness Clubs in Amityville. Among the owners were bodybuilders Paul Riedel and his best friend Alex Algeri.
(Photo by Michael Benson)

The location at the rear of the fitness club, where the murderer and the victim came together in a hail of bullets. Alex Algeri managed to stumble back into the gym before he collapsed. It would be days before the shooter realized that he'd killed the wrong man. *(Photo by Michael Benson)*

The killers parked their minivan on the dark side street and waited for their target to emerge from the back of the building. This is the view of the kill spot from the parking spot on Park Avenue where the hit men lay in wait. *(Photo by Michael Benson)*

View of the back of the gym where Ralph Salierno and Scott Paget waited in the dark. When Alex came out the back door, the shooter moved swiftly across the parking lot, got within point-blank range, and filled Alex with lead. *(Photo by Michael Benson)*

Here's the famous so-called "Amityville Horror" house, where Ronald DeFeo slaughtered his entire family. The house is only four blocks from Dolphin Fitness Clubs, where Alex Algeri was murdered—and the last thing the village people wanted was another infamous murder within Amityville's borders. *(Photo by Michael Benson)*

Ketcham's Creek, where the murder weapon was found. One smart cop found a rock that weighed about the same as a handgun, tossed it into the creek from a moving car, and began searching at the spot where the rock kerplunked into the water. The gun was found almost immediately. *(Photo by Michael Benson)*

Brunswick Hospital, where Alex Algeri died. The facility has since been transformed into a psychiatric hospital and the emergency room area has been closed. *(Photo by Anne Darrigan)*

Sal Algeri, the victim's father and the original "Papa Smurf," talks to a reporter from WPIX-TV outside the Riverside, New York courtroom. *(Photo by Robert Mladinich)*

Leonora Ferrari *(right)* is Alex Algeri's mother. She was on a cruise at the time of the murder ad was informed of his death by ship personnel.
(Photo by Robert Mladinich)

Alex's brother and sister react with relief after both juries returned guilty verdicts. *(Photo by Robert Mladinich)*

The victim's brother comforts his mother in the hallway outside the Suffolk County courtroom. *(Photo by Robert Mladinich)*

Private Investigator Jay Salpeter worked hard for Lee Ann Riedel's defense team. Here he points at a news item regarding his most famous case, in which a man fed his child to the family dog. *(Photo by Robert Mladinich)*

Suffolk County Assistant District Attorney Denise Merrifield speaks with the Algeri family moments after Lee Ann Riedel's sentencing.
(Photo by Robert Mladinich)

Lee Ann met Paul Riedel while tending bar at The Carousel, a strip joint in the Long Island town of Huntington. *(Photo by Robert Mladinich)*

A five-shot Colt detective special, very similar to the one used to kill Alex Algeri. *(Photo by Robert Mladinich)*

The victim, Alex Algeri, as he appeared during his senior year of high school on Long Island. *(Photo by Grace Mainey)*

In high school, Alex played football and lacrosse. Mononucleosis, however, kept him from playing sports during his senior year.
(Photo by Cailin Murtha)

Defense attorney Bruce Barket fought hard to win Lee Ann Riedel an acquittal, but he didn't put her on the stand. *(Photo by Robert Mladinich)*

The ambulance carrying Alex Algeri screamed past this gazebo on its way from Dolphin's Gym to Brunswick Hospital. The gazebo is in the heart of Amityville and gives the town a wholesome, small town appeal. *(Photo by Robert Mladinich)*

Mangano Funeral Home where Alex's body was laid out. According to Sal Algeri the line was around the block with people wanting to pay their respects to the popular victim. *(Photo by Robert Mladinich)*

Alex is buried in at St. Charles Cemetery on Conklin Ave. in Farmingdale, just a few miles from the gym. At the gravesite Sal planted a memorial tree and put a stone in front of it. Every year at Christmas he and his wife celebrate Alex's life by decorating it. *(Photo by Robert Mladinich)*

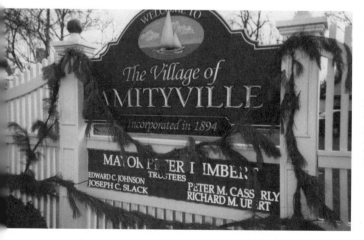

At the time of Alex Algeri's murder, just about everyone had heard of Amityville. It was a great place to live, but that didn't have anything to do with its fame—or infamy. *(Photo by Robert Mladinich)*

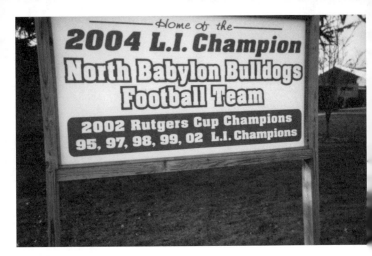

The intended victim attended North Babylon High School where he was a football superstar, setting school records that stand to this day. Though recruited by college football powers, an injury prevented him from furthering his career on the gridiron. *(Photo by Robert Mladinich)*

Lee Ann Riedel with all three of her boys: Christopher, Nicholas and baby Zachary. *(Photo by David Armanini)*

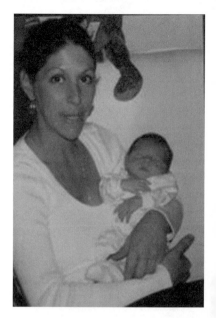

Lee Ann, shown here with son Zachary, wanted everyone to know that, no matter what else she might have done, she was always a good mother. *(Photo by David Armanini)*

At Zachary's christening, Lee Ann is joined by her brother James and Father Martin, who performed the ceremony. *(Photo by David Armanini)*

Lee Ann couldn't be happier as she cuddles with baby Zachary.
(Photo by David Armanini)

Christopher, Nicholas, and Lee Ann. *(Photo by David Armanini)*

Christmas, Paul took a trip to Arizona with his younger half-brother, Christian Miller, and Alex Algeri.

The object was to "take care of" a troublesome employee out there. When Paul returned, he had huge bags of marijuana with him, very impressive to the boy who had never seen any kind of drugs before.

Paul hadn't shown off the bags of weed. Chris had stumbled upon it by accident when he was scrounging around looking for a duffel bag for storing his football equipment. He found a bag filled to the brim with pot. According to Chris, there was even a brown vial of cocaine in there.

He didn't squeal and still doesn't think his mother knows why Paul went to Arizona or that there were large quantities of illegal substances being stored in he house when she and Paul lived together.

During this time Chris often accompanied Paul when he went on his errands. He went to the gym, to a tanning salon, which Paul part-owned at that time, everywhere. He knew everyone Paul knew, and they knew Chris. People began to think that Paul was Chris's father.

One day Chris accompanied Paul Riedel to a check-cashing place in Amityville, which was owned by a friend of Paul's named Johnny La. La was probably short for something, but Chris didn't know what. Chris watched as Paul gave Johnny the drug-filled duffel bag.

Two weeks before Christmas of that year, Lee Ann, according to her son, had some "surgery on her ovaries." She was in bed recovering for a while, and during that time, Chris said, Paul wasn't nice to her at all. Paul never tried to comfort her. At one point he said that he was going to pay for all the medical bills, but he never did.

Even though Lee Ann was still having trouble getting out of bed, Paul threw a Christmas party at their house and invited three of his buddies. They were Philly

Monte, who was arrested for selling guns, and whose father owned Monte Sanitation; Mike Sini, who owned a string of Dolphin Fitnesses; and Bret Holla.

While the party raged downstairs, and Lee Ann remained in her bedroom upstairs, Chris recalled Paul repeatedly standing at the foot of the stairs and yelling up. "You could at least come down and say hello," he was saying.

Eventually Lee Ann gave in. She came downstairs and she sat on the couch with everyone, even though the doctor had warned her that she should stay in bed. That night Paul told Chris's uncle Jamie that he—that is, Paul—was a very powerful man. Very powerful. He had the power to make men disappear.

Uncle Jamie hadn't a clue as to why Paul would tell him this. Chris later theorized that it was one of the techniques Paul used to frighten people, to nip potential problems in the bud.

Paul bought an extraordinary number of Christmas presents. On Christmas Day Lee Ann and Chris received "everything they could have dreamed of." The summer before, Chris had his bike stolen, and now he had a new one, a full-suspension Trek mountain bike. The stolen bike had been built by Chris himself, on the cheap, with parts he could find here and there. Now he had one of the world's greatest bikes.

Chris noticed that his mother was changing. She was growing increasingly subservient, growing comfortable with her space beneath Paul's thumb. Lee Ann and Paul had known each other for approximately five months at that point.

"I guess I'd never seen her get yelled at by a man before," Chris commented.

It was around then that Chris learned that Paul had gone away for a few years. Sing Sing. According to

Chris, Paul put a shotgun to an undercover cop's head. He used to rob drug dealers and he got stung.

Along with bitching about how he busted his balls to put dinner on the table, another favorite subject of Paul's whining was his supposedly abusive childhood. According to Paul, his mother used to beat him. His dad was never around.

According to the teenage Chris Armanini, there was only one reason that Paul Riedel hated his mother, and that was because she was the one who had said it was Paul's voice on an FBI recording when he got arrested.

Sometime around Chris's twelfth birthday, his biological father, Craig, called him on the phone from California. Chris had no idea how the man got his number. They spoke for hours. A couple of times.

Craig said that Chris should have an opportunity to meet his real dad, that he was going to send Chris airplane tickets so he could fly out to California. Then one time Craig called and Paul answered the phone. That was it for Craig. Paul bawled Craig out. Called him a piece of shit.

"He told Craig that I didn't need him anymore. I had him, Paul, and that was good enough," Chris said. Craig didn't call back after that. The plane tickets never arrived, but Craig did send Chris balloons on his birthday.

A week before Chris's twelfth birthday, Paul and Lee Ann got into a fight. They were making a ruckus and Uncle Jamie came up from the basement to see what was going on.

Uncle Jamie charged into the master bedroom just in time to see Paul hurl Lee Ann across the room. Jamie started to come to Lee Ann's defense, but Paul said he'd stab him in the back of the neck if he got involved.

Although there was no stabbing, Paul picked Jamie up by the head and threw him against a wall. While all of this was going on, Paul's half brother, Christian, was in the other room playing a video game.

Christian was a lot younger than Paul, maybe still nineteen when this happened. He called the cops. Christian gave the police operator the information quickly, then hung up.

Paul's brother knew that he would be in big trouble if Paul caught him on the phone. By the time the cops got to the house, Paul was down at the door to meet them.

"Get the fuck out of my way," Paul allegedly said. "You little bitches can't do a thing." With that, Paul got in his car and drove away. The cops were left standing at the door, mouths open.

"The police didn't do a thing, for some odd reason," Chris Armanini remembered.

On March 19, 1998, Lee Ann and Chris split for Florida. "In fear of our lives," Chris said. Uncle Jamie moved out, too. He ended up living with his sister for a while; then he, too, moved to Florida.

After staying in Florida for a brief period, Lee Ann and Chris returned to New York to get their stuff from the Carle Place house. Paul had moved in with Lee Ann and Chris, so everything belonged to the Armaninis.

They arrived at the house when it was empty, apparently with a U-Haul truck and some friends to do the heavy lifting. Chris remembered the moving crew being his mother, grandmother Pat Armanini, his uncle, and his uncle's two friends.

Paul arrived as the stuff was being taken out. Lee Ann and Chris were inside putting things into boxes. Paul made a dramatic entrance.

"If one more box gets moved, I'll have everyone here killed," Paul said.

Threatening family members was one thing—Paul had a lot of hot air. But to say something like that in front of the uncle's two friends, whom Paul had never met, took some cojones.

The family continued to pack, thinking Paul was full of it. Paul didn't become violent, but he walked around with such a glare of hatred on his face that he scared everyone. The family left without retrieving Lee Ann's stuff.

After that, Lee Ann and Chris went to Chris's great-grandmother's house in Mineola. That was where Chris lived until the 1997 to 1998 school year finished. During the time that Lee Ann lived with her grandmother, Paul wooed her and convinced her to come back to him.

He promised to change. Of course, Paul was living all by himself in her house, the house Chris grew up in and used to live in with his mother and uncle. "He had complete control," Chris remarked. Lee Ann told her son that it was going to be all right, because Paul was sorry and he was changed.

Paul said that he found a beautiful house for sale on the Great South Bay in Babylon. Paul said they were going to buy everything brand-new. Her stuff and the old house? Sell it.

Paul bought the new house in Babylon in his own name, Christopher recalled. Now he didn't have to worry about living in someone else's house. Now Lee Ann and Chris were living in his house.

Chris thought it was sometime in 1999 when they moved into the new house and he officially became a rich kid. It was beautiful waterfront property.

"We had it all," Chris remembered. "Boats, cars, Jet Skis, motorcycles."

Around the same time Paul bought some storefront property, and built a Dolphin Fitness Club in Amityville. Paul and Chris would visit the construction site in Amityville daily. At that time Chris became friends with Paul's partner in the fitness club, Alex Algeri.

"Al was a really straight-up guy. He worked in the union as an electrician, and really didn't get into any bad stuff with Paul," Chris said.

Chris felt isolated by his new home. Although the new house was luxurious, Lee Ann and Chris were now, as Chris put it, "thirty-five minutes from our family and lives."

One night, sometime in 1999, Lee Ann and Chris had plans to go to Roosevelt Field to do some shopping. This was a mega mall not far from where the Armaninis had lived previously. But when they went to the driveway, they found that their 1998 Cadillac Eldorado was gone.

They called the police to report the car stolen. While the cops were there, Paul showed up and acted shocked that a car had been stolen from right in front of his house.

Paul later admitted that he'd had the car stolen and taken to a chop shop in Deer Park to be converted into parts. Lee Ann and Chris had to get around in a rental car for a while until Paul bought them a new Cadillac. Now the car was in his name, too. Complete control.

Later that year Lee Ann got pregnant by Paul and she was ecstatic. She couldn't have been happier. Paul acted kind of happy, but not nearly as much as Lee Ann.

Paul thought more about business—and business was booming. The gym in Amityville was the number one moneymaking Dolphin Fitness Club on Long Island—and that was saying something because there were quite a few.

It was around this time, according to Chris's recollection, that Paul began to stay out late and not come home until the next day.

"My mom swore up and down that he was having an affair," Chris said.

Lee Ann started to follow Paul. She found out that Paul didn't have a girlfriend. Instead, he was going to some guy's house. She found out that the guy was named Robert Passantino. They called him Rubber Rob, but Christopher didn't know why.

It was a house full of wiseguys and wiseguy wannabes, all smoking crack. Lee Ann confirmed that Paul was a drug addict when she found a crack pipe in his pants pocket.

Paul was an extremely functional drug addict, too. He had all the money in the world—he bragged that he was raking in $50,000 a week. He didn't have to worry about the cost of his habit like most junkies do.

Once a visibly pregnant Lee Ann went into the crack house and tried to pull Paul out physically, but if Paul didn't want to go, he wasn't going to go. It made no difference how much tugging Lee Ann did.

Lee Ann was shocked by this. She had never done any drugs in her life, according to her son. "She didn't even drink," he added.

Chris said that he felt very protective of his mother and did his best to keep her from going out looking for Paul. "Just leave him wherever he is," Chris begged. Lee Ann would say that Paul needed help, and if no one else was going to try to help him, she would. She said she could never leave him.

The drug problem got worse. On the night Lee Ann went into labor, Paul wasn't there. He was out with his crew doing drugs. On Mother's Day that year Paul had a couple of friends over to the house and they were downstairs doing "scoops," which Chris thought was a form of the party drug gamma hydroxybutyrate (GHB).

Lee Ann and Chris were upstairs asleep in their respective bedrooms. Later that night Lee Ann was awoken by the sound of someone downstairs puking. It was Paul, on his hands and knees, in the foyer, heaving his guts up, ODing on the scoops.

Lee Ann, all one hundred pounds of her, dragged him into a shower. She said he stopped breathing at one point. She had to slap him to snap him out of it, and he came back. She saved his life. The next day, though, Paul remembered none of it and claimed that Lee Ann was lying.

It was June 2000 when Paul first physically abused Chris. Lee Ann and Paul were on the floor of the living room playing with baby Nicholas. Chris, Paul seemed to feel, was the odd man out.

Paul kept asking Chris if he didn't have someplace to go so he would be out of Paul's sight, and Lee Ann explained that she didn't let Chris go out on school nights, so he really had no choice but be home. Paul told Chris to get some hobbies. Chris said something back to Paul.

"Don't you ever fucking answer me back. Now go to your room," Paul said. And Paul got up and chased him up the stairs. About halfway up the stairs Paul hit Chris in the back of the head.

Chris ran into his room and locked the door. Lee Ann came up with the baby, and Chris let her in. They relocked the door, which by Chris's estimate was about 2½ inches thick. Paul now was the only one on the outside.

"Open the fucking door," Paul screamed.

"Paul, the baby. Paul, the baby," Lee Ann yelled from the other side of the door.

Paul started to punch the door. His fist went through the door twice, and with the second punch, the door flung open. Paul went for Chris.

"You're a big man. Come on, you pussy. Stand up for your mom. Come on. Come on. What are you going to do, you little bitch?" Paul screamed at the teenager.

Paul then left the house, saying that if they were still there when he got back, he was going to put them all in their grave. Lee Ann and her two boys moved into Lee Ann's father's house for about a week.

Paul continued to phone in death threats while they were there. Once Paul said he was on his way over to

Chris's grandfather's house to do some clobbering and the cops had to be called.

Paul, a little more reasonable now, agreed to let Lee Ann and the boys live in his Babylon home while Pat Armanini, Lee Ann's mother, visited from Florida. She was coming up for a few days to say good-bye to her father, Chris's great-grandfather, who was on his deathbed. Paul promised that he wouldn't bother them in the house while Chris's grandmother was visiting.

It was on the second day of Pat's visit to the Babylon house that Chris had what he later called the most frightening experience of his life. Paul called up while Pat, Lee Ann, Chris, and the baby were having dinner. Paul, who had gotten himself all fired up, said he wanted everyone out.

"Paul, my mom is only staying for a few days," Lee Ann said. "She'll be gone by Thursday." Paul started in again with the death threats, and for a second time Lee Ann had to call the cops and they came to the house.

Paul called when the cops were on the way and he told Lee Ann that he hoped she had the whole precinct coming to protect her, because there was nothing any of those cops could do to keep him from getting to her. While the cops were still there, Paul showed up. The cops wouldn't let him in the house.

The police officer said, "Why don't you just leave them alone for a few days." Paul agreed. Paul left and picked up one of his hoodlum friends. Together they drove to Chris's uncle David's house.

Paul said to Chris's uncle, "People are going to start disappearing and I'm going to start with you." The uncle waved his hand and said he didn't want to get involved. Paul then threatened to kidnap Nicholas, the baby, and left.

He returned to Babylon. The Armaninis were expecting him, however. Uncle David had called and told them Paul was on his way to pay another visit. For a time Paul parked on the street out in front of the Babylon house and lay on the horn. Either this was intended as a warning or it was just a childish way to be annoying.

Inside the house everyone was terrified. They had once again retreated into an upstairs bedroom, and they had pushed furniture—a table and some chairs—in front of the door, to help keep Paul out.

Barring the bedroom door was a regular thing when Paul was out doing drugs. He came home mad from his drug binges and Lee Ann always wanted to make sure that he crashed someplace other than in a bed with her.

Lee Ann, huddled in that bedroom with her mother and two sons, called the cops from the bedroom—the second such call of the day. The cops came. Paul began to scream that they were "cop-callers," as if that were the dirtiest word he could think of.

The police came and asked if there were any weapons in the house. Lee Ann showed them Paul's shotgun, which was underneath his side of the bed. Paul had shown Chris that gun lots of times. Cops took the shotgun and left the house. They left a patrol car out in front of the house for the rest of the night to make sure they weren't bothered.

That weekend, after Chris's grandmother returned to Florida, Chris went to live with his grandfather and his wife for a few days. Just to get away from things. When he got back, he was stunned to learn that Paul had convinced Lee Ann to take him back.

Lee Ann told Chris that Paul deserved another chance. He had problems. She said Paul had promised to get help for his problems.

"I truly did not want to go back to that house with him," Chris said, "but I did it for my mother and my little brother." Chris promised himself that if Paul did "one more act of stupidity," he was not going to stand for it.

At first, like usual, Paul was nice. He told Chris that he was sorry for all the things he had said and done to him, that he was going to give it his all to make them a happy family.

That lasted for about three days. Then Paul returned to the crack house and any hopes of becoming a happy family popped and sizzled like the crystals in his burnt glass pipe.

Lee Ann waited until the end of the 1999 to 2000 school year and again headed down South with her boys. "My mom truly wanted to leave Paul and start a life with her children," Chris recalled.

Paul didn't make it easy for them to get away. According to Chris, he harassed them daily while they were in Florida. Paul got a court order that said Lee Ann and the baby had to go back to New York. Chris stayed in Florida.

Chris's grandmother's girlfriend, Liz, introduced Chris to a guy named Ralph Salierno, aka Rocco, whom she knew through a guy named Larry Ortolano, from the World Gym in Delray.

Liz had gotten some guys to hang around and help Chris and his mom whenever they needed. They provided a little protection. Chris remembered that he spent Christmas, 2000, in New York. He flew up there and spent the holiday with his mother and his baby brother.

The big news in January 2001 was that Paul's business partner, Alex Algeri, a guy Christopher knew and liked, was shot and killed. Some folks thought Paul did it, but it was obvious Paul was afraid in the wake of Alex's death, afraid for his life—certain that those bullets were meant for him.

In February, Lee Ann once again reconciled with Paul and convinced him to come down to Florida with them. Paul was better down in Florida. Paul and Lee Ann would still sometimes have arguments, but nothing major—at least not until that summer.

During that time Paul must have decided that he wasn't big enough, because he began to take a new steroid, actually a human-growth hormone, called Serostim. Paul and Chris used to go to a shooting center in Palm Beach, where Paul would test out his new handgun.

Paul had plans. To go with his Amityville fitness club, Paul was going to build another one in Westbury, another town in Long Island. During the summer of 2001, Paul took Lee Ann and her sons back up North. Paul wanted to oversee the demolition that was starting in Westbury for the new facility.

During the New York visit Lee Ann said that she wanted to take Nicholas to see her father, who lived twenty-five minutes away. Lee Ann's dad hadn't seen his grandchildren in more than a year.

"That started World War three," Chris said. "Paul didn't want my grandfather around Nicholas. I don't know why. I guess I'll never know why. He and my mom had a big fight about it in a parking lot."

Lee Ann was holding the baby and Paul was screaming into her face that he was going to kill her if she took the baby "there." Lee Ann, still holding the baby, worked her way into the backseat of a car and locked herself in.

Chris, fourteen by this time, decided he was going to come to his mother's aid, but he was predictably ineffective. Paul swatted him away as if swatting a fly and told him he'd knock every tooth he had out of his fucking mouth if he tried to get in his way again.

According to Chris, he refused to back down, and luckily for his smile, the police showed up at that point. By this time the cops knew Paul by his first name. Lee Ann and her boys went to her father's house to spend the night.

Lee Ann stayed on at her dad's house. Chris flew back to Florida the next day. Down there Chris spent a couple of days with his uncle; then Paul and Lee Ann flew down to Florida. They acted like nothing had happened—but Paul and Chris weren't speaking to one another.

A couple of weeks later, one of their cars was broken into and some CDs were stolen. Whoever had broken into the car apparently hadn't looked under the driver's seat because Paul's Beretta .380 was still there. According to Chris, the gun came from a friend of Paul's, Rubber Rob, who dealt coke.

More to disrupt Paul's sense of equilibrium than anything else, Chris claimed that he stole some stuff from Paul a couple of times. Paul always seemed to know Chris was the thief—and Chris always confessed and returned the stuff he'd taken. But more than ever, the two couldn't be comfortable in the same room together.

"Rob got the gun brand-new from his brother who's a cop in Suffolk," Chris said.

After Paul left, Chris moved back in with his mom. In December 2001, Chris's new baby brother, Zachary, was born. After that, Chris only saw Paul on a very limited basis. In 2002, Paul decided he wanted to see Nicholas, so he would fly down to Florida, pick up Nicholas, and then they would fly back together the same day.

Once when Paul was picking up Nicholas, Lee Ann's dad came along for the drop-off. Seeing his father-in-law again set Paul off. Paul tried to call the man out to fight him and eventually hit him on the side of his head. Unfortunately for Paul, he did it in front of a traffic cop, who arrested Paul.

Paul ended up spending a night in jail, and Chris's grandfather pressed charges, but as far as Chris knew, nothing came of that. And that was how the situation stood when Lee Ann's attorney had a private detective find out what he could about Paul Riedel, and an affidavit from Chris was typed up and signed. Chris still saw Paul briefly every once in a while, but only when he was in New York to see his brother Nicholas.

Chapter 30

Paul's World,
According to Lee Ann

At some point Lee Ann's lawyer, Bruce Barket, asked Lee Ann to write down what she thought was Paul's legal history, time spent in jail, laws that she knew he had broken, things like that.

Lee Ann's writing was not as prolific as Christopher's, but it was no doubt better informed. In at least one case it corrected and clarified stories of which Paul's stepson had—one might suspect—only partial knowledge.

She wrote in an attractive feminine hand, with perfect parochial penmanship on a wide-ruled sheet of loose leaf: "(I *think*) 1986-87, Paul was in prison (Sing Sing/Attica) for 6 or 8 years. He took a plea."

Both of the prisons Lee Ann mentioned were maximum-security facilities where law and order placed only its most dangerous criminals. Attica State was far upstate, south of Lake Ontario, between Buffalo and Rochester. Sing Sing was the nickname of the prison in Ossining,

New York, in Westchester County, not far from the Hudson River, only twenty or so miles north of New York City's northernmost borough, the Bronx.

Lee Ann continued, "I was told he used to set up drug deals, then rob them. This particular time it happened to be an undercover officer. His mother told me he held a gun to the officer's head while the officer was pleading for his life."

According to Lee Ann, the undercover policeman with Paul's gun pressed to his head was wired, and the entire incident was recorded. Lee Ann wrote that Paul's mother had heard the tape and was appalled and haunted by it.

"She told me she heard the tape of the officer crying and begging Paul not to kill him," Lee Ann wrote.

Lee Ann then listed all of the crimes she could remember Paul committing, or had heard of Paul committing, either through Paul's bragging or some other source. She wrote that, "in '99 I started dating Paul. He had a bookie business. Sports."

Up until this time, investigators into Paul's background had noticed a pattern: Paul seemed to be a sadist, who enjoyed scaring the shit out of people, whether it be hurling verbal threats or holding a gun to someone's head. But, and it was a big *but*, he didn't seem like he had a penchant for actual violence. That changed with Lee Ann's next statement.

"On the last night of Paul's parole (from the armed-robbery charges), we all went out to celebrate. Paul got into a bar fight," she said. "Paul ended up hurting a guy, but there were so many people around, no one realized he even did it."

Paul had learned a lesson in prison, according to Lee Ann. Instead of stealing the money from the guys who were selling pot, it was much easier just to sell the pot. However, Paul lacked the patience to sell small amounts of pot to users.

The former football star had long exhibited a pumped-up sense of entitlement. He thought big. He wanted to make mega bucks all at once. That meant making a huge pot buy and then selling slices of that pie to distributors. He made one purchase, four or five sales, and he was done. The profit margin would be huge.

"Paul sold pot with some guy Bobby in Arizona. *Big* pot deals!" Lee Ann wrote. So this would seem to indicate that the trip to the Southwest to "take care of a guy"—the trip that Christopher had construed to involve whacking someone—was more likely a big, big business deal. In this statement she did not use Bobby the pot dealer's last name, but in another interview she revealed it to be Minucci (pseudonym).

"Paul also did business for a guy named John [last name deleted] who was in jail for killing a Mexican during a drug deal. Paul was always bringing money over to John's girl. She was Bobby's cousin," she wrote. In the margin of the paper she wrote that she wasn't writing Bobby's last name, but that private investigator Jay Salpeter already knew it.

Lee Ann said that she had told the police all of this. Then she told them that Paul also made money with car insurance fraud. As Christopher apparently had described correctly, Paul would arrange to have his own car stolen so that he could collect the insurance without actually losing the car. After noting this, Lee Ann mentioned that the police she had spoken with had told her that they already knew about the insurance fraud business.

"Paul's parole officer George Bengis told me Paul had a big cocaine deal that a guy named Vinny Lombardi ended up in jail for," she wrote. She added that a lot of that illegally gained money had gone into the gym. "He put everything in my dad's name so the IRS wouldn't look at him. I know Paul was doing a lot of things. He never would tell me. I guess he was afraid I would tell."

Chapter 31

Grand Jury

Back in February and March of 2003, a Suffolk County grand jury had listened to the case to decide if Ralph Salierno and Lee Ann Riedel should be indicted for first-degree murder in the death of Alex Algeri.

One of the star witnesses during this process was the man whose testimony was most essential for the prosecution of Lee Ann Riedel: Michael "Big Balls" Fiaccabrino.

Fiaccabrino told the grand jury that he was thirty-three years old and was a resident of Florida. His questioner asked if he'd been charged or pleaded guilty to a federal narcotics case in Florida. Big Balls said that he had. He admitted that he'd pleaded guilty recently to "intent to distribute five hundred pounds of marijuana." The guilty plea, they established, was part of a deal Fiaccabrino had made, a deal that included cooperation with the investigation of Alex Algeri's murder.

The deal also called for Fiaccabrino's maximum term to be ten years, minimum of five, with a chance that he might be able to serve some of that time in a halfway house rather than a prison. His chances of making it into that halfway house were directly proportional to the level at which he cooperated with the prosecution in this murder case, as well as with other drug cases in Florida.

Other than that five-to-ten range, he said, no other promise was made to him regarding his prison term.

He was asked if his testimony came "in exchange for hope from the court you will, in fact, receive a more lenient sentence from the federal court." Fiaccabrino said yes, that was the case.

His plea agreement stated that in exchange for a lenient sentence—in fact, the statutory minimum—he would "provide truthful and complete information and testimony, and produce documents, records and other evidence, when called upon by the district attorney's office."

Also that he would "appear at such Grand Jury proceedings, hearings, trials, and other judicial proceedings, and at meetings, as may be required by this Office."

And that he would, if requested, "work in an undercover role to contact and negotiate with others suspected and believed to be involved in criminal conduct, under the supervision of, and in compliance with law enforcement officers and agents."

That agreement had been signed on January 6, 2003, by Fiaccabrino and his attorney, Charles Garret White, and by Donald F. Chase II, the assistant United States attorney.

When asked for details regarding his arrest, Fiaccabrino said he had been arrested in an undercover narcotics case in which an individual wore a wire. A federal agent had taped the witness making a deal to sell 465 pounds of weed.

"Isn't it true that you, in fact, while being recorded, spoke about your friend Randy and this murder in Suffolk County. Is that right?"

"Yes, I did."

Fiaccabrino said that he had made the statements before he knew he was the focus of a federal probe. He acknowledged that among the statements he made were those about Mr. Salierno and what he had done in Suffolk County. Fiaccabrino said that was true.

"Do you know Ralph Salierno?"

"Yes."

"How long have you known Ralph Salierno?"

"Probably since the ninth grade."

"When you say in ninth grade, was that in New York?"

"Eastchester, New York."

"Did he go by any other name than Ralph Salierno?"

"Pretty much Rocco."

"Did he go by the name Randy as well?"

"Rocco, Randy."

Fiaccabrino said he'd moved to Florida thirteen or fourteen years before. Randy moved to Florida maybe five years before. At that point Fiaccabrino and Randy often found themselves working out at the same time at the gym. They both worked out—lifting weights, that is—five or six times a week. Afterward, they went to a lot of restaurants, nightclubs, and stuff like that.

Fiaccabrino testified he also knew a guy in Florida named Larry Ortolano. He knew Larry from back in the Eastchester days, too, but mostly from the World Gym in Delray Beach. Randy knew Larry, too.

The witness said he knew Richie Pollack. He'd known him for about six or seven years. Unlike the others, who had grown up in the same vicinity up North, Fiaccabrino met Richie Pollack in Boca Raton, Florida. Fiaccabrino said he was the guy who introduced Richie to Randy. That was probably in 1999.

Through Randy, Fiaccabrino said, he'd met Lee Ann. He said Lee Ann met Randy through Larry Ortolano.

Fiaccabrino testified, "He met Lee Ann through Larry, but it was for a business thing, that she wanted her husband's legs broken and a major beating thrown on him because he was abusive, and stuff." There'd been a meeting at Lee Ann's mother's house to discuss what to do about Lee Ann's bad relationship.

According to Fiaccabrino, he and Randy were lifting weights one day during the summer of 2000 when Larry came up to them and told them about Lee Ann and how they were willing to pay for someone to do something to Lee Ann's husband. Ralph agreed to a meeting.

Fiaccabrino later learned that the meeting had taken place. He was under the impression that someone named Michael Salvaggio had been at the meeting with Lee Ann, Pat, and Liz, as well as Richie Pollack and Ralph Salierno. Big Balls was alone in this opinion. Everyone who was actually at the meeting had been interviewed and not one had mentioned the presence of anyone named Salvaggio.

Asked what the meeting had been about, Fiaccabrino said, "Pretty much it was about Paul Riedel, Lee Ann's husband." Randy told Fiaccabrino there'd been a couple of meetings, and he'd agreed to do the job.

At the third or the fourth meeting, according to what Randy said, Richie Pollack and Mike Salvaggio had a falling-out. There were money issues. They dropped out of the deal. That left only Randy still interested in doing the job.

Richie and Randy also had a falling-out at around that time, Fiaccabrino said. Richie had "kind of a crush" on Lee Ann, and Randy didn't like that. Randy told Fiaccabrino that Richie "pussied out. . . . He couldn't handle the wiseguy stuff."

Fiaccabrino was asked if there came a time during the autumn of 2000 when Randy told him the plans regarding Paul Riedel had changed. Fiaccabrino said yes.

"From a beating, legs broken," the witness testified,

"it escalated into murder. They wanted Paul Riedel killed. Lee Ann and her mother, Pat, did."

"That was what Randy told you?"

"Yes."

Randy told Fiaccabrino that he was going to get $50,000 up front and another $50,000 after the job was done. Lee Ann was supposed to have the money in a safe-deposit box in New York.

After a while, Randy told him, he started to think that Lee Ann didn't have access to that $100,000 in the safe-deposit box because it was in Paul's name. He started to talk to her about property Paul owned. There were, he was told, two to four gyms and the whole thing was worth something like $750,000. When Paul was dead, she would inherit the money.

Fiaccabrino said he met Lee Ann at Pat's house in the summer or fall of 2000. While there, he heard Lee Ann and Randy discussing Paul's murder.

"Would you tell the grand jury what you heard Lee Ann saying?"

"She would break down and cry and say, 'I can't handle this anymore. *I want him fucking dead.*'"

"What did Randy say?"

"He said, 'Don't worry. I'll take care of it.'"

"Did you ever hear Randy and Lee Ann discuss what they were going to do with the money after Paul was dead?"

"Yes, Lee Ann said that they were going to use the money to buy a house together," Fiaccabrino testified.

Fiaccabrino said that Lee Ann also had said that they were only going to spend part of the money on a house to live in and the rest was going to go toward a house to grow marijuana in. Fiaccabrino remembered Lee Ann's mom was interested in a piece of the marijuana business.

The witness said there was a time when he and Randy were headed to the gym and they had to "get some information from Lee Ann. We stopped over there real quick," the witness said. "She gave him a picture of Paul and, like, a sheet of paper that I thought was, like, directions."

Fiaccabrino admitted that he had not read what was on the sheet of paper. Randy's only comment was that the information was for "the New York trip." By this time Fiaccabrino knew what the "New York trip" was. He knew this was the trip Randy was making to "take care of Paul." Fiaccabrino was asked and verified that he understood that "take care of" was a euphemism for "kill."

When Lee Ann handed the photograph and the piece of paper to Randy, she said something along the line of "here's the stuff you will need," according to Fiaccabrino's recollection.

"Now did there ever come a time when Randy asked you to help him in killing Paul Riedel?"

"Yes," the witness said. The proposition had come sometime around Thanksgiving, maybe the beginning of December 2000. "He knew I was broke. He offered me three thousand to drive, just drive him to New York, and he would kill Paul. All I had to do was drive."

"After he asked you to do this, what, if anything, did you tell him?"

"I said, 'You're eff'ing crazy,'" Fiaccabrino said, bleeping himself. "'I don't want to be part of nothing like that.'"

Randy also wanted Fiaccabrino to use his credit card to rent a van for the New York trip. Fiaccabrino again told him he was crazy. "Then he asked me if I knew anyone who would use their credit card to rent the van. He said there was five hundred dollars in it for anyone who agreed to do that for him."

"Did Randy ever tell you whether, in fact, he got somebody to do that?"

"Yes. He said Larry Ortolano or one of the coworkers rented the van for him."

"Did Randy also ask you to help him find a gun in any way?"

"Yes, he asked if I could find him a gun and I told him I would make some calls, but I never really made calls because I didn't want anything to do with it. He wanted a thirty-eight and I just never came through. I told him no, after a while."

Randy told him he had tried to get a gun for the trip from someone named Joe, in Miami, but that had fallen through. Fiaccabrino said, "I guess maybe toward the end of December, he told me he got the gun from Michael Scauzillo with a connection with the crime-connected Albanians in New York."

Fiaccabrino testified that he knew Michael Scauzillo and that he lived in Eastchester, New York. The witness had met him, but he wasn't good friends with him. He wasn't one of the guys who had relocated to Florida. He'd stayed in New York.

The witness was asked what he meant when he said "the Albanians," and he replied, "They're a bunch of lunatics that run around the Bronx."

"What kind of gun did he say he had?"

"Thirty-eight snub nose."

"Was this a semiautomatic or a revolver?"

"All I know is a thirty-eight pistol. I think it was a revolver."

"Did Randy ever discuss with you who was going to accompany him on the New York trip?"

"Yeah. Another guy from the gym, Scott Paget." Randy said that Scott had accepted the $3,000 offer to drive the car. When Randy was missing from the gym for a few days, Fiaccabrino correctly assumed that this meant Randy was taking the New York trip.

Fiaccabrino next heard from Randy when he and Scott were on their way back from New York. Randy called Fiaccabrino on his cell phone. Fiaccabrino asked Randy how things had gone and he said it went good.

Randy was laughing and giggling, saying that Scott had been really nervous and had smoked four or five packs of cigarettes on the way there. Randy said he would see Fiaccabrino the next day at the gym.

That same day—apparently January 17, 2001— Fiaccabrino also received a phone call from Michael Scauzillo, up in New York. It was a brief conversation. Scauzillo said Fiaccabrino should log on to the Internet and search for Dolphin Fitness and any assaults that might have taken place. When Scauzillo said "Dolphin Fitness," Fiaccabrino knew what he was talking about, but he didn't go on the Internet at that point.

Randy was back in the gym lifting weights the next day, just like he said he would. But he couldn't get into it. Too nervous. Salierno cut his workout short. Randy and Fiaccabrino left together and went to Fiaccabrino's father's house.

It was while at his dad's house that the witness finally logged on to the Internet and looked up the Amityville shooting, as Scauzillo had suggested he should the previous day. Randy was eager to see the news, too. He wanted to make sure the guy was dead.

That was when Randy learned that he had shot and killed the wrong guy. Randy "kind of freaked out." According to Fiaccabrino, Randy said, "Holy shit, it's the wrong guy. I'm gonna end up in fucking jail."

"Did Randy ever explain to you or talk to you about how the murder actually took place?"

"Yes, he said Scott drove the van. They had zipped-up hooded sweatshirts on. They were parked near the rear entrance to the gym. Scott waited in the car. Randy got out of the car. A gentleman came out of the club, which he thought was Paul Riedel, and he went into the glove compartment of his SUV. Randy came up to him, said,

'Hey, Paul.' The guy turned around and he shot him three or four times in the head and chest and neck area. He was making gasping noises, fell down, started crawling."

Then they got out of there. Scott was still driving. They took a couple of quick lefts and got stuck at a light. They heard police cars coming and stuff. They went to a close body of water, ditched the gun into the water.

Fiaccabrino said that he had been to Amityville once, maybe fifteen years before, but he wasn't familiar enough with the geography around there to know which body of water Randy was talking about when he talked of disposing the gun.

"Did there ever come a time shortly after the murder that Randy had spoken to Lee Ann on the telephone in your presence?"

"Yes. We were at a hotel in Miami and he didn't hear from her for about five days. He was kind of nervous, so he called me from his cell phone and she was in New York at the time."

"Why did he call her on your cell phone?"

"He didn't want to call her on his own cell phone. He didn't want any trace of calls to her."

"After that, did you ever hear Randy and Lee Ann discussing the murder?"

"Yes, Lee kind of freaked out, saying, 'You killed the wrong fucking guy.' Stuff like that."

"What, if anything, did Randy say in response to that?"

"He said you should have gave [*sic*] me a current picture." Lee Ann, according to Fiaccabrino, had complained about how hard it was to go to Alex's funeral and look Alex's girlfriend in the eye.

The next thing Fiaccabrino heard about the murder came when Randy said the cops were talking to people. Michael Scauzillo had gotten a call from a guy named

Michael Alexander. Alexander told Scauzillo that Randy should watch his ass because the Suffolk County police were looking for him and they knew everything about the murder.

Also questioned by the grand jury was Larry Ortolano, who was allegedly the first man Liz Budroni had approached when she was looking for someone to help with her girlfriend's daughter's marital problem.

The witness stated that his full name was Lawrence Oliver Ortolano, that his occupation was "venture work in the stock market," and that he lived in Boynton Beach, Florida. He was told that he was under oath, and that the grand jury was investigating the murder of Alex Algeri.

Ortolano was told that witnesses who gave testimony to the grand jury received immunity, unless they explicitly had waived immunity ahead of time—or if their self-incriminating evidence was gratuitous or nonresponsive to a question.

In other words, it was possible for a grand jury witness to incriminate himself, but only if he did so while answering a question that hadn't been asked. As a result of these rules, Ortolano would not be allowed to invoke the Fifth Amendment as he would if he was testifying in a jury trial. He would not be able to refuse to answer a question on the grounds that he might incriminate himself.

It was then explained to the witness that he was not immune from criminal-contempt charges if he was purposefully evasive in his answers. In other words, he would not be allowed to answer a question with "maybe yes, maybe no."

Ortolano was informed that he had the right to consult with an attorney before he answered any questions.

He told the court that he was not currently represented by an attorney, nor did he wish to delay the proceedings so he could get one.

If the witness did seek to testify with the legal assistance of an attorney, it was explained, the attorney would have to stay outside the courtroom. Following a question, the witness would have been allowed to consult with the attorney outside and then return to the witness stand to answer the question. The attorney, however, under no circumstances, would have been allowed to stay inside the courtroom while the witness was questioned.

At that point the main questioning of the witness began. He said that before he moved to Florida, about four years before, he lived in Westchester County, just north of New York City, in New York State. His first home in Florida was in Boca Raton. He subsequently moved to Lake Worth.

He said that while he lived in Westchester County, he knew a person named Ralph Salierno, who also went by the name Randy. He knew Randy because they both worked out at a gym called the East Coast Fitness Center, Yonkers, New York.

Randy was about sixteen years old when they met. Randy moved down to Florida while the witness was still in New York. After Ortolano moved to Florida, he became reacquainted with Randy because they both worked out at the Delray World Gym, in Delray Beach, Florida. Randy, the witness said, was a member of the club.

"And in addition to seeing him at your gym, did he occasionally come to your place of business as well?"

"Yes, he did. My company at the time was making motion pictures. We made three motion pictures, so he used to come by and say hi."

The witness then acknowledged that while in Florida, he was introduced to two men whose names were Richie

Pollack and Michael Fiaccabrino. Randy had introduced the witness to them, and Ortolano knew them as guys who "hung out" with Randy.

"Did Michael Fiaccabrino also work out, lift weights, at the Delray gym?"

"Yes, he did."

"Did you also know a person by the name of Scott Paget?"

Ortolano said that he had. Scott was another friend of Randy's, and Randy had introduced them. Scott, Ortolano said, worked out at one of the World Gyms in Boynton Beach.

"And do you know Michael Scauzillo?"

"Yes, I do."

"And how do you know Michael?"

"Michael, I know from living in Westchester County. He lived in Westchester. I know Michael Scauzillo for about ten years."

"Did there come a time, sir, that you met a woman by the name of Liz Budroni?"

The witness said there had. He met her at the Delray World Gym, where Liz also worked out.

"And did Liz Budroni ever approach you, and ask you to help her with regard to a problem?"

"Yes, she did."

"Could you tell us what Liz Budroni was asking you to help her with?"

"Basically, I was working out early in the morning and you have conversations with people at the gym. Like, it's social. You meet people. And I met Ms. Budroni there. She had a real heavy New York accent. She's from the Bronx or Brooklyn. She curses a lot. She is just fun to talk to. She was just a real character. In the midst of the gym she started telling me about her niece. That she was in a very bad relationship with her husband—"

"Let me stop you for a moment. What did she want done?"

"Someone to go to the husband and rough him up and beat him up—or threaten him or do something rough to him."

"To help the girl? This was the husband of a niece of hers?"

"Yes."

"Did she talk to you about any payment or anything?"

"She said that he has a lot of money, and they have a big house. You know, there would be some type of monetary reward, basically, for the service of helping them, and then she directly asked me."

"Asked you what?"

"To do that. To help her niece rough this guy up. And he lives over here in Long Island. And I looked at her and I said, 'I don't do anything like that. I'm a businessman. That's what I do for a living.'"

"After you told her that, did she ask you anything else?"

"If I knew anybody that does anything like that."

"And what did you tell her?"

"I said yes, I do actually. I do know somebody who collects money and . . . you know."

"What, if anything, did you tell Liz Budroni next?"

"I told Ms. Budroni that I would ask if this person would help her out with her problem with her niece."

"Did you give her a name of a person at that time?"

"Yes. His name was Randy Salierno."

"And after you told Liz this, what if anything did Liz do next?"

"Liz gave me her phone number and she said if he's interested, have him give a call."

"What did you do with the phone number?"

"I took the phone number, until I ran into Randy Salierno again."

The witness was asked if he remembered when these conversations occurred. It took him seconds of thought, but he finally came to the conclusion that the conversation had occurred at the beginning of the summer of 2000.

"How long after that conversation with Liz Budroni before you next ran into Randy?"

"It was about a week, maybe less, that I ran into Randy and told him."

"And when you ran into him at the gym, what, if anything, did you tell him?"

"I just told him the story. That the woman that I met, a character, a street-smart woman, very street-smart woman, and the problem that her niece was having, and would he be interested in something like that? And I gave him the number for him to call her."

"In addition, did you mention the money as well?"

"I told him what she had told me, about the house, and the guy, and everything like that." The witness said he gave Liz's phone number to Randy at that time. Randy was with his friend Michael Fiaccabrino as this conversation took place.

"What, if anything, did Randy say to you after you gave him the phone number?"

"He said he would look into it."

The witness said that he next saw Randy about a week or two weeks after that. Randy had come to Ortolano's office for a visit and with him were Michael Fiaccabrino and Richie Pollack.

"What, if anything, did Randy discuss with you at that time?"

"He said he went to see Liz and that she was exactly how I described her. A real character, real street-smart woman. And they talked about the problem of the niece and her husband, and the whole situation with the house, and the money and all of the things that went along with that.

Randy said that he was going to take the job, basically. He said he would try to help out."

"At that time, Richie agreed to that as well?"

"Yes."

The witness said that neither Randy nor Richie said where the meeting with Liz Budroni had taken place, nor did they say who else had been at the meeting. Ortolano verified that he, himself, had not been at the meeting.

The witness said that after the conversation in his office, about a month passed before he next spoke to Richie. Richie Pollack came to Ortolano's office alone, without Randy. Richie said he had backed out of the job to help Liz Budroni's niece.

Ortolano said, "Richie said he wasn't involved in that job. Basically he said to me that he wanted to get away from that type of work—and away from Randy. The reason Richie had come to me was to repay a loan. I had lent Randy and Richie five thousand dollars apiece, and Richie had come to pay me. He was moving, leaving the state, to go with his father, but he paid me back."

"With regard to Randy, did there come a point in time when he came to your office and he asked you to help him in any way?"

"Yes. Christmas of 2000. He came to my office and he wanted me to rent a car for him. He said something was wrong with his car and he needed a credit card. I didn't have a credit card, so I didn't think about it. He asked a couple guys, thirty or forty people in my office. One of the guys in my office, Jimmy Dasler, knew somebody at Enterprise [Car Rental]."

"Did your office do a lot of business with Enterprise?"

"Yes, we did."

The friend at Enterprise was Lucas Schmitt (pseudonym). Ortolano was asked if Randy had agreed to give Lucas any money in exchange for his help, and the witness said he had. The friend was to receive $500 for helping Randy rent a car.

Ortolano said that there was no further discussion of renting a vehicle that day, and that he next saw Randy a couple of days later. This time Randy was in the company of Scott Paget. Randy and Scott were in a rented van.

Ortolano said, "Randy told me they went up to New York, and they were sleeping in the van and they were traveling. He said he wanted to get the van cleaned, inside and out. I asked him, 'Why inside and out?' And he said, 'You just don't want to know. You don't want to know.'" Ortolano said it had been his experience that people didn't go out of their way to clean rented vehicles before returning them.

"Was he bringing this van back to you?"

"He was bringing the van back so that Lucas could clean it and return it."

"From the time that Randy had come back with Scott Paget to today's date, has Randy Salierno ever made any other admission to you about anything with regard to coming up to New York?"

The witness said that he had not. Asked specifically if Randy had ever talked about murdering anyone on Long Island, Ortolano said he had not. The questioning then returned to the van. Ortolano said he referred Randy to a gas station half a block away that would give it a thorough cleaning. It was an Amoco station and Ortolano knew the Russian guy who worked there. The van was cleaned and brought back.

The witness was asked to step outside the presence of the grand jury for a moment and some discourse took place off the record. Then the witness was brought back and was reminded that he was still under oath.

It was established that the story of the rented van that needed to be cleaned took place in January 2001, which of course was the same month in which Alex Algeri was murdered.

Ortolano subsequently learned that Randy Salierno had moved back to New York. Randy had not told him that in person, but he learned it from another source.

"And when was the next time you saw him?"

"Well, I was coming out of World Gym around six-thirty, seven o'clock. It was dusk and he was getting out of a car in the parking lot, and he looked, you know, like, kind of like wild. And he asked, 'Did anyone come and talk to you?' And I said, 'Why would anyone want to come and talk to me?' He said, 'Has anyone talked to you? The police, or the FBI? Has anyone come and talked to you?' I said, 'Why would the police or the FBI want to talk to me?' We went back and forth. He was upset and very loud. He was getting very agitated. I didn't know what he was talking about. I didn't know what was going on, and he said he borrowed a friend's car to come down here, and that he was leaving tonight, but he needed to see me to find out if anyone had talked to me."

"Did you subsequently find out he got arrested?"

"Yes."

"And that was after you saw him in the parking lot?"

"Yes."

"So he was not in police custody when he asked you if anyone had spoken to you."

"No, no, no."

"About how long after you saw Randy in the parking lot, did you learn that he had been arrested for murder?"

"About a week and a half."

The witness originally estimated that the meeting in the parking lot had taken place in June 2002, but upon being reminded that Randy Salierno was arrested in the middle of April 2002, he said that the parking-lot meeting had taken place closer to the beginning of April.

That concluded the grand jury testimony of Larry Ortolano.

On March 17, 2003, at 9:52 A.M., the grand jury handed down a three-count indictment on Lee Ann and a two-count indictment on Rocco. Rocco was charged with murder in the first degree and conspiracy in the second degree. Lee Ann's indictment included those counts, but added murder in the second degree.

The first-degree murder charged that Rocco and Lee Ann had, while "each aiding the other and acting in concert with another person known to the Grand Jury, on or about January 17, 2001 . . . with intent to cause the death of Paul Riedel (the last name was misspelled as "Reidel" throughout the indictment, but will be corrected here), did cause the death of a third person, to wit, Alexander Algeri." They did it by "shooting him with a gun." The motive was stated as "the receipt or expectation of receipt of anything of pecuniary value."

Count Two stated that Lee Ann had aided and acted in concert with Rocco with intent to cause the death of Paul, but Alex had been shot instead. Count Two left out the alleged cold-blooded motive.

Count Three stated that Lee Ann and Rocco had conspired with the intent to commit a Class A Felony, in this case a murder.

To justify their decision to indict, the grand jury, as was customary, listed the "overt acts" attributed to the accused in testimony heard by the panel. That list consisted of:

1. Lee Ann and Rocco met in Florida during the summer of 2000 and there made a business deal in which Lee Ann would pay Rocco to physically assault Paul.

2. Several weeks later, Rocco and Lee Ann met again in Florida and this time discussed the murder of Paul Riedel. The agreement was that Rocco would kill Paul, and Lee Ann would give Rocco something of monetary value.

3. Around that same time Lee Ann gave Rocco a photograph of Paul to assist in murdering Paul.

4. At that same time Lee Ann gave Rocco directions to the places on Long Island where Paul worked, lived, and hung out. Among those locations was the murder site, the gym Paul co-owned with the eventual victim.

5. During January of 2001, Salierno and Paget also came to a financial agreement. Salierno agreed to pay Paget $3,000 to participate in the murder of Paul Riedel. Paget's duties were to drive from Florida, where they were, to Long Island, New York, where the murder would occur. The payment also included driving duties for the return trip to Florida.

6. That same month Salierno and Paget obtained a van for the trip up North.

7. On January 17, 2001, Salierno and Paget killed Alexander Algeri at the Dolphin gym in Amityville, New York.

8. The final overt act was that after the murder, Salierno did pay Paget $3,000, signifying that the job had been accomplished.

On April 11, 2003, as part of the "discovery" process—whereby the prosecution makes available to the defense the evidence it intends to use—prosecutor Denise Merrifield was deposed. The deposition was made in response to a March 30, 2003, defense request for materials above and beyond what had already been provided.

She stated that she was a Suffolk County assistant district attorney (ADA) assigned with the prosecution of Lee Ann Riedel. The request had been made for all oral and written statements provided to the police by Lee Ann Riedel and Ralph Salierno, as well as the grand jury testimony of those individuals.

Merrifield replied that copies of all oral and written statements by Lee Ann Riedel were being provided to the defense, although she protested that this action was redundant, as those materials had been sent previously to the defense.

She said that she was also sending Salierno's statements, oral and written. She did not complain that these had been provided previously. She said that she was unable to provide transcripts of Lee Ann or Ralph's grand jury testimony because neither had ever testified before the grand jury.

In response to an apparent request for this information, Merrifield then itemized the contents of Lee Ann and Ralph's pockets at the times of their respective arrests. They couldn't have traveled lighter. Salierno had a wallet, $15 in cash, and one set of keys. Lee Ann had her Florida driver's license, a yellow ankle bracelet, and a library card.

Also provided to the defense were the laboratory and scientific tests. Merrifield wrote: "Photographs of the case, including autopsy photographs and the crime-scene video, are available for viewing at a mutually convenient time."

The prosecution said that they would be glad to provide the defense with tapes of police band radio calls and 911 calls concerning the case if the defense supplied a blank tape to dub those recordings onto.

The defense had requested complete details of any agreements the prosecution had made with their witnesses. Merrifield said that the agreements would be explained in court before those witnesses testified, but noted that "at this time" the people were requesting a court order to "conceal the identity of these individuals and their agreements."

The risk of physical harm and/or intimidation outweighed the usefulness of discovery, Merrifield said. Merrifield pointed out that Salierno was a dangerous man, even when incarcerated.

According to the Suffolk County Correctional Facility, Salierno had not been a model inmate since his arrival on murder charges. He had threatened several people's lives over the prosecution of this case, and he allegedly had assaulted a fellow inmate regarding information provided to the police against him.

"Thus," Merrifield wrote, "there is concrete evidence that disclosure of the identity of individuals who have cooperated and provided evidence against the defendant would result in serious harm to these people."

Merrifield acknowledged that the defense had asked for the defendant's driving record, but the prosecutor pointed out that, by law, she was not obligated to supply driving records to the defense.

Since turnabout is fair play, most of the time when it comes to the law, Merrifield ended her deposition with a request of her own, which was referred to as the "Reciprocal Demand," that the defense release to her the results of any psychiatric, psychological, or physical examinations that had been performed on one or both of the defendants.

The people also requested to borrow any photographs, drawings, or tapes that the defense hoped to introduce. The prosecution explained that it would need to "inspect" such materials.

Merrifield's last request was for transcripts of any statements that the defense witness had made to the defense attorneys. She then signed the affidavit. It read, "Denise Merrifield, Assistant District Attorney, Homicide Bureau." The affidavit was then stamped and signed by a Suffolk County notary public.

Chapter 32

A Dual Trial—Sort Of

Riverhead is a sleepy town in Suffolk County, located at the divergence of Long Island's north and south forks. Much of Suffolk's law and order headquartered itself in what was known as the Alfred M. Cromarty Courts Complex.

In the complex is a police station, a jail, a courthouse, with various courtrooms and judges' chambers, and the district attorney's headquarters that contained the office's homicide, major crime, family crime, appeals, and narcotics bureaus, as well as administrative offices.

The courts complex was located at the intersection of County Road 51 (Riverhead-Moriches Road) and County Road 98 (Nugent Drive), approximately four miles south of the Long Island Expressway on Exit 71 and eight miles north of Sunrise Highway on Exit 61.

Lee Ann and Rocco were to be tried together. Well, sort of. Only one trial would be held, but two separate juries would determine the former lovers' fates.

The panel determining Salierno's fate was called

"Jury A." Salierno's panel featured nine men and five women. Two of the men were black; the other twelve members were white.

Lee Ann's jury was "Jury B." And both juries would not see precisely the same trial. Many times testimony would be given in the presence of one jury, but not the other.

Because of this, both juries would spend a lot of time in a pair of rooms, sealed off from everything, especially what was going on in the courtroom while the codefendant's case was being argued by one side or the other.

Because of the double jury (and their alternates), the trial had to be held in a cavernous courtroom—Suffolk County's largest—big enough to accommodate everyone. Each jury was assigned its own court officers, had its own television monitors with which to view evidence, and had its own waiting/deliberation rooms.

The double-jury system, though rare in most regions, had become fairly common in Suffolk County in cases where more than one defendant was to be tried simultaneously. Between 1990 and 2004, eight major trials in Suffolk had used double juries.

According to the law, a defendant can't implicate a codefendant, so each jury would only hear the parts of each admission that were relevant to its case. In this case, evidence included defendants making statements that involved others charged with the same crime. One jury had to leave.

It might have been more efficient than holding two trials, back to back, but no one could deny that the dual-trial system was awkward. As *Newsday* columnist Robin Topping pointed out, there were "delays as the two panels file in and out, depending on the evidence being heard, and different defense lawyers question witnesses. Prosecutors must give two opening and closing statements—one for each jury—and the judge must carefully keep track of which panel hears what, to avoid a mistrial."

Was it still easier on the taxpayers' dollars than two separate murder trials? Prosecutors and defense attorneys disagreed.

John Collins, head of the homicide bureau for the Suffolk County District Attorney's Office, said, "The main benefit is judicial economy. While a dual-jury trial may take six weeks, you can rest assured that trying the two defendants separately would take longer, maybe nine or ten weeks."

Bruce Barket countered this opinion by saying, "It's confusing, it's time-consuming, and it's a minefield for reversible error." By that, he meant that the system had the strong potential of causing legal mistakes that would necessitate that the case be retried.

A Huntington, New York, defense attorney named Christopher Casser, who was not involved in this case, but had participated in double-jury trials in the past, agreed with Barket. Casser said that two-jury trials "sacrifice fairness for expediency. Defense lawyers with inconsistent theories end up turning on one another, creating almost a second-prosecutor situation."

Seth Muraskin said that his job was complicated by the double-jury trial, and that he would have preferred that his client, Ralph Salierno, and Barket's client, Lee Ann Riedel, be tried separately. The double-jury system, he said, made it more difficult for him to prevent his client from being tainted by his codefendant.

"If you throw so much mud against the wall, something has to stick," Muraskin commented. "I would rather it was my own mud as opposed to other people's mud."

In New York State the double-jury trial system did not have a substantial history. It dated back only to 1987. The first case involved a drag-racing incident that had resulted in a fatality. Two drivers were tried simultaneously before separate juries for criminally negligent homicide. Both drivers were convicted, but the cases went to the state court of appeals. One of the challenges stated that the trial had been unconstitutional because of the double jury. The court of appeals, however, upheld the constitutionality of the trial, but nonetheless warned against the indiscriminate use of double juries in the future.

"Multiple juries are to be used sparingly and then only after a full consideration of . . . the defendant's due process rights," the court of appeals ruled.

A note to readers: The comings and goings of the juries may not always be expressed in this re-creation of the trial. As a rule, unless otherwise stated, Lee Ann's jury, Jury B, was not allowed in the courtroom as Seth Muraskin was cross-examining prosecution witnesses on Salierno's behalf, and Salierno's jury, Jury A, was not allowed in the courtroom when Barket was cross-examining witnesses on Lee Ann Riedel's behalf.

On Sunday, February 15, 2004, two days before the trial started, Bruce Barket decided that he needed to know more about Mike "Big Balls" Fiaccabrino, the guy who was originally offered the job of driving the van from Florida to New York so Ralph Salierno could shoot Paul.

Lee Ann's defense attorney sent a fax to his private investigator, Jay Salpeter. He gave Salpeter the subject's name and nickname, his date of birth, and his last-known address. He gave him the docket number of Fiaccabrino's indictment, and the name of the judge who had handled the case.

Barket said that Mike wasn't the only member of the Fiaccabrino family who knew Paul Riedel was to be hit. According to Barket, Mike's father, Frank, also knew that a hit had been ordered.

The fax concluded: "Prior to his arrest, Mike Fiaccabrino is on tape telling a criminal investigator that Lee Ann either 'inspired' or 'conspired' the whole thing. Obviously, there is a world of difference. I have listened to the tape and it sounds like 'inspired' to me. But the Feds, of course, have it as 'conspired.' He does not say how he knows this. Perhaps it is what Ralph told him or what he assumed because of all the money Lee Ann was reputed to obtain on Paul's death."

Chapter 33

Merrifield's Opening Statements

After two juries were chosen, the trial began on February 17, 2004, three years and one month after Alex Algeri's murder. Presiding over the trial was Judge Louis J. Ohlig.

Judge Ohlig was a friendly, down-to-earth man, with a folksy way about him.

Ohlig liked people to know that he was not just in control of his courtroom, but that he knew everything that was going on in it. When he heard a sound he didn't recognize, his ears perked.

"Is that a new cough?" he'd ask, making everyone laugh.

When Ralph Salierno was brought into the courtroom, his friends and family had to do a double take to recognize him. He was wearing a suit, which was odd enough for Salierno, but odder still, he was wearing glasses.

Police officers who had attended many criminal trials

couldn't count the number of times they had arrested a suspect with perfect vision who showed up at trial wearing eyeglasses. Seasoned courtroom observers suspected immediately that Salierno did not actually need eyeglasses, but was wearing a pair with clear glass. This is a common trick designed to make a defense attorney's client look less dangerous.

Throughout the trial a regular in the courtroom's spectator section was David Armanini, Lee Ann's father. He was a man with exceptional posture, whose body language communicated pride. He always stood very straight with his chin up, almost defiantly up. By not bowing his head and by always presenting a proud posture, he was supporting his daughter physically. She, too, held her head up, and throughout the trial she would wear her hair in a perky ponytail.

Leading the prosecution team was Denise Merrifield, whose demeanor in and out of the courtroom was like night and day. Out of the courtroom the attractive assistant district attorney was almost coquettish, in the courtroom she was a hard-boiled professional. Merrifield delivered the opening statements for the prosecution. She had to deliver her statement twice, once for each jury.

To Jury B she said, "Lee Ann was a very cunning woman. Cunning and manipulative. And she felt trapped in an unhappy marriage, so she left the Babylon home she shared with her husband. She took their son, Nicholas, and one hundred thousand of his money and left for Florida.

"While down there, embroiled with hate for her husband, she contacted several Florida mobsters. The defendants met in her mother's home. She asked, 'Can you beat up my husband?' One of those mobsters was Salierno. He suggested that instead of just beating her husband up, that they 'whack' him. She agreed.

"The defendants at that point contracted with each

other to kill her husband. She agreed to pay him one hundred thousand to do the job. The original deal was fifty thousand up front and fifty thousand after the murder. She and Salierno later fell in love and decided instead to buy a house together from Paul Riedel's inheritance, an inheritance they never got a chance to collect. On December 24, 2001, Lee Ann bore Salierno a son."

Merrifield told the court that Salierno had an accomplice in the killing of Alexander Algeri, a guy named Scott Paget, who had already pleaded guilty to the murder charges against him. She described how Salierno and Paget had driven to New York and had set an ambush for Riedel in the parking lot behind the gym he owned.

She tried to explain the tragic case of mistaken identity. How could the killers get it so wrong?

"They were both big guys, both Italian men, and both had the same Yukon," Merrifield said. Both men also had similar haircuts and goatees, she noted.

Summing up, Merrifield promised that prosecution witnesses would say that Lee Ann, her mother, and her mother's female lover hired Salierno and Paget to "put a beating" on Paul, so that he wouldn't be tempted to come down South and try to cause trouble or get his money back.

There was good reason for Lee Ann's concern, Merrifield noted. Paul was a troublemaker to begin with, and he already had reacted poorly to Lee Ann's departure. He had hired a New York lawyer. A New York court order stated that Lee Ann could not take the boy more than fifty miles from home. That meant *Paul's* home.

The outcome of a nasty custody battle would determine whether or not Lee Ann would be able to take her son more than fifty miles away from Paul Riedel. To Lee Ann, fifty miles didn't seem like nearly enough.

She quickly determined that moving to New York was going to make a continued romance with Rocco impossible. The only alternative, and she thought it was quite a clever one, was to lure Paul down to Florida. That way she could be with Rocco and still be within fifty miles of "home."

The lure was Lee Ann's promise of reconciliation. Paul went for it. Despite the fact that she had split and taken the kid, he went for it. Lee Ann told him her bun in the oven was his, and that made him want to be near her even more.

In the meantime, the plot to "beat up" Paul, witnesses testified, evolved into a murder plot. Paul's court order said that if he lived for six months in another state, all future custody hearings would have to be held in that state.

On the six-month anniversary of Paul moving to Florida to be with his wife and son, Lee Ann told Rocco that she wanted her husband taken care of—permanently. The timing was too perfect, Merrifield said, to be a coincidence.

Prosecution witnesses, she said, would testify that Lee Ann had been very upset that Alex Algeri had been the victim of the attack. She told one witness that facing Algeri's girlfriend was the toughest thing she'd ever had to do in her life.

Prosecution witnesses testified that Algeri, who happened to drive the same car as Paul Riedel, was simply in the wrong place at the wrong time. Salierno shot him to death while he was retrieving music CDs from his car.

It would become clear through the testimony of prosecution witnesses that Rocco may have been a huge man physically, but he was a mental midget.

After Algeri's murder, Rocco regularly told the patrons of the strip joint where he worked that he had "killed people" and that sometimes he got the "wrong guy."

One of the most damaging prosecution witnesses would be a junior-high-school teacher who had heard Rocco make a series of admissions while bragging to strip joint customers.

Chapter 34

Barket:
"They Got It Wrong"

Bruce Barket also gave his opening statement on February 17, 2004. He said there was a better explanation for the events of January 17, 2001, than those offered by the prosecution.

Lee Ann's defense attorney said it was clear that the motive was not profit at all. It was jealousy. Salierno had heard rumors that Lee Ann and Paul Riedel were attempting reconciliation and this had driven him over the edge, into a murderous rage. Salierno had been obsessed with his client. He wanted Paul Riedel dead.

About Salierno, Barket said, "He is as guilty as sin."

Barket's key point was that "my client is no Lady Macbeth. If Lee Ann was so cunning, then why did the killers show up at the gym on a Wednesday when Wednesday was Paul Riedel's day off?

"I believe that the prosecution, in their sincere efforts to exact justice in this case, simply got it wrong," Barket said. "They got it wrong because she is not involved. The evidence, quite simply, does not point toward Lee Ann having any involvement in this case. Lee Ann is not the cunning, manipulative woman the prosecution would have you believe she is. She is not the Lady Macbeth that's being painted by the prosecution. She is, rather, a classic abused woman, who picks the wrong man, time after time."

Barket apparently had psychoanalyzed Lee Ann and had come to a conclusion about why her taste in men was so poor.

"I believe her problems started when her mother left her when she was only eleven years old to live with her gay lover," Barket said.

Barket said that murder had been the last thing on her mind when she first met with Salierno.

"She merely wanted protection, in case Riedel came looking for her," Barket explained.

He told the jury that the evidence would show that the Riedels were attempting reconciliation at the time of the murder. He told the court that there was no conspiracy in this case. This was a case of one man acting on his own.

Lee Ann's jury got to hear all about Barket's theory, which placed responsibility for Algeri's death on Salierno's shoulders, and Salierno's shoulders alone.

"This is the story of a man's obsession with a woman. The murder was Salierno's evil and murderous attempt to eliminate his rival," Barket concluded.

Salierno's jury sat in their waiting room during Barket's presentation.

Seth Muraskin, Ralph Salierno's defense attorney, delivered the third opening statement of the day. He reiterated what he had earlier said outside the courtroom, that the so-called confession Salierno had signed had been beaten out of him and that he actually had been on a date in Westchester County, many miles from the murder scene, at the time of Alexander Algeri's demise.

Chapter 35

The Intended Victim

On the morning of February 23, 2004, tension was high in the courtroom as the intended victim, Paul Riedel, was called to the stand to testify. Everyone wanted to see if Paul and Lee Ann would make eye contact. They didn't appear to, although it's hard to believe that one, or maybe both, hadn't sneaked a peek.

Paul testified that he had met Lee Ann when she was working as a barmaid at a strip joint on Long Island. They'd fallen in love and gotten married. They had a baby named Nicholas; then they had marital problems. A lot of it was his fault. He was partying too much.

They'd split up. She left and took the baby. He was afraid that he wasn't going to get to see his son anymore. He might have hurled a threat or two. He might have made a phone call and yelled. He had a big mouth when he was high—although he didn't get high anymore.

There were a couple of attempts to reconcile, but none lasted very long. Sooner or later he'd lose his temper; then Lee Ann would be packing her bags again.

They were separated at the time of the murder, although Lee Ann wasn't in Florida. She'd been on Long Island, in fact, visiting her grandma. Paul testified that he learned about Alex's death from his wife. He'd been at a friend's house when it happened.

Right after the murder Lee Ann had talked him into going on vacation so they'd driven together up to New England. Lee Ann convinced him that the bullets had been meant for him and he was in danger.

Not long thereafter, he and Lee Ann had broken up for good. Divorce papers had been filed on both sides by the time Lee Ann was arrested. He didn't know, or even suspect, that Lee Ann had been behind the shooting in the gym parking lot until after she was arrested and reporters started shouting questions at him.

Yes, he knew that Lee Ann had taken up with a guy in Florida named Rocco. He didn't know much about him, just that a guy named Rocco was visiting Lee Ann and going places with her whenever Paul wasn't around, visiting his kid.

When Denise Merrifield's direct examination of the intended victim was complete, Paul Riedel was cross-examined by Bruce Barket on behalf of Lee Ann Riedel, and by Seth Muraskin on behalf of Ralph Salierno. The cross-examination lasted the rest of the day and Riedel was visibly fatigued by the time Judge Ohlig adjourned court for the day.

Barket wanted Jury B to realize that the "mistaken identity" portion of the prosecution's scenario might have been valid—but that was still no indication that Lee Ann was guilty of murder. He established that Riedel was a man of many enemies by asking Riedel what he thought when he heard that the best man at his wedding, and the godfather of his son, had been shot and killed in the parking lot behind the bodybuilding gym they co-owned.

Paul told the court that as soon as he heard about the

shooting, "I knew it wasn't for Alex." He realized immediately that he had been the intended target.

"Who did you think was behind the shooting?" Barket asked.

Paul replied that he didn't know, but that was what the question was, as far as he was concerned: Which of his enemies had tried to bump him off?

Was it the two mobsters he bounced out of his gym for harassing a female patron?

Was it the drug connection that had accused him of being a police informant?

Riedel didn't think so, but he considered the possibility that he might have been someone connected to his bookie, to whom he owed $24,000. He'd had harsh words in a restaurant with a captain of the Gambino crime family a few days earlier. Had that been enough to get him eliminated? he wondered. But Riedel did not say that he suspected his wife to be behind the murder.

Having established that Riedel knew several people who were both prone to violence and who might have a reason to hurt him, Barket moved on. Now he attacked Riedel's credibility.

"Isn't it true that you have dealt cocaine in the past?" Barket asked.

Riedel acknowledged that it was.

"And isn't it true that you were using cocaine heavily at the time of Alex Algeri's murder?"

"Yes, sir."

"And isn't it true that you were using anabolic steroids at the time of the murder?"

"Absolutely not."

"Pardon me?" Barket said, pretending not to hear.

"I did not and do not use anabolic steroids," Paul Riedel replied.

Barket's brow was furrowed as he asked, "Isn't it true

that you once told a judge that steroid use led you to deal drugs?"

"I might have said something like that, yeah," Riedel said.

"Now you deny using steroids?"

"Yeah. I just said that to the judge because I was charged with selling cocaine and I thought that might get me a lighter sentence."

"So you lied to a judge to get something you want?" Barket asked.

"I'm sure you know it's done, Mr. Barket," Riedel replied.

"Actually, I don't, sir," Barket said.

During his cross-examination of Riedel, Barket brought up the fact that Riedel was found to have hidden $280,000 in two different locations. Muraskin asked him why he had done this.

"I did it so I could pay a contractor. I was going to have a new gym built."

"Why would hiding copious amounts of cash help you pay a contractor?"

"That's just business. The contractor gives a better price for cash," Riedel replied.

"Just business," Barket echoed, smiling. "So why did you hide it in two locations?"

"You don't want to have cash lying around in your own name," Riedel answered matter-of-factly.

"No further questions," Lee Ann's defense attorney said. Judge Ohlig called for a short break.

When court reconvened, it was Seth Muraskin's turn to cross-examine the intended victim. Jury B had left and Jury A had taken its place.

As had Barket, Muraskin tried to divert attention from his client, and hopefully create "reasonable doubt" in the mind of a juror or two, by running through the list of enemies Riedel had acquired. Muraskin wondered why the first suspect was not his bookie, to whom he owed $24,000.

"The debt was no big deal, that's why," Riedel said. "Doesn't everyone know a bookie?"

Chapter 36

Big Balls

Then the prosecution put Michael "Big Balls" Fiac-cabrino on the stand. His testimony to the grand jury had helped get Ralph and Lee Ann indicted. Now the prosecution hoped it would help get them convicted as well.

Fiaccabrino spent three days on the stand: February 24 through 26, 2004. He told the court that he'd been a childhood friend of Salierno's from New York. Like Rocco, he'd relocated to Florida.

Fiaccabrino testified that the plan had not started out as murder. He said that a mutual friend had approached Salierno with a "business opportunity," that he knew a woman who wanted "her husband's legs broke and a major beating thrown on him."

"The plan then changed?" Merrifield asked.

"Yeah, then they planned to set Paul up for a drug arrest," Fiaccabrino said.

"How were they going to do that?"

"The plan was to plant a kilogram of cocaine in the

diaper bag of Riedel's son so that he would get arrested at the airport. That way Paul would be out of their lives for twenty years," Fiaccabrino testified.

Fiaccabrino gave credibility to Paget's tale when he testified that Rocco had offered him $3,000 to drive from Florida to New York and back again. But Fiaccabrino, who was running a marijuana-growing operation, steadfastly refused to be an accomplice to murder. He did, however, arrange through an intermediary for Salierno to do a "paperless" rental of a minivan with which to do the job.

Fiaccabrino told the court that after the murder, Salierno—whom he called Randy—told him that he had waited with Scott Paget in a van behind the gym until a man came out and went to the passenger side of a vehicle.

"Salierno told me he walked to the victim and said, 'Hey, Paul' before shooting him in the face, neck, and chest. He said he stood there and watched as the man crawled back into the gym."

Denise Merrifield asked, "Did Salierno tell you what he did as the man crawled back to the building?"

"Yeah," Fiaccabrino answered. "He made fun of the man gasping for breath."

Fiaccabrino did not limit his damaging testimony to Rocco. He pointed an accusatory finger at Lee Ann as well.

"You knew that Salierno was having a relationship with Mrs. Riedel?" Merrifield asked.

"Yeah. Yes, ma'am."

"How would you describe their relationship?"

"I don't know about her. He didn't like her that much. He told me he thought she was ugly, disgusting."

Barket's face reddened from behind the defense table, and he made his umpteenth "hearsay" objection of the day. For the umpteenth time Judge Ohlig overruled.

Barket believed the testimony to be perjury. It contradicted a previous statement by the witness. The defense lawyer knew that during an earlier statement to police, before he rehearsed his testimony with the prosecution, Fiaccabrino had said that Rocco Salierno loved Lee Ann.

Fiaccabrino testified that he had been present when Lee Ann gave a photo of her husband to Salierno—and immediately Barket began to seethe.

"Did Mrs. Riedel say anything when she handed Mr. Salierno the photo?" Merrifield asked.

"Yes," Fiaccabrino replied. "She said, 'I want him fucking dead.'"

Visibly angry, Barket objected that the testimony was hearsay. Judge Ohlig again overruled.

Barket's anger didn't have anything to do with hearsay, however. He didn't believe Lee Ann ever said that she wanted her husband dead, at least not in the context of hiring a hit man. He felt that Fiaccabrino was lying, his testimony all but written for him by the prosecution.

Barket knew he had to do something. This testimony, if believed, completely negated his attempt to paint Ralph Salierno as the bad guy, and Lee Ann as his innocent "victim." The direct examination continued.

"Did Mrs. Riedel specify how she was going to compensate Salierno for killing her husband?"

"Yeah. She said she would pay with the assets she would inherit."

Barket had had enough. He began in a somewhat civil manner. But that degenerated. He started out by saying that the assistant district attorney was engaging in "gamesmanship."

Barket said, "Denise Merrifield is attempting to deny my client a fair trial."

"You are coming very close to slander," Judge Ohlig warned.

"I'm not done," Barket said, on a roll now. "I think she's coaching witnesses to lie. Witness after witness has changed their testimony."

He pointed out the discrepancy between Fiaccabrino's testimony that Salierno thought Lee Ann was ugly, when in a previous statement he had said he thought Salierno was in love with Lee Ann. And he pointed out this change—from truth to falsehood—was hurting his client's ability to receive a fair trial. After all, why would Salierno kill to keep this woman from reconciling with her husband if he thought she was ugly and disgusting?

Barket knew that one thing Lee Ann had going for her was her looks. The lawyer wasn't convinced that every member of the jury liked his client, but he was fairly certain that all twelve acknowledged her physical attractiveness. Everybody had seen ugly and disgusting, and Lee Ann wasn't it.

Judge Ohlig invited Denise Merrifield to say a few words on her own behalf.

"I'm saddened to see that a fellow officer of the court would accuse me of allowing perjured testimony," Merrifield said.

"I also believe that Denise Merrifield is withholding the terms of Fiaccabrino's federal plea deal," Barket said. Barket had been unable to find out just how much Fiaccabrino was getting in exchange for his testimony against both defendants.

"I know that this witness has made a plea deal with the prosecution. He's charged with conspiring to purchase four hundred sixty-five pounds of marijuana, Your Honor," Barket said, gesturing at Fiaccabrino. Barket complained that he couldn't get access to electronic evidence against Fiaccabrino.

"The prosecution is making [it] difficult for me to get

audible copies of undercover tape-recorded conversations the Drug Enforcement Administration made of Fiaccabrino," Barket said. According to reports, those tapes contained Fiaccabrino talking about Salierno's version of the murder.

Then Barket moved for a series of mistrials based on this belief that the prosecution had withheld key information from him, and that the prosecutors had elicited false testimony from witnesses. The judge denied each motion.

"Ms. Merrifield, why hasn't defense been able to get a copy of the tape?" Judge Ohlig asked.

"Your Honor, Mr. Barket was supplied with the tape he is talking about. It was on a computer disc," Merrifield said, biting off her words a bit.

"I have put those discs in my computer. They do not open," Barket complained.

"Your Honor, it's not my fault if the disc doesn't work in his computer," Merrifield said.

"Perhaps if you give him another copy . . . ," Judge Ohlig said.

"I have given him several copies," Merrifield said.

Then the direct examination of Fiaccabrino continued. It was a considerably less relaxed courtroom than it had been when Fiaccabrino took the stand.

After the murder, Fiaccabrino testified, Salierno had asked him to retrieve an Internet article from his computer that stated that it was Alex Algeri who had been murdered in Amityville.

"Were you present when Salierno read the article about Algeri being murdered?" Merrifield asked.

"Yes, I was."

"What was Salierno's reaction?"

"He said, 'Holy shit! I shot the wrong guy.'"

Big Balls was also present, he testified, a couple of weeks later, when Lee Ann and Rocco had argued about Rocco's fatal mistake.

"She said, 'You shot the wrong guy, you stupid ass-hole,'" Fiaccabrino testified.

"What did Salierno say in response to that?" Merrifield asked.

"He said, 'You should have given me a better photo.'"

According to Fiaccabrino, Lee Ann then called Rocco a "fucking idiot" for killing the wrong man.

During Fiaccabrino's direct testimony there were frequent objections from Barket and Muraskin. They argued that testimony against one defendant amounted to hearsay against the other.

"Your Honor, both juries should hear it all because it is evidence of conspiracy between the two," Merrifield said.

Judge Ohlig overruled the objections.

Now Muraskin cross-examined Fiaccabrino.

"You made a deal with the prosecution in exchange for this testimony, did you not?" Muraskin asked.

"In exchange for my truthful testimony, that's correct, sir," Fiaccabrino said.

"In fact, you hope to avoid having to do prison time because of your appearance here today, correct?"

"Yes, sir."

"The term 'rat.' You know what it means?"

"Yes."

"That apply to you?"

"I would say so," Fiaccabrino said, without a hint of shame in his voice.

"The crime took place in January 2001, but you first discussed it with police in September 2002, is that correct?" Muraskin asked.

"Yes, sir."

"Why didn't you contact the police regarding your knowledge of this case sooner?"

"I was growing weed. I didn't need any more police around," Fiaccabrino said.

That answer briefly broke the tension that had enveloped the courtroom.

As expected, Barket's cross-examination of Fiaccabrino was lengthy. It stretched into Fiaccabrino's third day on the stand.

"According to Salierno, at their first meeting, what did Lee Ann say she wanted to do to her husband?"

"She said that she wanted his legs broken," Fiaccabrino replied.

"Did Salierno tell you that Paul Riedel had stopped taking drugs by the time of the murder?" Barket asked.

"No."

"Did Salierno tell you that Paul Riedel was going to parenting classes in an attempt to reconcile with his wife?"

"No, he didn't mention that. I heard he was an abusive, bad guy," Fiaccabrino said.

"According to Salierno, how did Lee Ann plan to pay for the hit?"

"He said she was going to pay with the proceeds from Paul Riedel's estate."

"Wouldn't it make more sense for her to pay with the hundred twenty thousand she had lying around?"

Before Merrifield could object that the question called for a conclusion, Fiaccabrino said, "I dunno."

Finally, a workable copy of Fiaccabrino being secretly taped was played for the court. As anticipated, Fiaccabrino discussed Salierno on the tape.

"They beat the confession out of him," Fiaccabrino said on the tape, referring to Suffolk County police and Ralph Salierno. "They beat him bad. They fucked him up. You should have seen it."

After the tape was finished, Barket asked Fiaccabrino, "Since you say, 'You should have seen it,' that you did indeed see the results of the beating you say cops put on Ralph Salierno."

"No."

"No?" Barket replied, a thick tone of incredulity in his voice.

"No, sir."

"You didn't see the results of the beating?"

"No, I did not."

"Do you know for a fact that there even was a beating, Mr. Fiaccabrino?"

"No, I guess I don't."

"You admit, do you not, that you knew about the plan to kill Paul Riedel before it happened, isn't that right?"

"Yes."

"Why didn't you come forward and tell police that you knew of a plan to kill someone?"

"I didn't want to get involved."

"Not even to save a life?" Barket asked.

"I didn't think about that," Fiaccabrino said. "I had my own problems."

When Fiaccabrino's cross-examination was over, Sal Algeri called his wife on his cell phone. She was in Florida recuperating from hip surgery.

"How did it go today?" she asked.

Thinking that Fiaccabrino's testimony assured future convictions, Sal said to his wife, "She ain't sung yet, but the fat lady's clearing her throat. This thing is over."

Chapter 37

Who's Bullying Who?

On Monday, March 1, 2004, both sides complained to Judge Ohlig that the other had committed improprieties over the weekend, attempting to intimidate and influence witnesses.

Seth Muraskin told the judge that Suffolk County police detective Pasquall Albergo and another policeman—whom he didn't name—had paid a visit to Salierno's alibi witness. Albergo was also the detective who had accompanied Detective Robert Anderson during the initial interrogation and subsequent arrest of Ralph Salierno.

Muraskin pointed out that the police had known of the witness's existence and importance since late 2003, but they had chosen the weekend before her testimony to pay her a visit.

"They were there to harass her, to intimidate her," Seth Muraskin complained.

Muraskin said that Albergo and the other detective located the witness, whose name was Tara Anzalone-Smith (pseudonym), and used strong-arm techniques.

"They walked into her apartment without permission and suggested that she was being paid by Salierno to lie on the stand," Muraskin said. "They said to her, 'Do you know we have him cold? What is Mr. Salierno getting you? What is he giving you?'"

Muraskin's accusation continued. The policemen paid a visit to the strip club where she worked. There they told her employer that they planned to charge her with a crime.

"That amounts to coercion, a misdemeanor," Muraskin said.

The judge turned down Muraskin's request for a mistrial. Reporters later tried to get the police department representatives to comment on the accusation, but all declined. A similar request of the district attorney's office did bring a comment.

"The detectives did not do anything inappropriate," Denise Merrifield said.

Accusations flew in the other direction as well. Prosecution witness Michael Fiaccabrino complained that he had received an unwanted visit at the Long Island hotel where he was staying from Jay Salpeter, the private detective who had been hired by Lee Ann's defense team. Fiaccabrino said that Salpeter "bothered him."

Salpeter had been more than just the defense lawyer's private eye. He also had functioned on occasion as point man for the "Free Lee Ann" PR campaign. He had even commented to the press about the case, always in sync and on point with Barket's message. Salpeter told Court TV that Lee Ann Riedel was no murderer. She was merely a woman who had moved to Florida and, while down there, had gotten mixed up with the wrong crowd.

"When all of this is finished," Salpeter said, "you will see that Lee Ann had no part in a murder or planning a murder. Lee Ann is guilty of making some bad choices in her life, and getting involved with the wrong men, but she is no murderer."

After a few days of testimony reporters had learned who liked to talk and who didn't. After a while they left Lee Ann's father alone. David Armanini had been a regular at the trial, along with Lee Ann's stepmother, but he'd had little to say to the press.

Armanini politely turned down all requests for interviews. He did make one comment to Court TV, saying, "I am confident that Lee Ann will be acquitted and freed from jail. Through the Blessed Mother and her Divine Son, my daughter will be proven innocent."

Chapter 38

"Lee Ann Was All I Had"

Later that same Monday, Paul Riedel gave his first interview with the press, speaking with Lisa Pulitzer, of the *New York Post*. He was candid and admitted offhandedly that he and Alex, who had been buddies, had had an argument in the days before the murder.

So when Alex got whacked, everybody thought it was he who had done it. Paul said it was rough, and told the reporter how he had tried to attend the funeral of his son's godfather, but had been turned away angrily by the Algeri family.

Riedel explained that he'd known as soon as he heard Alex was dead that he, Riedel, had been the actual target. Who would want to shoot Alex?

Riedel said he had his own list of suspects back in those days, but that it would never have occurred to him in a million years that his wife was behind it. He had thanked Lee Ann for standing by him, and later he felt like a fool about it.

He recounted how he and Lee Ann had met while she

was a waitress at a strip joint on Long Island, how she had gotten pregnant with her second child, and he had done the right thing and married her. He explained how Lee Ann had left him after the baby was born because he was partying too much, and how her splitting had served as a "wake-up call" for him.

He said that he tried to win her back, but he was forced to file for divorce after their relationship failed to improve. He said he and Lee Ann reconciled in December 2000 and she had agreed to move back to Long Island with him. That was about a month before Algeri was gunned down in cold blood.

Riedel told the reporter that he had been a tearful mess in the days after he learned his friend had been killed, but he didn't remember that kind of emotion from Lee Ann.

He said he was an emotional wreck after Alex was shot. He knew he was the prime suspect, and that only added to his stress. He said that he turned to Lee Ann for comfort.

Of course, by the time of the interview, he realized that Lee Ann was one of the few people in the world who knew Paul Riedel was innocent. He said that he was questioned regularly by the police in the months following the crime.

For weeks he'd been subjected to surveillance, Riedel complained. One or more cops shadowed him as he went about his daily life.

He discussed testifying at the Suffolk County Criminal Court in Riverhead the previous week, and how it had been an emotional experience for him. He couldn't believe that he was testifying against his own wife, and he could not bring himself to make eye contact with her in the courtroom.

The subject of the interview shifted to four-year-old Nicholas Riedel at that point. Paul noted that he now had full custody of his son and was doing his best to be a good father.

Pulitzer asked if he knew Lee Ann was cheating. He said a relative had told him a guy named Rocco had been hanging around, but Paul didn't believe him. He said he didn't believe Lee Ann had cheated on him until after she was arrested.

Chapter 39

The Direct Testimony
of Scott Paget

On March 3, 2004, the prosecution's most important witness, Scott Paget, the driver of the van, took the stand. He was testifying as part of a plea agreement he had made with the prosecution.

Paget told the court that it was indeed he who had driven the van, but it had all been Salierno's idea. Salierno was the actual killer.

In his testimony Paget referred to Ralph Salierno as "Randy." He said he met Randy at the World Gym, in Delray Beach, Florida, and that he saw him from time to time in strip clubs, such as Diamonds, Wild Side, and Flashdance. Paget, who like many of the figures in the story was a muscular weight lifter, admitted that muscle had been in his job description as well. He had collected debts for loan sharks to help support his drug habit.

He said that he had known Salierno for a couple of

months when Randy offered him a moneymaking proposition.

"Randy asked me if I had a problem going to New York with him to clip someone," Paget told both juries.

"Did you understand what he meant by 'clip'?" Merrifield asked.

"Yes, I did."

"What did he mean?"

"He meant 'kill,'" Paget replied.

"Who did Randy want clipped?"

"He said the girl he was with wanted her husband out of the picture. He offered me money."

"How much money?"

"Three thousand dollars."

Lee Ann's lawyer objected that this was hearsay evidence, but the judge overruled him.

"Did Randy tell you why his girl wanted her husband out of the picture?"

"Yeah, he said that the husband was an asshole and she would get his money."

Paget said that it was Salierno who acquired a .38 snubnosed revolver.

"He was unhappy with the size [of the gun]," Paget testified. "He was going to be wearing gloves, so it was going to be difficult handling it."

Paget said it was Salierno who rented the white minivan they would use.

"He made all of the arrangements for the trip north," Paget said.

They drove north for twenty hours on January 16, 2001.

"Did you make any stops?" Merrifield asked.

"Yes, ma'am."

"How many?"

"Two."

"What were the stops for?"

Paget recalled that one of the stops was to pick up a wool cap for Salierno and the other was to pick up New York State license plates for the minivan. The plates would be put over the existing plates on the van. They then followed directions that Salierno said he got from Lee Ann and drove to Paul Riedel's gym in Amityville.

"He had to tell me where to go. I'd never been to Long Island before," Paget said.

Paget testified that he parked the van so that he and Salierno could get a clear view of the gym's rear door and Paul Riedel's black SUV. Less than a half hour later, a man exited the center and walked toward the SUV.

"What did you know about the man you were there to kill?" Denise Merrifield asked.

"We knew that he was tall, muscular, and Italian-looking," Paget replied.

"Did you have any information about his vehicle?"

"Yeah, the directions said he drove a black Yukon with a Dolphin gym sticker on it."

"Did you know that Alex Algeri fit the same general description as Riedel and drove the color and make of car?"

"No, we didn't know," Paget said, sadness evident in his voice. It was clear that he felt awful about the error he and Salierno had made.

"How was the lighting behind the Dolphin gym when you arrived that night at about seven-thirty?"

"The lighting was very bad. It was hard to see," Paget replied.

"What did you do after you arrived at the gym?"

"We backed the van into a parking spot and we waited."

"How long did you have to wait?"

"About twenty minutes."

"What happened then?"

Paget testified that he saw a man who fit the description of their target come out the back door of the gym and go to the black Yukon in the parking lot, which was only a few steps away from the door.

At that point, Paget testified, Salierno said, "That's him."

Paget testified that Salierno jumped out of the van alone and confronted the man.

"I heard him say, 'Paul!' I heard a series of shots after that, three or four shots," Paget testified. "Randy then climbed back in the van and yelled, 'Go!' As we were making our getaway, we passed a police car racing toward the bodybuilding gym."

"What did you do after leaving the gym?" Merrifield inquired.

"We drove for about a mile down a road called Merrick Road."

"What did you do after you drove a mile?"

"I stopped the van and pulled over. I got out of the van and threw the gun into a creek."

They also made stops to get rid of Salierno's clothes. The New York State license plates were removed from the van, revealing the Florida plates underneath. The New York plates were thrown away.

Paget remembered, just as Salierno had, that they got lost on the way back, but eventually found the George Washington Bridge. That got them out of New York—at last—and on the road to Florida. Paget said that he and Salierno spoke little on the return trip to Florida.

"Did Salierno pay you for your participation in the murder?"

"Yeah, he paid me as soon as we got back to Florida," Paget replied.

"Did he pay you in cash?"

"Yes, ma'am. He gave me thirty 100-dollar bills, and then he went to get a tan at a tanning salon down the street."

"When did you learn that the man who was killed was not the intended target?"

"Not until the next day." On the day after the murder, Paget testified, he and Salierno had visited the office of a friend, Big Balls Fiaccabrino. Salierno, Paget said, wanted to find out if the Long Island murder had made the newspapers. He went online and checked the Internet.

"Randy downloaded an article off the Internet that said it was Alex Algeri who had been murdered," Paget said.

Other witnesses had stated that Salierno had been upset when he learned that the murder victim had been Algeri instead of Riedel. Paget disagreed.

"He seemed amused," Paget testified. "He just looked at me. He was stone-faced. He sort of smiled, threw the paper at me, and said, 'I got the wrong guy.'"

"As far as you know, have you ever met Paul Riedel?" Merrifield asked.

"No, but I did run across him once," Paget replied.

"Tell us about that."

"Two months after the murder, by coincidence, I noticed a black Yukon with New York plates in the parking lot of the Florida gym where I was working out. I later found out the truck belonged to Paul Riedel."

"Did you tell anyone about seeing Riedel's Yukon in the parking lot of the Florida gym?"

"Yeah. I told Salierno. He said maybe we should kill Riedel while he was in Florida."

"What did you say to that, Mr. Paget?" Merrifield asked.

"I said no. I didn't think it was a good idea," Paget replied firmly.

That concluded the direct examination of Paget. It was late in the day, so Judge Ohlig ruled that cross-examination of the witness would begin the following morning, Thursday, March 4.

Chapter 40

Paget Cross-Examined

Under cross-examination by Seth Muraskin, Paget admitted that his current story had undergone many changes over the months. Paget admitted that he originally had denied ever being in New York with Salierno.

When he finally did admit to making the trip, he initially said that he thought it was another collection job for a loan shark. He gave a written statement, but it was not nearly as detailed as the testimony he had offered on behalf of the prosecution.

Paget's next version of the story was that he knew the trip was being made to kill someone and that he had received $3,000 to share the driving duties.

With Jury A in the jury box, Salierno's defense attorney, Seth Muraskin, had Paget go over in detail all of the changes his story had undergone.

"The closer we got to the trial, the more detail you provided, isn't that the case?" Paget admitted it was. Muraskin then made sure the jury understood that Paget would benefit from his cooperation with the prosecution.

Paget's agreement with the prosecution said that in return for his cooperation during this trial, and a guilty plea at his own arraignment, he would receive a reduced sentence of eighteen years to life.

"This is your bargain. You say this and we're going to give you eighteen-to-life, right?" Muraskin said, holding up the written plea agreement.

"Right, eighteen-to-life for my truthful testimony," Paget replied.

Jury A was dismissed, but Jury B was present in the courtroom while Lee Ann's attorney, Bruce Barket, cross-examined Paget.

"Mr. Paget, isn't it true that you are a regular cocaine user?" Barket asked.

"Yes," Paget conceded.

"And aren't you a regular drinker of GHB?" the defense attorney inquired.

GHB is a "party scene" drug used to get high. In higher doses it has been used as a "date rape" drug as well. On the street the drug is most commonly referred to as G, but it is also called Gamma-OH, Liquid E, Fantasy, Georgia Home Boy, Grievous Bodily Harm, Liquid X, Liquid Ecstasy (although it is *not* Ecstasy), Scoop, Water, Everclear, Great Hormones at Bedtime, Soap, Easy Lay, Salty Water, G-Riffick, Cherry Meth, Organic Quaalude, and Jib.

Paget admitted that yes, he was a regular drinker of GHB.

"Isn't it true that you've done work as a collector for loan sharks?" Barket asked. Paget said it was true, but when asked, he said he was not familiar with the term "the vig," which is slang for the amount of weekly interest (points) on a loan from a shark.

"Mr. Paget, when did you meet the defendant Ralph Salierno?"

"May 2000."

"Where did you meet him?"

"In a gym."

"What were you doing for a living at the time you met Salierno?" Paget asked.

"I was working security at nightclubs," Paget said.

"When you say security, you mean that you were a bouncer?"

"That's right."

"And when you say nightclub, are you referring to a strip joint?"

"Yes."

"Which strip joint were you working at when you met Salierno?"

"I'm not sure. I left one job around that time and started another."

"What were the names of the places you worked at during that time?"

"One place was called Wild Side. The other was Flash-dance," Paget said.

Barket had Paget reiterate that in January 2001, Salierno offered him $3,000 to drive to New York to "murder an individual."

"How did you tell Salierno that you agreed to take the money in exchange for driving the car?"

"I said, 'For three grand, maybe I can help,'" Paget replied.

As Paget drove the van up to New York, he testified under cross-examination, Salierno showed him a .38 snub-nosed revolver. Salierno, Paget said, showed him how he was going to conceal one license plate by putting a phony one on top of it. After they got away, they would take off the fake plate and throw everyone off the trail—if there was a trail.

Paget said that he and Salierno had left Florida in their rented minivan on Tuesday, January 16, and that they had gotten to New York in twenty hours.

"Isn't it true that your appearance was different in January 2001 than it is now?" Paget inquired.

"Yes, I had facial hair, a goatee. I had a little more hair on top, too," the balding Paget said, smiling.

Paget then told Barket how his arrest had come about, how cops had called his mom and asked her to relay a message. Paget had been led to believe that police needed to speak with him because of an incident he had witnessed in a strip joint. But when Scott got to the police station, he realized he had been deceived and that he actually was about to be questioned about the Amityville hit.

Paget recounted how the day after the murder, he and Salierno drove to Big Balls Fiaccabrino's office in a warehouse and there retrieved an Internet article that said the wrong man had been murdered on Long Island.

Barket—using the police report resulting from Detective Anderson's interrogation of Paget, as well as Paget's written confession—had Paget go over his previous statements, point by point, establishing that Paget was a person who did not always tell the truth, especially if he was speaking with members of law enforcement.

Paget admitted that at first he had told Detective Anderson that he only had been to New York once, in 1988. He said he'd been to Brooklyn visiting a girlfriend.

"Why did you lie about this?" Barket asked.

"I was trying to downplay my involvement," Paget said. Later in the interview with Anderson, he admitted that he'd been in New York as recently as 1996, this time visiting another girl. Anderson asked him point-blank if he had been to New York with Randy Salierno and he said no. During the Florida interrogation Paget admitted that he had gone out on loan collections with both

Randy Salierno and Mike Alexander. (It was through Alexander that Long Island police first heard the name Scott Paget.)

At one point, according to the transcript of that interrogation, Paget said, "Listen, what if I did take a ride with him at one time or another? What do you want to know? I might have information you want to know, but need to know where I stand. Are you going to arrest me?"

During that interview Paul finally got around to admitting his involvement in the murder. He said, "Most of what I told you guys is true, with the exception of certain things."

Paget's written confession, Barket strongly noted, did not mention that Salierno had gotten instructions on how to find Paul Riedel on Long Island from Lee Ann.

Judge Ohlig interrupted Barket as he was making this point. The judge noted that Paget didn't mention the instructions from Mrs. Riedel in his written confession because the police did not ask him about that.

Barket responded sharply, "Judge, with all due respect, I don't think the court should be doing redirect [examination] for the prosecution."

Barket later moved for a mistrial because of the statement made by Judge Ohlig, but it was, predictably enough, denied.

"I've never been accused of not giving a defendant a fair trial—or of being biased—in my twenty-eight years on the bench," Judge Ohlig said. (According to *Newsday*'s Andrew Smith, Ohlig's claim should come with an asterisk. Less than two years before, two defense lawyers publicly accused Judge Ohlig of pressuring one defendant in a child molestation case to implicate his codefendant. Ohlig denied he had done this, then recused himself from the case.)

With Barket still cross-examining, Paget described driving to New York, where Randy directed him to a strip mall. Randy directed him to drive to the rear lot and look for a black SUV. It was there. They parked and saw a man exit the gym and go to the black SUV. Randy got out of the minivan. Just before the shots were fired, Paget said he heard Salierno say, "Paul." Then there were anywhere from three to five shots. Randy ran back, got into the van, and said, "Go."

Barket, of course, wanted Jury B to think of the crime in terms of a jealous man shooting someone he thought was his rival—rather than as a murder-for-cash scheme, as the prosecution had painted it. Toward that end the defense attorney got Paget to say that Randy continued to think of Paul long after the botched attempt to kill him. Randy had asked him to see if he could find out Paul's routine. The implication was that Salierno was still thinking of whacking Paul Riedel, even during a period of time when he was not in extensive communication with Lee Ann.

Again asked about his plea bargain, Paget said, "I did drive the car. I did not pull any trigger." By cooperating with the prosecution he would be out of jail while he was still too young to collect Social Security.

Then Barket got to the crux of his cross-examination. He wanted to show that Lee Ann had nothing to do with the murder, and that it was not Lee Ann who was pulling Salierno's strings, as the prosecution was contending.

"After the murder, did you ever discuss the shooting with Salierno?" Barket asked.

"I did not."

"Did you ever encounter Paul Riedel after the shooting of Alex Algeri?" Barket asked.

Paget said that he had. He ran into Paul in a gym in Florida. "When I told Randy about it, he was surprised. He did not know that Lee Ann and Paul had moved to Florida."

That concluded Bruce Barket's cross-examination of

the man who had ridden shotgun during Alex Algeri's murder. Denise Merrifield informed Judge Ohlig that she had a few questions in redirect.

Merrifield established that at the time of the murder, Scott Paget legally owned a 9mm gun. Scott said that he wanted a gun after 9/11, but admitted that he first applied for a license in May 2001.

Merrifield then took Paget over familiar territory again. How it had come about that he had made a plea agreement with the prosecution. The agreement, Paget testified, had been made in November 2002.

The prosecutor made Paget reiterate that the Suffolk County DA's Office had never made any promises to Paget, that it was Paget who approached the DA's office with info, not the other way around.

"Were you ever promised that you would not be charged with murder?" Merrifield asked.

"No, I was not," Paget said.

"You were arrested on April eleventh, correct, the same day you were interrogated by Detective Anderson in Florida?"

"That's correct."

"At that time, did you know whether or not Ralph Salierno was under arrested for the murder of Alex Algeri?"

"I did not."

"No further questions," Denise Merrifield said. Judge Ohlig looked at Barket.

"I have a couple of questions on recross," Barket said.

"Proceed," the judge said.

Bruce Barket again emphasized his theory that Paget and Salierno had been responsible for Algeri's death, and that his client had had nothing to do with it.

"Your knowledge of Lee Ann Riedel's involvement in this crime came from the very person who paid you three thousand dollars to help him commit the murder, the person who you say pulled the trigger, the same person who said you pulled the trigger, yes?" Barket asked.

"Yes," Paget said.

"Isn't it true that all of your information of how Salierno and Lee Ann had intended to profit from a scheme to kill Paul Riedel came from Salierno, and from Salierno alone?" Barket asked, enunciating especially well so the jury would know that an important point was being made.

"Yes, that's true," Paget said.

That established, Barket took his last few questions to further hammer away at the witness's credibility. He made Paget repeat again that he had taken cocaine and GHB regularly.

"Isn't it true that two months after you got your gun, you OD'd on cocaine and GHB?" Barket asked.

It was true. Paget explained that he had passed out outside his car and the gun was in the car. He had not been arrested in that incident.

Barket made Paget admit that there were aspects of Paul and Lee Ann's relationship to which he wasn't privy.

"I didn't know everything," Paget conceded.

Referring to the month of the murder, Barket asked, "Did Salierno tell you that in January of 2001, she had reconciled with her husband?"

"No."

"No further questions, Your Honor," Barket said, and Judge Ohlig told the witness that he could step down. Paget was immediately gathered up by his guards and returned to his cell.

Chapter 41

The Schoolteacher

On the morning of March 5, 2005, Denise Merrifield stood behind the prosecution table and said, "Michael Cunningham (pseudonym) to the stand."

Cunningham, like many of the men involved in this case, was thickly muscled. He had bleached blond hair, a Fu Manchu mustache, and an earring in his left lobe. He was wearing a suit and black-and-white wingtip shoes.

Cunningham said in a deep, clear voice that he was thirty-three years old and had a bachelor's degree in political science. He had attended both the University of Florida and Florida Atlantic University.

In addition to his poli-sci major, he triple-minored in education, social science, and math. He currently was employed as a ninth-grade math teacher from Boynton Beach, Florida. He didn't look like a schoolteacher. More like a night owl.

"Before I begin the pertinent questioning of this witness," Merrifield said, "I want to note that he has vowed ahead of time to take the Fifth if he is asked any questions about drug use." Then she asked the witness: "Do you know a man named Scott Paget?"

He did. In fact, he and Paget went way back. They had met in 1990 or 1991 in college. They were roommates for 1½ years when both attended Florida Atlantic.

"Did there come a time when you and he stopped being roommates?" Merrifield asked.

There had, and it hadn't occurred under the best of terms, either. "I had to ask him to leave—on account of his drug addiction," Cunningham said.

Merrifield asked and was told that Scott drove a Tahoe during his college career.

"His mother bought it for him," the schoolteacher recalled.

Though they stopped being roommates, they continued being friends, and Cunningham was asked what he knew about Scott Paget's employment history following his collegiate career.

"He worked at an exercise equipment store, then as a bouncer," Cunningham said.

"Did you know a man by the name of Ralph Salierno?" Merrifield asked.

"Yeah, but I didn't know him as Ralph. I knew him as Randy," the schoolteacher replied.

Merrifield asked how Cunningham had met Salierno and the witness said that Scott Paget had introduced them. They were all in an "adult nightclub." After that, Cunningham said, he saw Salierno regularly.

"I saw him in adult nightclubs, in the World Gym in Boynton Beach and Delray Beach," Cunningham said.

"To your own personal knowledge, did Scott Paget once purchase a weapon legally at a Lantana, Florida, pawnshop?"

"Yes, he did."

"And what kind of a weapon was that?" Merrifield asked.

"It was an automatic," the schoolteacher replied.

Merrifield's questions then launched Cunningham into a story that would be the meat of his testimony. Sometime in the summer of 2001, before Salierno moved to New York, Cunningham had been drinking with Scott Paget and Ralph Salierno in a joint called Club Diamond.

Cunningham didn't remember how it started, but Salierno got into an argument with someone Cunningham didn't know. "Randy said to this guy, 'You don't know me. You don't know anything about me. I kill people.' Salierno then turned to Paget and said, 'If I get the right guy.'"

"What was Salierno's facial expression as he spoke those words?" Merrifield asked.

"He was grinning—grinning and smirking," Cunningham responded.

"What did you do when Salierno joked about getting the right guy?"

"I looked at Paget and he looked at me, and then we looked away and didn't say nothing."

"Did Ralph Salierno or Scott Paget ever discuss the murder of Alex Algeri with you?"

"Yes, they both did. Paget discussed it with me; Salierno talked to Paget about it in front of me."

"What did Salierno say to Paget in front of you about the murder?"

"He said he felt sorry for the next people who rented the van they were in. That they stunk it up with BO and flatulence," Cunningham replied.

Cunningham said that Suffolk County police officers first spoke to him about his knowledge of Algeri's murder, on April 2, 2001. Two weeks later, Cunningham repeated his statement in New York. This time he had two attorneys with him.

"Did you enter into an agreement at that point?" Merrifield asked.

"Yes, I agreed that I would testify and you-all agreed that I wouldn't be prosecuted for anything I might have done."

That concluded the prosecution's direct examination. The cross-examination of the schoolteacher was short and sweet.

Seth Muraskin asked, "Are you currently under the influence of cocaine?"

"No," the schoolteacher said, his face showing concern. There weren't supposed to be drug questions.

"OK. Do you have a history of cocaine abuse, Mr. Cunningham?"

Merrifield objected, noting her earlier statement that the witness was going to plead the Fifth to any questions pertaining to his drug use. Judge Ohlig sustained Merrifield's objection and the line of questioning about the schoolteacher's drug use was cut off.

Muraskin had no further questions, and Bruce Barket said he had no questions for the witness, as he had offered no testimony that was damaging to Lee Ann.

Chapter 42

The Mystical Discovery of the Gun

Merrifield called Sergeant Raymond Epps, the man who had found the murder weapon, to the stand. He was a clean-cut man—clearly all business, all professional. Even before his testimony began, spectators could see that the jury liked Sergeant Epps. He identified himself as the supervisor of beach and boat operations for the Suffolk County Police Department's Marine Bureau.

Under direct examination, Sergeant Epps told the court he was a fourteen-year veteran of the department. He was the executive officer in his bureau, which meant he was second in charge. Because of his rank— he had been a sergeant for five years—he was in charge of most dive operations.

On December 6, 2002, Detective Robert Anderson requested that Epps's bureau perform an underwater search. The job was to search the bottom of a stretch of creek for anything metallic.

The search was to be of the bed to Amityville Creek, which was eighty-one feet wide as it ran along Montauk Highway. The divers, following the New York state troopers manual, would use underwater metal detectors. These metal detectors had three settings: high, medium, and low. For this search the machine was put on the medium range.

The search began on December 10, 2002, four days after the initial request. Divers determined that the creek varied in depth from one foot near the edges to nine feet in the middle.

Sergeant Epps explained that searches such as these involve dividing the area to be searched into small squares, which they called a grid. Each diver was assigned certain squares in the grid, and when all of the squares were searched, they knew they had given the search area complete coverage. The sizes of the squares in the grid, Sergeant Epps explained, depended on the clarity of the water.

"Big squares for clear water, little squares for murky water," he said.

Nothing was found that first day. Or on the next attempt. Or on the one after that. Subsequent dive-and-search operations were held on December 16, 17, and 22—and another on January 3, 2003. At that point the searches stopped.

"Why did they stop?" Denise Merrifield asked.

"Because of weather conditions," Sergeant Epps replied. "It was getting colder and the divers were hampered by ice."

"Did the search of the creek resume at any point?"

"Yes, we searched again on March 31, 2003."

"Did the search resume in the same stretch of Amityville Creek?"

"No, we resumed our search in Ketcham Creek, about one mile east of the previous site."

Sergeant Epps said that they were trying to piece together the location of the gun based on the story of one of the men involved in a murder, that he had hurled a gun from the road. Having decided that the new location was a viable alternative to the Amityville Creek, which had been searched so thoroughly during the early winter, Sergeant Epps had an idea.

He found a rock that was approximately as heavy as a handgun. Riding in the passenger seat of a police car, he chose the spot from which he thought the gun might have been hurled—as best as he could based on the story of the witness—and heaved the rock into the creek as far as he could.

There was a big splash and the ever-growing concentric circles in the water marked the spot where the rock had *kerplunked* its way into the creek. He decided to start there.

Soon thereafter, using the underwater metal detector and a clam rake, he found a gun at the bottom of Ketcham Creek buried in two feet of mud. Merrifield then produced photos of a clam rake and asked him if it was the one he had used. Sergeant Epps said it was.

"What kind of gun was it, Sergeant Epps?" the prosecutor inquired.

"It was a five-shot Smith and Wesson revolver with five casings in it," the witness replied.

"What condition was the gun in?"

"Poor. It was encased in mud and dirt. There were barnacles growing on the handle."

"What happened to the gun after it was discovered?"

"It was kept in a bucket of the water it was found in, and turned over to the Crime Scene Unit."

"Did that conclude the [Suffolk County Police Department] Marine Bureau's search of Ketcham Creek?"

"No, Detective Anderson asked us to return on April 4, 2003, for an additional search. We did a thorough search of the area and found nothing further," Sergeant Epps said.

The gun had been found very quickly after Epps hurled his big rock, in the first place Epps had looked. Detective Anderson wanted to make sure that nothing had been overlooked in Ketcham Creek.

"No further questions, Your Honor," the assistant district attorney said.

"Mr. Muraskin," Judge Ohlig said.

The defense attorney for Ralph Salierno, predictably, wanted to know more about the hurling of the big rock. Epps had expected this from the moment they found the gun in the way they had. It was just good police work, he knew, but it had happened too easily. He knew that some were going to doubt his word. Some might think that it had to be true because the cop would have made up a better story if he were lying. Others might just find it far-fetched. Throwing a heavy object from the open window of a moving vehicle is an imprecise location technique, for certain. Imagine throwing two rocks on separate drive-bys and trying to hit the exact same spot twice in a row? It would be very hard, and the odds would be good that the two rocks would land nowhere near one another. Yet Sergeant Epps precisely located the lost gun in two feet of mud by throwing a rock from a moving car. Did it have to be true, or was the sergeant just a bad liar? Muraskin wanted to get to the bottom of it.

"How fast was the car going when you threw the rock out the window?" Muraskin queried. His voice increasingly dripped of sarcasm as this line of cross-examination proceeded.

"Approximately thirty-five miles per hour," Sergeant Epps replied.

"And how far from the road did the rock land in the water?"

"The distance from the car to the gun's location was twenty-eight feet."

"Isn't it miraculous that the rock landed where it did?" Muraskin said, glancing at the jury to make sure they noticed how incredulous he was. His voice now drenched in sarcasm, Muraskin asked Sergeant Epps about his qualifications to locate a gun by hurling a big rock out the passenger-side window of a moving motor vehicle.

If Sergeant Epps was annoyed or troubled by this line of questioning, he did not let on.

"What, you have never had any special training in physics?" Muraskin questioned.

"No."

"And you have never had any special training in the relationship between weights and distances?" the defense attorney posed.

"No."

"No further questions, Your Honor," Muraskin said, believing he had made his point.

The witness was excused. Sergeant Epps's story may have been on the wild side, but there was nothing wild about Sergeant Epps. He had been a very professional, believable, trustworthy witness.

Spectators couldn't help but feel that Muraskin had picked the wrong target to discredit. The defense attorney had looked worse because of his sarcasm, and Epps looked more than ever like the poster boy for good police conduct.

Chapter 43

Liz and Larry

Elizabeth Budroni, the lover of Lee Ann's mother, testified for the prosecution. She had been granted immunity by the prosecution in exchange for her testimony.

She said, "Lee Ann was very upset." Referring to Paul Riedel, Liz said, "She was frightened of him. He hadn't been nice to her. He talked to her real mean and she wasn't happy."

Addressing both juries, Liz admitted that she had gotten together with Lee Ann and her mother and decided they should "recruit" someone to "scare" Paul Riedel. If necessary, they decided, maybe even beat him up for emphasis.

Referring to Lee Ann, Liz said, "She didn't want him hurt badly. Just beat."

"Is it true that you carry a book about New York mobsters with you?"

"That's true."

"Could you share with the court why you do that?"

"So I can point out to people my relatives who are in the book."

"So you, Pat, and Lee Ann decided to scare Paul Riedel, correct?"

"Correct."

"Who did you first contact about doing the job for you?"

"A guy by the name of Larry Ortolano. I saw him at my gym and I knew him from Little Italy."

"Why did you approach him in particular?"

"I figured he had Mob ties," Liz said.

"What did Larry Ortolano do?"

"He referred me to Ralph Salierno," Liz said.

The prosecution then called Larry Ortolano to the stand. Like Liz Budroni, Ortolano had been granted immunity from prosecution in exchange for his testimony. He told the court who he was, spelled his name, and said that he was forty-six years old. By this time the court was growing used to seeing huge men testify. Ortolano—like Salierno, Riedel, and Paget—was big and muscular. Ortolano was also bald, and his muscles bulged so much that his dark blue suit strained to contain them.

"What do you do for a living, Mr. Ortolano?" Merrifield asked.

"I am an investment banker," he said.

"Is it true you recently spent a year in a federal prison?"

"Yes, it is."

"What were the charges?"

"I was convicted of stock fraud conspiracy."

"Do you currently possess a credit card?"

"No, ma'am."

The juries got the idea. Ortolano was stretching the

truth a bit when he referred to himself as a banking investor.

"You are a big guy, have you ever made money from using your strength?"

"No, but I get mistaken for a nightclub bouncer all the time," Ortolano bragged.

"Why did Liz Budroni call you when she wanted someone to lean on Paul Riedel?"

"I don't know. She's the first person to ever ask me to use my muscle on someone."

"How did Liz Budroni go about asking you to use your muscle?" Merrifield asked.

"She was exercising on the treadmill next to me. She said her niece was being abused and harassed by her husband. She said her niece was in a very bad relationship with her husband and she wanted someone to talk to him, to scare him, to rough him up, or something of that nature," Ortolano said.

"Did you have any contact with Ralph Salierno following the murder of Alexander Algeri?"

"Yes, I did. I don't remember how long it was after the murder, but some time."

"And what, if anything, happened?"

"Salierno came to see me at my office. I asked him what he wanted and he asked me if I knew of a place where he could have a rental van thoroughly cleaned before returning it. I asked him why he needed the van cleaned and he said, 'You don't want to know. You don't want to know.'"

Chapter 44

Anderson Takes the Stand

On Tuesday, March 9, 2004, Detective Robert Anderson took the stand, and with Merrifield's questioning guiding him along, he ran down the history of the case's investigation. Anderson testified that mistaken identity had not been the investigation's first theory as to what happened.

"You originally believed that Alexander Algeri had been the true intended victim of the murder, isn't that correct?"

"Yes, it is," Anderson admitted.

"What were some of the first avenues the investigation took?" Merrifield queried.

"We looked into possible organized crime connections involving Algeri. We checked into a gambling debt owed to Algeri. There was a rivalry with another gym, and then we investigated a jealous-boyfriend angle," Anderson said. "All of these were negative. Another theory was that Algeri's business partner had been falsely accused of being a police informant. Once I verified that Paul Riedel was not working undercover for law enforcement, we discounted that theory as well. The only motive left was the mistaken identity."

"When did you receive the break in the case?"

"About five months following the murder."

"In what form did that break come?"

"Nassau County police received an anonymous tip to the effect that Paul Riedel had been having difficulties with his wife, Lee Ann," Anderson replied.

"Was there another important break?"

"Yes, on November 11, 2001, New York City detectives arrested a grand larceny suspect named Michael Alexander. Alexander told police that he was a friend of Salierno's and offered information about the Algeri murder. Some of the information that Alexander provided did turn out to be false, but he did supply police with Scott Paget's name."

Throughout this latter part of Detective Anderson's testimony, Bruce Barket repeatedly objected on the grounds that Alexander was not testifying and therefore could not be cross-examined. His objections were overruled.

Judge Ohlig said, "I'm not going to tell the prosecution how to try their case."

Barket responded, "With all due respect, Judge, that's your job."

Anderson then testified about his initial interrogation of Salierno, about how Rocco had tried to lie, but the suspect slowly realized that the cop already had all of the answers to the questions he was asking.

Anderson recalled telling Salierno for the first time that a junkie had already spilled the beans, that he already knew all about the murder of Alex Algeri. He recalled the look of defeat on Salierno's face when he pulled out the photo of Scott Paget.

"I wanted to prove to him we weren't bluffing," Anderson testified. The detective told the court that Rocco had confessed to knowing all along that the road trip from Florida to Amityville was for the purpose of committing murder; he then wrote a six-page confession to the same effect.

Salierno's written confession was identified and entered into evidence. That ended the direct examination of Detective Robert Anderson.

Anderson was cross-examined on Friday, March 12, by Seth Muraskin. In anticipation of this damning evidence against his client—Anderson's testimony and Salierno's confession—Muraskin had made statements both in and out of court that left no doubt that he felt Salierno's confession had been beaten out of him.

That beating, Muraskin believed, was administered by the "notorious" Suffolk County Police Department, a department known for its unusually high confession rate in murder cases. Because of complaints of police brutality during interrogations, Muraskin pointed out to the jury that the Suffolk County police had been the subject of various state investigations that had spawned numerous reports in the media.

Now Muraskin cross-examined Anderson on this point. Referring to Salierno's six-page written confession, Muraskin asked, "Was that statement written out before Ralph Salierno was brought to police headquarters?"

Anderson responded with a question of his own, "Now, isn't that a silly question?"

"How did you get him to sign it?" Muraskin asked.

"I didn't get him to sign it. He did it," Anderson answered.

"Where did the interrogation of Ralph Salierno take place?"

"In our interview room."

"About how big would you say the interview room is?"

"About eight feet by eight feet."

"Does it have windows?"

"No, it does not."

"When you put on your black gloves, were they leather?"

"That's a silly question."

He asked Anderson if he had punched Salierno during the interrogation. He asked if he had kicked him. He asked if he had knocked Salierno off his chair and then repeatedly kicked him.

"Did you grind the heel of your shoe into Salierno's genitals?" Muraskin asked.

The lead investigator denied it all, until he was clearly angered by the defense lawyer's tactics.

"Have you ever been accused of assaulting a defendant before?" Muraskin asked.

There was a two-second pause and then the detective replied, "In the past a defense attorney like yourself will allege anything, yeah."

Muraskin asked if Detective Anderson would prefer videotaping confessions in the future.

"Yes, I would," Anderson said. "I would prefer it because then people like you couldn't stand up there at that podium and fire the false bullets that you are firing."

In redirect examination the ADA asked if it was routine for police to mistreat suspects until they confessed. Anderson replied that it wasn't the routine at all, and that the contrary was true. Merrifield asked why this was.

"It makes more sense to treat defendants properly," Anderson replied. "We want to continue to have their cooperation so they'll talk about the crime."

* * *

Bruce Barket then cross-examined the witness. He did not attack the manner in which police convinced Ralph Salierno to confess. Barket made Anderson reiterate that Paul Riedel was a man with many enemies, many of whom had the inclination to commit murder.

Anderson was forced to mention again that Riedel had antagonized a Mob figure, had owed a bookie a sizable sum, failed to convince his drug buddies that he was not a police informant, and had been feuding with a rival gym.

The cross-examination became nasty when Barket asked about a minor point.

"I'll take your word for it," Anderson said skeptically.

"God forbid I tell the truth," Barket replied, wide-eyed with sarcasm.

"It would be nice of you to tell the truth," Anderson said, and the hostile exchange continued.

Chapter 45

Weighing the Taint of Hearsay

During the prosecution's case it was Barket who offered the most objections, who seemed to be most appalled by the way things were going.

It was Barket who regularly put on the record his belief that Judge Louis J. Ohlig had regularly committed "prosecutorial mistrial" and repeatedly asked for a mistrial. Barket, with these accusations, apparently was trying to build a case with which to, if necessary, win Lee Ann a reversal or a new trial in appellate court.

Both Barket and Muraskin, however, had been vocal in and out of the courtroom about their belief that the trial was being mishandled. Both disapproved of the double-jury system and felt that it was making it more difficult for their clients to receive due process. Both lawyers felt that their clients were being unfairly tainted by the other.

Muraskin said, "There are a lot of things coming out

that have to be tied to Lee Ann, and for my purposes, what Lee Ann does or doesn't do is irrelevant and muddies the water."

Both attorneys had called for a mistrial due to the hearsay evidence being allowed by Judge Ohlig against their respective clients. Hearsay evidence, because it is a witness saying what he heard another person say, constitutes evidence from someone who can't be cross-examined. If those hearsay statements were made by one or the other of the defendants, no cross-examination can take place because the defendants cannot be forced to testify to anything that might tend to incriminate them. Under normal circumstances hearsay evidence is not allowed, but in this case Judge Ohlig had allowed it after Denise Merrifield successfully argued that such evidence was necessary in order for her to prove a conspiracy between the defendants.

Muraskin told *Newsday* columnist Robin Topping that Judge Ohlig's hearsay rulings would be among those challenged in a court of appeals.

Chapter 46

"That's Just Liz"

On Monday morning, March 15, 2004, with Jury B in the jury box, Detective Sergeant Edward Fandrey took the stand for the prosecution against Lee Ann Riedel. Fandrey told the court that he had interviewed Lee Ann two days before Rocco was arrested and that she had denied ever wanting to have her husband killed.

The interview, Fandrey said, took place at Lee Ann's Florida home in April 2002, fifteen months following the murder. At first she denied it, but she eventually admitted to first meeting Salierno when he was invited to a meeting with her mother and Elizabeth Budroni. At that meeting, Lee Ann conceded, the possibility of Rocco "beating up" Paul Riedel was discussed.

"Did there come a time when you asked her if money was discussed at the meeting?" Merrifield asked.

"Yes, there did. Mrs. Riedel said that the subject of a price for the job never came up," Fandrey replied.

"What was your response to that?"

"I said, 'That's incredible.' But she insisted. I said, 'Lee

Ann, the way it's supposed to work is that when I ask you questions, you are supposed to tell us the truth and not wait until you know I know it, and then tell us reluctantly.'"

During the interrogation, Fandrey said, Lee Ann continued to deny that she had ever wanted her husband killed. Fandrey said that it appeared to him that she was using her children as an excuse not to answer questions. "Whenever we got to a question she did not want answered, she would say that one of the children needed tending to." The children at that time were a toddler and an infant, two years old and three months old, respectively.

"What made you think that this was a technique she was using to avoid answering questions?"

"The children did not appear to need tending to," Fandrey said. "I mean, they were not crying or anything."

Fandrey said that following the question-and-answer period with Lee Ann, she had prepared a written statement. In the statement, which was identified by the witness and entered into evidence, Lee Ann said that Liz Budroni, during their first meeting with Rocco Salierno during the summer of 2000, had stated that someone ought to "break Paul Riedel's legs."

Lee Ann acknowledged that she and Paul were separated at the time of that first meeting with Rocco, but discounted the importance of Liz Budroni's comment.

"Liz is always going off like that. That's just Liz," Lee Ann had said.

Later, according to Lee Ann's written statement, a fellow named Richard Pollack had offered to "whack" Paul Riedel. Lee Ann wrote, "I said I didn't want him killed. He's the father of my kids."

During cross-examination Bruce Barket asked, "In that written statement, did Lee Ann acknowledge that she and Paul Riedel reconciled twice after you met Ralph Salierno?"

"No."

"In the written statement, did she mention that she and Paul Riedel were together when Algeri was killed?"

"No."

"You testified that you thought Lee Ann was using her children as an excuse not to answer questions."

"That's right."

"You believed that she was saying they need tending to when you thought they didn't, is that right?"

"Yes, sir."

"Detective Sergeant Fandrey, are you an expert of some sort in child care?"

"No."

"Are you familiar with all of the key signs of a child needing tending to?"

"No."

"So it is possible that the children required attention without you knowing it."

"Sure, that's just the way it seemed to me at the time."

"No further questions."

The prosecution concluded their case soon after, and it was the two defense attorneys' opportunity to call witnesses.

Chapter 47

Salierno's Alibi Witness

On Tuesday, March 16, 2004, Seth Muraskin's key defense witness took the stand. She was the buxom and attractive stripper who, as Muraskin had promised for weeks, would provide Ralph Salierno with an alibi. And she was more than just a key witness, she *was* Muraskin's defense.

The woman raised her hand and promised to tell the truth, the whole truth, and nothing but the truth. She then stated her name—Tara Anzalone-Smith—and spelled it slowly for the court reporter's benefit.

"How old are you?" Muraskin asked.

"I'm twenty-seven," she replied.

She testified that Salierno could not have been the killer because he had been with her on a date at the time of the murder.

"It was like our first date, having dinner together," Anzalone-Smith said.

"About how long were you with Mr. Salierno on January 17, 2001?" Muraskin asked.

"About thirteen hours," she said.

"Where did he pick you up?" Muraskin asked.

"At the bar where I was working at the time, a place called Pretty Woman," she said.

"What time was that?"

"He arrived at about four P.M., and he stayed until I finished work at about five-thirty," she replied.

"What happened then?"

"We left Pretty Woman together and went to a restaurant to eat," the exotic dancer said.

"Do you remember which restaurant you went to?"

"Yes, it was a place called Artie's."

"Where is Artie's located?"

"On City Island," she replied, referring to a small island filled with many restaurants on the Long Island Sound, not far from the Bronx coast.

"You were with Mr. Salierno at Artie's on City Island at seven-thirty that evening?"

"Oh yes."

Now, as far as Muraskin was concerned, it was established that their date took place during the murder, so Salierno could not have been anywhere near the crime site.

"Where did you go after you dined?" the defense attorney asked.

"We went to a few bars. We were out until about three forty-five A.M."

"You were with Mr. Salierno that entire time?" Muraskin asked.

"Yes, I was."

"What did you do at three forty-five on the morning of the eighteenth?" Muraskin asked.

"He took me to my home, which I share with my mother and my daughter," she replied.

"He dropped you off at your home?"

"No, he came in and stayed until five-thirty or six

in the morning. Then I asked him to leave. I wanted to make sure he wasn't still there when my mother woke up."

"No further questions," Muraskin said. His body language showed confidence. His client was innocent and he had just proved it.

There must have been a temptation on the part of the prosecution to ignore this witness, to pretend that they simply did not hear. But, when asked, she said, yes, she had a few questions for the witness.

"Ms. Anzalone-Smith," Merrifield said, "how can you be so sure of the date of your outing with Mr. Salierno?"

"I'm sure," Anzalone-Smith replied. "We dated for a little more than a year and that's my anniversary."

Now Merrifield might have regretted her choice to cross-examine. She cut her questions short, dismissing the witness with a small wave of her hand. There was little to gain. The less the jury saw of this witness, the better.

The woman would remain alone in her contention that Salierno was with her on the night of the murder. Muraskin was putting a near-impossible weight on the uncorroborated word of this Bronx-born dancer. It was her word against thirty-five prosecution witnesses.

Chapter 48

"I Noticed Bumps on His Head"

In Muraskin's mind, he had convinced the jury that his client was many miles from the murder scene at the time of the shooting, so he attacked what he believed to be Salierno's coerced confession.

After Ralph Salierno's alibi witness stepped gingerly down from the witness stand, Muraskin called Steven Wilutis, of Miller Place, Long Island, to testify. Wilutis, it was established, had been Ralph Salierno's attorney before the defendant retained Muraskin.

Wilutis said that he saw Salierno in the days following his initial interrogation and confession.

"How did Mr. Salierno appear when you saw him?" Muraskin inquired.

"Mr. Salierno appeared as if he had been mistreated," Wilutis replied.

Muraskin spoke slowly: "What signs of mistreatment did you see?"

"I noticed bumps on his head, almost like welts, above the hairline and on the back of his head," Wilutis replied.

Muraskin had no further questions. This time Denise Merrifield was eager to cross-examine.

"Mr. Wilutis, do you know how those marks on Mr. Salierno's head got there?" the ADA asked.

"No, I do not."

"You were not there when this individual voluntarily spoke to the police, were you?" Merrifield asked.

"No, I was not—if he did," Wilutis replied.

"You do not know for sure that those welts were not caused by other inmates in the Suffolk County Jail, do you?"

Wilutis admitted that he did not. Merrifield had no further questions. Wilutis was allowed to step down. Muraskin then informed Judge Ohlig that the defense rested. Judge Ohlig turned to Bruce Barket and asked if he was prepared to begin his defense. What followed was one of the trial's most stunning moments.

Many spectators in the courtroom had been looking forward to Bruce Barket presenting his case. Much of the speculation outside the courtroom among the spectators had been: Will Lee Ann testify on her own behalf?

So there was an audible moan in the courtroom when Barket announced that he did not intend to call any witnesses. He stated that he believed he didn't need to.

"The prosecution had failed to meet the burden of proof," Barket proclaimed. They had offered no credible evidence that Lee Ann was guilty of anything, so there was nothing for him to defend.

With all three sides of the case having rested, court was adjourned. They would reconvene the following

Monday morning, at which time the closing arguments would be heard. The attorneys and their staffs would have the weekend to prepare.

Outside the courtroom, while many were still chatting about Barket's decision not to put Lee Ann—a seemingly sympathetic figure—on the stand, Muraskin, ever the optimist, was the one talking to the press.

Muraskin told reporters, "I think the case went as well as it could have for us. We got enough out of every individual witness that we wanted to. Hopefully, I will be able to tie it together in my closing statement. I'm not pulling things out of the hat and creating science fiction, but hopefully, the jurors listened. Hopefully, they will see that it makes sense and they will acquit Ralph Salierno."

Chapter 49

Barket Sums Up

It was Monday morning, March 22, 2004, the day the closing arguments were to start, and the weather had turned gorgeous. It was a glorious day. According to the calendar, it was officially spring and Mother Nature had responded with a cloudless blue sky and a new mildness in the Long Island breeze.

Seth Muraskin came to the courtroom early, about 9:20 A.M., before court began, and he spoke to Lee Ann's family. Although he represented the other defense in the case, he wanted to let them know there was no ill will. He patted her father, David Armanini, on the shoulder and said good luck.

Muraskin then left the courthouse, not sticking around to listen to the other lawyers speak.

At 10:00 A.M., Judge Ohlig called the court to order. For nine minutes the court took care of preliminary business. At 10:09 A.M., Bruce Barket stood before Jury B and began his closing argument.

He explained that in all trials the defense gave the first closing argument.

"This morning, I am going to speak to you first, and Miss Merrifield for the prosecution is going to go second," Barket said.

Barket tried to introduce into evidence some graphs and charts for the jury. He said that much of his summation involved a timeline, and the visual aids might help the jury understand what he was saying.

Judge Ohlig, however, threw Barket's plans for a loop. The judge ruled that the charts could not be entered into evidence because they were not based on information that was in evidence. Barket argued that he was about to enter the information into evidence in his summation.

The judge ruled that Barket's point was moot. Since the summation had not yet been delivered, the information was not yet in evidence, and so the visual aids would not be allowed. Barket was seething.

Barket later would have harsh words about the judge regarding this moment—he would call Judge Ohlig "beyond awful"—but then, in front of the jury, Barket held his tongue and continued with his summation.

"I want people to like me," Barket said. "But I know that no matter how hard I try, there may be people in the world who don't like me. There may even be a juror or two who doesn't like me, and if that's the case, I'm sorry—but I would ask those jurors who don't like me—for whatever reason—to not take their dislike out on my client. No matter how you feel about me, it should have nothing to do with the guilt or innocence of Lee Ann Riedel.

"I've done everything I could to represent her the best I can. This case is not about me. I have faith in the facts of this case. Not so much faith in my own personality. Judge Lee Ann Riedel on the facts and you will find her not guilty. Judge her on what you think about my personality, I don't know.

"In order to find Lee Ann guilty, you must find that the evidence points to her guilt beyond a reasonable doubt. Beyond a reasonable doubt. Is there proof without any reasonable doubt? The answer is unequivocally no. The case against Lee Ann Riedel suffers from a lack of credible evidence."

He pointed out that the jury cannot look at the fact that Lee Ann Riedel did not testify in court on her own behalf as evidence of her guilt.

"You can't hold that against her," Barket said. "She didn't testify because there was no need for her to. There was no credible evidence for her to defend herself against."

Barket explained that he had called no witnesses in Lee Ann's behalf, he said, because she didn't need any. The prosecution, he claimed, had failed to show that his client had had anything to do with the murder.

"This is not a close case. There is a lack of any credible evidence that implicates Lee Ann Riedel in this murder. We rested immediately because I know, and you know, there is not proof beyond a reasonable doubt," Barket said.

Barket told Jury B that there were three charges against Lee Ann Riedel: first-degree murder, second-degree murder, and conspiracy to commit murder. Barket wanted to convince the jury that the prosecution didn't really expect the jury to find Lee Ann guilty of first-degree murder. After all, she obviously had not pulled the trigger and had been many miles away from the murder when it occurred.

They had put those other charges in there thinking that the jury might, as Barket put it, "throw the prosecution a bone." He urged them not to do this. "Do not compromise," he said.

Barket argued that his client had merely wanted someone to protect her in the event her estranged husband came looking for her in Florida, where she had fled with some of his money. Salierno carried out the killing on his own without her knowledge.

Barket said, "Salierno was an obsessive, manipulative man. He took it upon himself to kill Paul Riedel so that he could have Lee Ann all to himself."

During his moving summation he said that he was proud of his work as an attorney, even though he regularly pleaded with juries to show leniency to his guilty clients.

"In this case, however," Barket maintained, "I have had the privilege of defending a doting mother of three whom I genuinely believe to be innocent."

Barket wanted the jury to understand that, considering how wrong they had been about Lee Ann Riedel, it was ironic that they had been so right when it came to everything else about the case. There were great aspects of the prosecution's case that Barket believed to be true, that he would have conceded to from the beginning.

For example, he believed that Ralph Salierno really had paid Scott Paget $3,000 to drive to Amityville and shoot Paul Riedel. He had no problem with that. And he had no trouble with the prosecution's theory that Ralph Salierno had set out to kill Lee Ann's husband and had shot her friend Alex by mistake. Barket had no doubt that this also was the absolute truth. But the prosecution's theory that Lee Ann had paid Ralph Salierno to kill her husband—that, Barket explained, was where the prosecutor's theory fell apart.

Barket said there were three reasons why the prosecution got their case so right when it came to Ralph Salierno, yet so wrong when it came to Lee Ann Riedel.

"The first reason is that they made an unwarranted assumption," Barket said. In other words, he explained, they assumed that just because she was having an affair with one of the murderers, she must have been in cahoots with that murderer and had a hand in the murder.

"The prosecution's theory demands a leap of faith regarding my client's character. Just because she once tried to hire protection from her violent husband, and just because she had an affair and a child with the man she hired to protect her, does not mean that she hired him to kill her husband," Barket said.

The second reason, Barket said, was that because Lee Ann and Paul were having marital problems, that this was a sufficient motive.

"The truth was that Lee Ann was attempting to reconcile with her husband at the time of the murder," Barket said.

The third reason was that the police—and then the prosecution—believed the lies of a series of low-life characters who had everything to gain by lying about Lee Ann's guilt. He named names: Paul Riedel, Scott Paget, Big Balls Fiaccabrino. The list went on.

"They all had a motive to testify falsely," Barket said. "Police gave the investigation over to those who committed the crime."

Barket asked the jury why they should believe Scott Paget. The man—who could forget?—had admitted to being a party to the murder himself. Had he not admitted to loading the gun that Ralph Salierno used to end Alex Algeri's life?

"These witnesses who have testified against Lee Ann Riedel, who have offered the only evidence pointing toward Lee Ann's guilt, all had something to gain. Ladies and gentlemen of the jury, I want you to ask yourselves a question when you consider the testimony offered by the prosecution's witnesses: What were these witnesses most concerned with, the truth or saving themselves?"

Barket took on the credibility of Paul Riedel next.

He pointed out that this was a man who, although he claimed to be an honest businessman, once met someone in a bar—someone who just so happened to be an undercover cop—and he pointed a gun in the man's face so that he could rob him and have two ounces of cocaine to sell.

Barket reminded the jurors that Paul Riedel was a man who said he never used anabolic steroids to enhance his physique. Yet when he was on trial in 1989 for robbery, he admitted to using steroids.

"He said that his wife left him in July 2000 for no reason. This is a man who has had ongoing problems with the law. He once fired a shotgun into the lawn of an ex-girlfriend. He once intimidated one of Lee Ann's ex-bosses by waiting outside his house.

"He was a big man and was used to intimidating people. It was a part of his lifestyle. He sometimes got what he wanted by frightening people for it. He had had a physical altercation with Alex Algeri a few weeks before the killing," and, Barket said, Riedel's other business investors wanted out of the gym.

The lawyer then ran down for the jury a timeline of Lee Ann's activities during the all-important spring and summer of 2000, a full six months before Alex's death. He expressed his regrets that the court was not allowing him to use his visual aids, which he had hoped would help the jurors see the timeline clearly. But, despite that, he was going to do his best to make Lee Ann's activities clear to them.

Barket reminded the jury that on June 5, 2000, Paul and Lee Ann had a fight over his drug use. During that same month she had taken Paul's shotgun and given it to the cops. Then she'd taken the kid and some of Paul's money and split.

She needed to get away. She went to her mom's place in Florida. She hadn't been there long when the threats started. Paul could be a scary guy. He was used to getting his way by being a scary guy.

The threats became so bad, Barket said, that on July 3, 2000, Lee Ann had to get an order of protection against her husband. It was served two days later. This meant that Paul was not allowed to get within a certain distance of Lee Ann or any member of her family.

If Paul was caught by the police defying the terms of the order, his arrest was mandatory. In other words, police would be obligated to arrest Paul even if Lee Ann told the cops she chose not to press charges.

By this time Lee Ann was pregnant again—a pregnancy that would end in a miscarriage.

Barket noted that Paul had made enemies down in Florida, and not just with Lee Ann, who had to go to court about the problem. Paul Riedel, in his own testimony that the jurors heard with their own ears, admitted to meeting with Ralph Salierno, Liz Budroni, Pat Armanini, Lee Ann's mom, and Richie Pollack, the friend of Rocco Salierno's who was the initial liaison between Rocco and Lee Ann.

Lee Ann had felt a lot of support from her friends. Richie Pollack, Liz Budroni, and Ralph Salierno had all said words to the effect that "if Paul comes by, we'll come over." They were afraid for Lee Ann's safety. Pollack, Barket said, had a crush on Lee Ann.

Barket ran through the multitude of enemies that Paul had accrued during the weeks and months before Alex was shot. There was a gambling debt. There were mobsters who thought he was an informant. There were some other tough guys he'd angered as well.

"So do you think Lee Ann had a good reason to be afraid of Paul Riedel? You've seen him, all six-foot-seven of him. Now imagine him on cocaine, or crack—or steroids!" the defense attorney exclaimed.

Continuing with the timeline, Barket said on July 17

Paul Riedel convinced his wife that he had stopped taking drugs. With that deception, Paul persuaded Lee Ann to go back to New York with him.

That reconciliation lasted about three weeks. It didn't take Lee Ann long to figure out that Paul's claims of being off drugs were highly exaggerated. On August 7, she packed her things and returned to Florida. On August 17, they once again took a crack at reconciliation. Lee Ann, Paul, and their son had a nice day together.

"Lee Ann was trying to make it work," Barket said, underlining his point. She wasn't ready to give up on Paul. She wasn't sure that she wanted to live without him. She was a long way from wanting to see him dead.

On August 25, Lee Ann filed for divorce. As a condition for visitation rights, Paul was ordered to attend parenting classes. He would also have to undergo periodic drug testing.

In the fall of 2000, Paul got clean. He went to his classes. He showed up for and passed his drug tests. Lee Ann "begged, pleaded, hoped, and prayed" he'd get off drugs. The man she had hoped Paul could become, he had.

"The best of Paul Riedel came out, but this came after she fled to Florida in August, where she began to see Salierno," Barket said.

In November 2000, Barket reminded the jury, Lee Ann returned to Paul $95,000 of the cash she had taken.

"If Lee Ann were hatching a plot, why did she return money?" Barket asked the jury, his palms turned upward. "Those are hardly the actions of a woman who is plotting to have her husband murdered."

Lee Ann was the one who was thinking reconciliation. She saw her husband as a sort of Jekyll and Hyde, a man with a split personality. There was the nice Paul. That was the guy with whom she had fallen in love. Then there was the mean Paul. That was the guy she was afraid of.

Every time Lee Ann decided to give Paul another chance, Barket explained, it was because she thought Paul's bad side was going to go away forever and she could be with Paul's good side. That way they could live happily ever after.

With those dreams still swirling in her head, the lawyer argued, there was no way she could have considered killing Paul as an option.

Barket pointed out that the Riedels' attempted reconciliation during the autumn of 2000 was not the final attempt. In a lot of ways there were signs that the breakup wasn't working out. On December 8, 2000— only slightly more than a month before Alex Algeri's death—Paul Riedel withdrew the divorce petition he had filed the previous August.

Barket then forced the jury to contemplate the sloppiness of the murder. The killers not only shot the wrong guy, but they showed up at the gym on a night when Paul Riedel was not even supposed to be there.

"Paul Riedel never, never works on Wednesday nights," Barket said. "Wrong place, wrong time, wrong night. Killed the wrong man. A colossal blunder."

Barket's argument was that this sloppiness would not have been there if Lee Ann had actually been in charge. The sloppiness, the fact that Salierno and Paget got it so wrong, was evidence that Lee Ann had nothing to do with her husband's murder.

"What was Lee Ann's reaction when she heard that Alex Algeri was murdered?" Barket asked rhetorically. "She immediately feared for Paul's safety. She tried frantically to get ahold of him, but she couldn't— because he was doing drugs with a friend."

Barket once again emphasized that it was Salierno alone who was responsible for the tragic error in the fitness center's parking lot.

"It was the fact that Lee Ann was attempting to reconcile with her husband that drove the defendant over the edge. Ralph Salierno killed Paul Riedel so that he could have Lee Ann to himself," Barket said.

When Salierno's plan didn't work, the Riedels once again reconciled. By the summer of 2001, according to the testimony of Scott Paget, Salierno had moved back to New York. He was no longer with Lee Ann. Lee Ann was with Paul.

He hammered away at the character of the prosecution's witnesses. Some of the damaging witnesses against Lee Ann were drug addicts. Some were facing prison time and had made deals and had something to gain by testifying.

Barket reminded the jury that they heard the prosecution witness Michael "Big Balls" Fiaccabrino on audiotapes saying that Lee Ann conspired the whole thing. Big Balls was Salierno's childhood friend, the guy who was originally offered the $3,000 to drive the Florida/New York round-trip.

Fiaccabrino, Barket said, was not a man known for saying the truth. Barket listed Fiaccabrino's known lies. He said that he had friends in the police department he could call. Turned out not to be true. Fiaccabrino said he'd had to get a lawyer because of the heat in the Salierno case, but he'd gotten no lawyer. One time he told the police that he got a gun from Albanians, those crazy guys that ran around the Bronx. The next time they asked, he said he got the gun from the Hells Angels, who had their headquarters in New York's East Village.

"So he's been known to play fast and loose with the truth to begin with," Barket said. "He admits to that. He admits to embellishing the truth. And in this case Fiaccabrino had a really good reason to lie. He was on a fast track to five to ten years in a federal pen for marijuana conspiracy."

Barket emphasized again, "There is a dearth of any

credible evidence that shows she's guilty beyond a reasonable doubt."

He returned to his own scenario regarding Alex Algeri's demise.

Barket said, "Salierno was in love with Lee Ann. In addition to emotion attachment, he also saw a business opportunity. Lee Ann would be his meal ticket. He thought Paul Riedel was richer than he was. Salierno mistakenly believed that Paul owned a whole string of gyms. He thought the intended victim owned more than one house."

In conclusion, Barket said, "I'm proud of what I do and worked hard to get where I am. Occasionally I get to participate in the freeing of an innocent person. Find her not guilty of all three counts. That's what the evidence requires and justice demands."

The argument had taken up much of the morning. Judge Ohlig called for the midday lunch break.

Chapter 50

"Two Years of Digging"

Denise Merrifield was in for a busy couple of days. She had to deliver not one but two closing arguments, one for each jury, one in response to each of the defense attorneys participating in the double trial.

She began the first of her two closing statements to Jury B at 1:15 P.M. on March 22, right after the lunch break. Merrifield began not with words but with a visual aid. Unlike Bruce Barket, she got to use her visual aid.

That was because her visual aid already had been introduced into evidence. It was the murder weapon—the gun Sergeant Epps had pulled from the muck at the bottom of Ketcham's Creek.

Merrifield held the gun up over her head, and then in front of her. She made sure that all of the jurors got a good look at it before she spoke.

"This thirty-eight-caliber revolver represents this murder case," she said. She told the jury that the murder weapon was found at the bottom of a creek miles from the murder scene. A metal detector needed to be used.

"Like the facts in this case, this gun was buried deep," she said. "It took two years of digging to get to the truth. It took digging through two feet of silt and mud to get to the gun. Yet, the gun—and the truth—were found."

She told the jury that without Lee Ann's say-so, there would have been no murder. Without Lee Ann's say-so, Alex Algeri would be alive today. It was she who induced the deadly action. "She didn't just think, 'I hate my husband,'" the prosecutor said. "She thought, 'I want him dead.' What this case is about is a murder for hire, but the plan backfired and they got the wrong guy."

Merrifield then took the jurors back to the night of the murder, to the scene of the crime, to a very-much-alive Alex Algeri, whose only mistake was leaving his place of work to get something out of his car.

"For that, he got killed," Merrifield said. "Imagine what Alex Algieri was thinking as he got shot, over and over again."

Lee Ann Riedel's defense team, Merrifield said, had gone to great lengths to assassinate the character of prosecution witnesses, in particular Michael Fiaccabrino. She suggested that those in glass houses best not throw stones.

Merrifield suggested that they compare the character of Fiaccabrino to that of Lee Ann Riedel, Rocco Salierno, and Scott Paget. Fiaccabrino, she noted, was offered $3,000 to drive the death van, but he turned the deal down.

"He said no. Lee Ann didn't say no. Salierno didn't say no. Paget didn't say no," Merrifield said.

Merrifield pointed out that Salierno had a photo of Paul Riedel with him when he traveled up North to commit the murder. According to Scott Paget, they had been supplied with a photo and instructions on how to get to places that Pail Riedel frequented. They got the photo and the information from Lee Ann.

The prosecutor told the jurors that they did not have to rely on the words of criminals that the white van had been in place, waiting in ambush for the victim, who turned out to be Alex Algeri. Truth was, there was another witness who was absolutely innocent and who had nothing to gain by her statements. Merrifield reminded the jury that there had been an eyewitness to the white van by the parking lot behind the gym on the night of the murder.

"The witness's name is Natalie Lynch," Merrifield said. "She said that the van had backed into place." This corroborated the testimony of Scott Paget, who had said the van had backed into place that night. Lynch had said that she felt nervous when she looked at the man in the van. She said the guy was a white male with a chubby face, about thirty to thirty-five years old, with short black hair. That, too, was in sync with the known facts of the case.

"That brings us back to the gun. The gun also corroborates the known facts of the case. Five shots were fired into Alex Algeri. After the murder weapon's discovery, the police crime lab technician examined the gun and found that it contained five casings. All five shots that hit Alex Algeri came out of this gun."

Merrifield told Lee Ann Riedel's jury that Lee Ann's version of the story didn't make sense. She would say that she and her husband were attempting reconciliation at the time of the murder, removing any motive she might have had. "But it makes no sense that she would attempt a reconciliation with her husband when just months earlier she sought an order of protection against him," Merrifield said.

The assistant district attorney told Jury B that Lee Ann Riedel moved back in with her husband after the murder simply for the sake of appearances. "She frantically sought out her husband after the killing of Alexander Algeri. It was only to avoid suspicion. She didn't want to appear to be Paul's enemy after the violence in the parking lot outside the Amityville Dolphin gym," she said. "She's very good at pretending."

The ADA told the jurors one more time how Lee Ann had left Paul Riedel during the summer of 2000 because she had grown tired of his partying, a euphemism for his cocaine addiction. She had gone to Florida and had taken $120,000 of Paul's money and Paul's son with her.

Merrifield told of how Lee Ann had been afraid, with good reason, that Paul would come looking for her, and how, because of this fear, Lee Ann had met Ralph Salierno through her mother's lover's connection at a local gym. The original plan had been to beat Paul Riedel up, but the plan evolved in August 2000 when Paul filed for divorce and got a court order forcing Lee Ann to live within fifty miles of her husband until the custody battle could be decided.

"She was pissed," Merrifield said. "She said, 'That's it. I want him dead!'"

The prosecutor pointed an accusing finger at Lee Ann as she spoke.

Merrifield then took on Barket's claim that Lee Ann's returning of $95,000 of the $120,000 she stole was evidence that she was not plotting to kill Paul Riedel.

"Why not return the money?" Merrifield asked the jury. "With Paul Riedel dead, Lee Ann figured to inherit that money anyway."

Taking on Barket's claim that Lee Ann's attempts at reconciliation with Paul Riedel was evidence that she was not plotting to kill him, Merrifield countered, "Lee Ann was pretending to reconcile with Paul Riedel in order to get him to drop the divorce case. After the murder failed, Lee Ann filed for divorce herself a few months later in Florida. This forced Paul Riedel to deal with his wife on her turf."

Addressing Barket's contention that the very sloppiness of the crime was an indication that Lee Ann Riedel was not involved, Merrifield said, "I don't have to prove that the murderers are smart. I just have to prove who did it. She did it with them."

Just as Bruce Barket's summary had filled the morning session, Denise Merrifield's closing argument to Jury B had filled the afternoon. Next up would be Seth Muraskin's argument, which would be delivered to Jury A.

But that was going to have to wait until the next day. Judge Ohlig ordered Jury B to be sequestered at a hotel during evenings for the remainder of the trial. Ohlig adjourned court for the day and told everyone to be back the next morning. For Denise Merrifield it was one closing argument down, one to go.

Chapter 51

"Ralph Salierno Didn't Do What They Say He Did"

Jury A filed in at 9:45 A.M. the next day—Tuesday, March 23, 2004. Their turn. They consisted of nine men and five women. All but one was white. There was one black male.

Salierno was already in the courtroom, looking about as studious as possible, wearing his dark suit and his black-rimmed glasses.

Salierno's defense attorney, Seth Muraskin, began his closing argument by thanking the members of the jury for their patience. Because of the special nature of the trial, the juries had been asked to get up and down a lot during the course of their testimony, and for putting up with that inconvenience, Muraskin thanked them.

He said, "Ralph Salierno didn't do what they say he did. He did not conspire with anyone to do anything. There's a lot you did not see. There is a lot you were not shown. There was no physical evidence to suggest or even link him to this crime. No DNA. No fingerprints. No bloodstains. Absolutely nothing. There's nothing that puts him where they want him to be."

Muraskin said that the story, as the prosecution told it, was fiction.

"It never happened," he said. "It was a confabulation based on snippets of fact and plenty of lies. And lies from whom? The biggest collection of drug addicts, drug dealers, convicted felons, rats, and liars."

All lies. The white van they had heard so much about? It didn't exist. There wasn't a shred of believable evidence that the van ever existed.

"Lucas Schmitt, who procured the van with his credit car, couldn't ID Salierno," Muraskin said. "They asked him about the guy who got the van and he described Paget."

Muraskin told the jury that Salierno's predicament had a lot to do with previous statements made by a fellow named Michael Alexander. Alexander was the guy who had been arrested for grand larceny by the NYPD, the one who had provided information during his interrogation, who was the first to supply authorities with the name Scott Paget.

And it was Paget, in turn, who had implicated Salierno. Yet, where was Mike Alexander? Everything hinged on Mike Alexander's word, and yet when they presented their case, he was not called as a witness.

"The silence coming from that chair is deafening. The prosecution benefited from Mike Alexander's absence," Muraskin said.

The defense attorney then turned his attention to a witness who did testify, Michael "Big Balls" Fiaccabrino— the guy who said Salierno gave him first dibs to drive the white van to Long Island.

"This guy testifies against my client, and suddenly, by

the magic of his cooperation, he gets a thirty-seven-month sentence," Muraskin said. The sentence may or may not have seemed too short to the jury. Three-plus years is a bit more than a slap on the wrist.

Muraskin then hit upon his favorite subject—the bogus nature of Ralph Salierno's confession under the grilling of the case's lead investigator, Detective Anderson.

"Police drove Salierno from Westchester to Suffolk, and never asked him if he wanted a lawyer," he said. His tone told the jury that the outrageousness was beyond comprehension.

Then he tried to communicate the ultimate creepiness and danger of an Anderson interrogation. "Imagine being in an eight-by-eight windowless room where Anderson is king. Imagine being in Anderson's world. Imagine being alone, cut off from the outside world," he said.

He asked the jury to believe his client's claim that it was Paget and not he who had pulled the trigger. He had only been speaking for a little more than a half hour, but he was through. He had tried hard, but had little with which to work. Either the jury believed Salierno's confession— or they did not. They believed Salierno's alibi witness— or they did not.

After Muraskin ended his argument, a class of high-school girls filed solemnly into the courtroom to observe the proceedings. They had missed the day's opening act.

Chapter 52

Merrifield to Jury A

Now prosecuting Ralph Salierno, Denise Merrifield began her closing argument to Jury A, just as she had for Jury B. She held the murder weapon up over her head and explained the analogy between digging up the facts of the case and digging the gun out of the Ketcham's Creek mud.

She said she was aware that the two men in that van that night told different stories. For the most part they were the same, but they differed when it came to one key point. Salierno said that Paget shot Alex Algeri, and Paget said that Salierno did it.

Merrifield told jurors that it didn't make any difference who pulled the trigger, so they shouldn't waste any of their valuable time deliberating over that issue. Salierno had confessed to the crime simply by admitting that he and Paget had gone to Amityville with the intention of killing Paul Riedel.

Who pulled the trigger? Didn't matter. But that didn't change the fact that only one scenario made sense, and that was the one in which Ralph Salierno fired the five bullets into Alex Algeri's neck and body.

Paget had nothing to gain by committing the crime. Rocco and Lee Ann, on the other hand, if all had gone as planned, would have had control of Paul Riedel's estate, estimated to be worth close to $1 million.

Merrifield said, "I'm not asking you to believe that confession at all—other than he admitted to being there with Scott." If the jury believed that part, and that part alone of Salierno's confession, she pointed out, then he was guilty of first-degree murder.

She repeated a refrain from her opening statement: "This was a simple murder for hire. When someone asks you to kill someone for them, and you say, 'OK, you need a job to be done, I'm your man,' that's murder for hire."

The prosecutor reminded the jury that this was not a simple crime. It was not a spur-of-the-moment thing. Despite the fact that it had been blundered horribly, there still had been quite a bit of planning to do.

"Salierno had to find a gun and a vehicle," she said. "He had to find someone to drive with him. Drove all the way from Florida, could have turned back anytime. They were on a mission to kill somebody and get paid for it.

"The other side has made much of the character of some of the prosecution's witnesses. I ask you, how could it be any other way? What kind of people do things like this—take money to kill another human being, to kill for a living?" she said.

Her witnesses weren't "Scout leaders, bakers, or even likable human beings." She noted, however, that their story, when taken as one piece, "rings true."

"What kind of friends are people like that going to have? I'm not saying that I like some of the witnesses I've called, or that I condone their lifestyle, I'm just saying that they are not lying," she said.

She accused the Salierno defense with disingenuousness in its closing argument that morning:

"They brought up Mike Alexander and asked why we didn't call him to the stand, and that it was a good thing that we didn't because his testimony would have hurt our case. My question to you, ladies and gentlemen of the jury, is: if Mike Alexander's testimony was going to help their case and hurt ours, why didn't they call him as a witness? He was available to the defense. The truth was that we had learned that some of Mike Alexander's statements to police and to the prosecution were untrue, and we are honor-bound not to call witnesses who we know have lied to us."

Merrifield then criticized Muraskin's style.

"Do you recall Mr. Muraskin's cross-examination of Sergeant Epps, the police diver who located the murder weapon? How sarcastic was Mr. Muraskin with Sergeant Epps?" Merrifield asked.

"Muraskin says that everyone is lying—everyone except his own client. He says that I'm having witnesses commit perjury to make my case. Please. If that were true, don't you think I would have had Lucas Schmitt pick Salierno out as the guy who had rented the van?" she challenged.

She noted that Salierno's story of being beaten until he confessed was also absurd. She showed the jury photos of Salierno taken after his confession, photos that showed no bruising or other signs of abuse.

Merrifield added, "Look at the size of that man. I don't think a Mack truck can make him do anything he doesn't want to."

Plus, she said, there were elements of Salierno's confession that subsequently had been proven to be true, and were direct evidence of his guilt in the murder of

Alex Algeri. For example, Salierno said in his confession that he had gone to see a friend in the Hunts Point section of the Bronx, and there he had purchased a second license plate to put over the van's real one.

The license plate was in case they were seen while making their getaway, so they could remove the outer license plate and become distinguishably different from the vehicle seen leaving the scene of the crime. Police would never have known about the extra license plate if Salierno had not told them about it, and when they checked it out, they found out that, sure enough, the story was true.

Merrifield said that it was Larry Ortolano who gave Richie Pollack the phone number for Pat and Liz. Why was Larry doing Richie a favor? It was because Richie and Rocco owed Larry money, so he was interested in them making a little extra cash so they could turn it over to him.

Rocco and Richie owed Larry $5,000 apiece, which they had borrowed to start a nightclub. And it was Larry whom Liz Budroni saw at a gym and mentioned that her girlfriend's daughter was having husband problems, and did he know anybody who took care of problems like that? Larry said he did. When Rocco needed a vehicle, he went to Larry first to see about getting one.

The defense and defense witnesses, she said, had told many lies during the course of the trial. But there were two that were whoppers: 1) Lee Ann had nothing to do with the crime, because she had everything to do with the crime, and 2) Paul Riedel had mobsters who were after him.

"I want you to remember who this trial is about," Merrifield said. "Alex Algeri."

Merrifield continued, "I want you to imagine what must have been going through Algeri's mind when he got into his black GMC Yukon at about seven twenty-five that night and was shot five times with a snub-nosed thirty-eight. He must have thought, 'Why is this happening? Why me?'"

She pointed at Rocco and raised her voice: "It happened because that man, right there, got hired to kill Paul Riedel and he's too stupid to find the right guy. I don't have to prove that he's smart, I only have to prove that he's the right guy."

She asked jurors to recall the six-page statement Salierno had signed soon after his arrest. She drew their attention to one detail that sealed Salierno's fate.

What was the proof that Paget's version of the crime was true, and Salierno's was not? It was in the details, Merrifield pointed out: "Salierno remembered that the interior light of Algeri's Yukon was on," Merrifield said. "If he had been sitting in the getaway car, parked on the street, and not near the Yukon, he could not have known that detail, a detail which was later confirmed by forensics."

Just how cold-blooded was the defendant? Merrifield said the key to that question was the amount of time the plan—the plan to take care of Lee Ann's "husband problem"—spent on the drawing board.

"Keep in mind how long Salierno had to change his mind and back out of the plan. The plan took months to evolve," she said. "But he never did change his mind. He just kept pushing ahead with the plan. That's cold. That's vicious."

Nearing the end of her argument, Merrifield attacked last, and hardest, Salierno's key defense witness.

"I want to talk to you now about Tara Anzalone-Smith. She was the stripper who said that Salierno couldn't have shot Alex Algeri because he was on a date with her at the time," Merrifield said, practically rolling her eyes. "This woman's testimony was insulting. Not only does her testimony stand alone in the face of all of the other evidence, but it is insulting as well.

"She complained because police came to see her to ask a few questions. She said that she felt 'violated' by this intrusion into her life. Violated? Violated? Do you know what this woman does for a living? She has customers put money in her G-string while she dances around naked. And that doesn't make her feel violated, but answering questions from the police does? Please."

Merrifield emphasized that there was no rush to judgment in this case. The arrest of Ralph Salierno had been the culmination of a two-year investigation, which involved teamwork between the Drug Enforcement Administration, the Suffolk County Police Department, the New York Police Department, and the Amityville Police Department—not to mention various law enforcement agencies down in Florida. She thanked the jury for their time and service, and once again reminded them to find Ralph Salierno guilty of the charges against him.

And that was it.

The trial had lasted five weeks. Thirty-five witnesses testified. For the entire five weeks Lee Ann Riedel had worn her hair in a ponytail. Although Lee Ann's mother, Pat, had not attended the trial, her father and her stepmother had. In fact, her dad and his wife had attended every day, always huddled close to one another, frequently holding hands.

Suffolk County district attorney Thomas Spoto announced that his office did not intend to seek the death penalty for Ralph Salierno—that, if found guilty, the maximum Salierno could get was life without parole.

Chapter 53

Juries A and B

The juries were given their instructions and subsequently were sequestered, cut off from all outside persons and media. Mostly, the juries had to be separated from one another. It was unlikely that the juries would come to a verdict at the same time, and knowledge of the first verdict couldn't help but influence the other. They began deliberation during the early morning of Tuesday, March 23.

While the jury was deliberating, a writer asked Barket his thoughts. The lawyer replied: "I hope they listened to every word, heard what every witness said and evaluate it. Hopefully, they'll listen to the law and consider the evidence. It's been a long trial. There is a lot to consider, but I feel confident that a reasonable person can't convict."

To a casual observer, a murder trial is quite entertaining. It is tense and often riveting, and sometimes it can be long and boring, but there is an urgency to the words of the players, since everyone in the room knows that there are people's lives on the line.

But the casual observer cannot imagine what the families and friends of the principals are going through. From the father of the victim to the father of the accused, the trial had become their universe. The decisions of the juries meant everything.

Jury B wanted some testimony read back. What exactly had Big Balls said? So the stenographer read back the words of Michael Fiaccabrino. He was the one who'd said Lee Ann called Salierno a "stupid bastard" for shooting the wrong man.

According to Big Balls's recollections, Salierno had yelled back at her: "I wouldn't have fucked up if you'd given me a better fucking picture!"

That was the part the jury wanted to hear. The dialogue rang true.

After Michael Fiaccabrino's testimony was read back, Judge Ohlig adjourned the court for lunch. By the time the spectators began drifting back into the courthouse for the afternoon, there were rumblings that Jury B had reached a verdict. But it was a false alarm. Lee Ann's father, David Armanini, was in the courtroom, as usual, his chin characteristically held proudly upward.

Steven Constantino, Paul Riedel's matrimonial attorney, was clearly a believer in Lee Ann's guilt. After Jury B asked for a second read-back, and another review of the charges, Constantino began chatting with a writer.

"She got a VOP (Order of Protection) in Florida," Constantino said. "Once you got that, you don't need Tony Soprano to stare down your husband. Just call the local police. They have guns, handcuffs, Mace, whatever they need."

Barket once again asked for a mistrial. Per usual, it was one of Judge Ohlig's statements that had him on his feet. Judge Ohlig had explained to the jury that they only had to consider one of the elements in the indictment—rather than all eight. As he had with all the others, Judge Ohlig denied Barket's motion for a mistrial.

During the long breaks in the action, while deliberation continued elsewhere, Barket appeared to be the most nervous man—both in and out of the courtroom. It wasn't acting. He couldn't stand still. He was pacing.

One reporter from the press section, trying to get the defense attorney to stay in one spot for a moment, struck up a conversation with Barket.

"How long have you been in practice, Bruce?" the reporter asked.

"Eighteen years," Barket said, almost adding a sigh. "Since 1986."

"All of that as a defense attorney?" the reporter asked.

"I've been a defense attorney for the last nine years," he said.

Referring to the current case, the reporter said, "You've got a shot."

Barket shook his head no. "No, I don't," he said. "It's done, it's over. They're convicting her right now. It's tough to watch such a winnable case slip away from you and you can't do anything about it." Then Barket added, "As tough as it is for me, she's a woman with three kids, who will be taken away from her. If ever this case gets tried again, it will be winnable."

Time moved through the hourglass a grain at a time—but eventually it got to be midafternoon. Outside the courthouse was Sal Algeri, the victim's dad. Sal was a bear of a man, just like his kid grew up to be. He wasn't tall, maybe five-ten. He had a big mane of white hair and a friendly, warm, welcoming face. His demeanor was paternal. He was, after all, the original Papa Smurf. He was a guy to whom people felt they could confide.

He would listen and they would feel better.

At that moment Sal might have been still just a tad shy of senior-citizen status at sixty-four years old, but it was clear he was a grandfather. Two grandkids came running up to him and he had a hug for each. One of Sal's grandchildren handed him a cracker. Revealing expert grandfatherly skills, Sal feigned a thrill at receiving the cracker, to the delight of both youngsters. Watching this, one couldn't imagine Sal being anything other than a great dad to Alex.

Sal's wife wasn't able to attend the trial because she was in Florida recovering from hip surgery. So he sat alone during most of the trial, and he was obviously pleased when he had family members there to keep him company—especially grandkids.

At 3:50 P.M., the jury wanted yet another read-back. One could almost hear the silent moan. This time they only wanted the explanation of the murder-one charge. Whatever disagreement or confusion they had had regarding the other two charges earlier apparently had been resolved.

Maybe it was a sign that the jury was making progress. Barket didn't look happy. He was more convinced than ever that they were convicting Lee Ann Riedel, right then and there. The wait was just torture, just a matter of prolonging the inevitable.

Constantino was once again available for chitchat. He was telling Paul Riedel's life story. The big guy still held football records at North Babylon High School. And football wasn't the only sport at which Paul excelled. "He boxed during his six-year prison stint in Clinton Prison. He had twenty-nine knockouts in prison," Constantino commented.

One writer asked about the change in Ralph Salierno's

physique. He was the incredible shrinking defendant. Constantino had stats that seemed to prove there was a lot less Rocco than there used to be.

"Salierno is five-ten. He used to be two hundred twenty pounds of muscle. Now he's down to one-eighty soft pounds," Constantino said.

His client, on the other hand, remained a fearsome human being, vying for "Baddest Man on the Planet" honors.

"If Mike Tyson came to Paul's house, he'd have a problem," Constantino said. "No way anyone could take him on, unless they had a gun."

About the victim, Constantino said, "Paul has two hundred photos of Papa Smurf, he's smiling in every one of them. He used to be designated driver for friends. Everyone loved him."

Chapter 54

"We Got One Today"

Later that day, March 23, 2004, after only four hours of deliberation, Jury A reached a verdict. An observer sitting in the spectator section, behind the defendant, couldn't help but look at Ralph Salierno—especially his head. He'd spent days looking at his back and noticed that the defendant's head was too small for his body. It was almost freakish, like the infamous photo of Lee Harvey Oswald where the head was superimposed. Maybe he'd been unable to juice up since he was in stir and he was losing massive bulk—starting in his head.

Salierno's jury found Ralph Salierno guilty of first-degree murder, second-degree murder, and second-degree conspiracy. His sentencing was scheduled for April 26. Salierno showed little emotion when the verdict was read. Those nearby the defense table could overhear Salierno thanking Seth Muraskin for his effort just before he was led from the courtroom.

Outside the courtroom, following the sentencing, Salvatore Algeri said, "Justice has been served. We got one today." Then, referring to the Lee Ann Riedel jury, which was still deliberating, the victim's dad said, "Hopefully, we'll get the other one tomorrow. Hopefully, we'll get two out of two."

Seth Muraskin said that it came as no surprise that the jury returned a guilty verdict against his client so quickly, considering the number of Rocco's former so-called friends who lied on the stand to get him convicted.

"He believes he'll be exonerated on appeal," Muraskin said of Salierno. "It's a sad state when anybody can come into the court and say anything."

Denise Merrifield explained that she couldn't comment as long as Jury B was still deliberating.

The tabloid press had fun at Salierno's expense. The *New York Post* referred to Salierno as "the Botch Killer." Writer Lisa Pulitzer described Salierno as a "love-struck hit man."

Chapter 55

"Can't I at Least Say Good-bye to My Family?"

Jury A had been quick to make up its collective mind. Jury B, not so much. For four days, everyone waited. At 11:15 A.M., March 26, the jury again wanted an explanation of the charges. Early signs that the jury was making progress were erased. They once again wanted definitions. Again, both first- and second-degree murder needed to be explained. The jury seemed to be losing ground.

As the judge went through the charges again, Lee Ann Riedel was in the courtroom, wearing a white sweater and gray slacks.

Until the afternoon of March 26, Lee Ann's jury deliberated. Six times they asked Judge Ohlig for a further explanation of first-degree murder. What is it? What isn't it? They asked to have lengthy chunks of testimony read back to them by the court reporter.

It took Jury B twenty-nine hours of deliberation over

four days. Then came the announcement: The jury
had reached a verdict. The jurors appeared drained and
fatigued from overwork and worry by the time—2:20
P.M., March 26—they slowly filed into the court to deliver the case's resolution. Lee Ann was already in
place, but none of the jurors looked at her as they
filed into court.

Lee Ann's father, who had looked sad throughout the
trial, now looked sadder than ever. To prevent any possible outbursts, three court officers stood behind Lee
Ann. Two court officers posted themselves in the vicinity of her father.

With the moment of decision again drawing near, the
stress-level difference between the principals and the
spectators was more apparent than ever. Those directly
involved in the case prepared to have their world ex-
ploded. Others chatted idly about their weekend, their
dinner plans, their children. . . .

The exception to this rule was Sal Algeri, who always
seemed pretty calm, but now appeared to be the calmest
man in the room. He looked forward to justice, he did
not dread it—and the difference was obvious in his
casual body language. Sal didn't look at the jury, however, but rather stared straight ahead.

Sal had met Lee Ann only a couple of times, and he had
never grown emotionally attached. He had been at Paul
and Lee Ann's wedding, and he had attended Nicholas's
christening, because Alex had been the godfather.

Sal thought Lee Ann seemed like a pretty nice person.
Smiling. Happy. Of course, a wedding and a christening,
those are happy times, and you only get to see one side
of a person. Only later had Sal learned that Alex had
been Lee Ann's sounding board, the one she came to
when she was having problems, the one she knew would
always listen when she was having marital problems
with Paul.

Now, in the courtroom, awaiting her verdict, Lee Ann was looking down at her feet. Her ponytail sagged.

But the chitchat came to a halt and everyone rose when Judge Ohlig entered. The judge asked the jury if they had reached a verdict and the jury foreman said that they had. The judge asked Lee Ann to rise, and she got to her feet, Bruce Barket at her side. Now she lifted her chin. She no longer looked at her shoes, but rather directly at the jury.

The jury foreman then said, "We find the defendant, Lee Ann Riedel, guilty of first-degree murder. . . ."

When Lee Ann first heard the verdict, she looked at Barket with a horrified expression. Barket may have assumed that this jury was going to convict her, but she apparently had not. She looked down at the floor again and began to shake, as if she were attempting to stifle her emotions. But there could be no stifling of the waves of emotion that rolled over Lee Ann.

Her crying started out quiet, but grew in volume as the proceedings continued. Her father, David Armanini, bowed his head. Lee Ann's stepmother, Maria, began to cry.

Barket now put his arms around Lee Ann in a full hug, hoping her sobbing would subside.

The jury also found Lee Ann guilty of the lesser charges: second-degree murder and conspiracy to commit murder. When the foreman was done reading, he sat down and put his head in his hands, apparently emotionally drained.

Barket looked at the jury and shook his head slightly. Lee Ann, by this time, was heaving uncontrollably. Judge Ohlig thanked the jury and then scheduled Lee Ann's sentencing hearing for April 28, two days after Salierno's sentencing hearing. By this time the sounds of Lee Ann's sobs were the loudest thing in the room.

As Lee Ann was being led away, she struggled for a moment and looked back tearfully over her shoulder.

"Can't I at least say good-bye to my family?" Lee Ann said, a pathetic sob in her voice. She was looking back at her dad and stepmother, who were visibly upset by the verdict and Lee Ann's demonstration.

The family of Alexander Algeri was quiet and stoic after the verdict was read. After a moment Algeri's mother, Leonora "Lee" Ferrari, and her sister Christine Stoll stood and embraced.

Outside the courtroom Sal Algeri, the victim's father, told reporters, "Justice was served completely. Unfortunately, it's sad to see another young life go to waste. But these two people did such horrible deeds that affected so many lives both physically and emotionally."

Sal added, "It's so tragic. I had to bury my son before I go. I didn't look forward to coming to court. I know he's with me in [spirit in] critical situations. Anger is only natural. He was a great son, always smiling. Everyone should have a friend or a son like him."

After the hearing Alex Algeri's biological mother said to one writer: "It doesn't close the book. I have emotional scars I'll carry the rest of my life. There's always someone missing from the dinner table on holidays. I can't speak to him again, hear his voice, or see his smile. He was a great uncle, great son, and a great brother. I miss him so much, it aches, every minute every single hour of the day."

Sal was asked how he would feel the next day and the day after that.

"I'll have the same feelings," Sal said. "Anger, sadness, and lots of love. There was not really a victory today. Nobody won or lost. I lost a son and so did the parents of the killers."

Someone asked, how often did he think of Alex?

"Do you remember that song, '(There's) Always

Something There to Remind Me'?" Sal asked, singing a little.

That was the way it was with Sal's head and Alex. There was always something there to remind him. Around the time of September and Alex's birthday, it would get worse.

Sister Christine said: "It's a little bit of relief, but no such thing as closure. He was my daughter's godfather. My kids miss their uncle terribly. Barket did a good job. I was a bit concerned after his summation. But it was only theory. Denise (Merrifield) did a fantastic job."

The Riedel family quietly left without speaking to the press.

Of course, Bruce Barket had a quotable quote: "Our justice system is not perfect and today the justice system stumbled. The case is hardly over. There will be an appeal and I have no doubt that Lee Ann will be cleared of these false charges."

Asked his opinion of Jury B, Barket replied, "I respect the jury system. I respect the jury process. I strongly disagree with the verdict."

Paul Riedel had not attended the trial, but his presence had been felt by the attendance of his lawyer and friends. After the reading of Lee Ann's verdict, Paul's lawyer, Steven Constantino, said, "Paul is very happy. This was justice for Alex. This whole case was about warped, sadistic greed. Among all the read-backs, not one was related to Paul. He was credible beyond a reasonable doubt. Paul would never raise his hand to a woman, but he'll kick the shit out of a man for good reason without blinking an eye."

Paul's friend Mark Barrett said, "Paul has been to hell and back."

Constantino arranged for some reporters to talk to Paul via phone. Paul said, "Alex was my best friend, my baby's godfather. He'll always be his godfather."

Paul did talk to a *New York Post* reporter at the Dolphin Fitness Club later that day. When the reporter found him, he was handing out free T-shirts to his customers that read "BIG AL: We'll always remember you."

Talking to the reporter, Paul disagreed with the statement that had been read for him earlier by his lawyer. Was it really justice for Alex?

"I feel like Alex will never get justice because he's not here," the intended victim said. "Alex Algeri was the best man I ever met in my life. He will always be my son's godfather and my best friend."

Lead prosecutor Denise Merrifield told the press that she gave the credit to Detective Robert Anderson, of the Suffolk County police. The lead investigator had stuck with the case and dug out the facts even after the trail went initially cold.

"It took a long time to dig out the truth," Merrifield said happily, repeating the theme of both of her closing arguments. "I'm just relieved these people are held responsible for what they did. We tried the case, brick by brick, until the house was finished. The trial took five weeks and included thirty-five witnesses. I'm glad they took as much time as they did. Now all people responsible for Alex's death have been brought to justice."

"Why do you think it took the jury so long to reach its verdict?" a reporter asked the prosecutor.

"Some jurors may have found it difficult to convict a woman who did not participate in the actual killing," Merrifield said. It would have been that very difficulty that would have necessitated six explanations of the charges by the judge.

The jury had made a collective decision to avoid the press following the trial. So, after its delivery of the verdict, it was escorted out the courthouse's side exit. The jurors were taken to a secure parking lot, where they were put into a series of cars and driven away.

In the next day's paper, the *New York Post* once again had fun with the case. L.I. WIFE GUILTY OF HIT AND MISSES, the headline shouted with tongue in cheek.

Two down, and one to go. Ralph Salierno and Lee Ann Riedel had both been found guilty of first-degree murder after a long and strange murder trial, but one of the persons responsible for Alex Algeri's death was still awaiting his day in court.

As expected, Scott Paget pleaded guilty to second-degree murder. This, along with his cooperation with the prosecution of Rocco Salierno and Lee Ann Riedel, was expected to earn Paget a comparatively lenient sentence.

Paget's lawyer, Ted Scharfenberg, of Holbrook, Long Island, described Paget as a good man who made bad choices. "He made a horrible choice to be friends with Ralph," Scharfenberg said.

Denise Merrifield, again representing the Suffolk County District Attorney's Office, said that it was sad that Paget's life had turned out the way it had. "He is an intelligent man with a college degree, but he threw away a promising life to help commit a murder," Merrifield said. "I appreciate, however, that he tried to make amends by cooperating with authorities."

Reporters who had covered Rocco and Lee Ann's trial found a remarkable difference in the courtroom atmosphere between those proceedings and Paget's day in court. The double trial was tense and emotional. In comparison, Paget's hearing was low-key.

Chapter 56

Paul and Sal on *Larry King*

On April 22, 2004, *The Larry King Show,* on the CNN cable network, featured Alexander Algeri's murder in one of its segments. Appearing on the show were Paul Riedel and Alex Algeri's dad, Sal. Larry King interviewed Paul all by himself at first, and then Paul and Sal together.

King asked Paul how the murder of Algeri had gone down. Paul explained that he and Alex had owned a club together. "It is a health, golf, and fitness club in Long Island," Paul said. Alex had been working and one of the girls from an aerobics class asked him if he would get a CD she liked. "So he went back to his car," Paul explained.

Paul told how the guy waited in the dark behind a Dumpster and just came out and ambushed him. Alex, though, was a really strong-willed man. "He made it back to the club. Just, he didn't make it," Paul said.

Paul told King that he was the initial suspect in the case because he was the business partner, and—well—everybody liked Alex. "He was just a really, really good guy," Paul said. "He wasn't unliked by anybody. So there wasn't no motive."

King asked how the case was broken, and Paul said it was because of a smart investigator named Robert Anderson. Paul displayed a working knowledge of Mike Alexander's arrest and how that led cops to Paget, who led cops to Salierno, and Lee Ann. About Anderson and the cops, Riedel said he was a "good investigator . . . diligent."

King asked how Paul first learned that Lee Ann and her lover were behind the attempt on his life. "I didn't learn it until the media came to my house and asked me about it," Riedel said. "They were like, 'How do you feel about your wife trying to kill you?' At first I thought it was a joke. Obviously, it wasn't a joke, because there were like five different media outlets there. The news was shocking, to say the least."

The TV host asked the intended victim what happened to Nicholas after the shooting. Paul told him that a full year passed between the murder and Lee Ann's arrest, so Nicholas continued to live in Florida with his mother. Paul explained that he'd been flying back and forth between Florida and New York the whole time.

Paul told Larry King how the wrong guy got shot, that he and Algeri resembled one another. "Except he was a lot better-looking," Paul said. They had the same kind of vehicle. Same bumper sticker.

"People ask me, 'Don't you feel lucky?' Because it could have been me taking that walk. I would never have asked him to do it. No matter what happens, that's a burden I'll always have to carry," Paul said.

King wanted to know Lee Ann's motive. Paul explained that he and Lee Ann were going through a custody battle with Nicholas. He said that Lee Ann understood that he was determined to play a part in his son's life, that there was no way he was going to stop looking for that relationship.

"She figured she needed me dead," Paul concluded.

Paul told King that he had testified at the trial, but he had not attended the trial as a spectator.

"It was something that I twisted and turned about," he said regarding his decision to testify. "I decided it was something that I needed to do for Al." He testified, he said, as to the state of his marriage and his complete history with Lee Ann. Toward the end of his segment on the show, he said he remained heartbroken for Alex.

"It was a bullet that was meant for me, and Al's gone," Paul said. "My son would have been without a father."

Bruce Barket did not appear live on the program, but he sent a quote for Larry King to read aloud on the broadcast: "While we pray for Mr. Algeri and his family, we will continue to work for Lee Ann's vindication. We are all aware that our judicial system is not perfect. Unfortunately, Lee Ann's first trial was littered with prosecutorial misconduct and judicial errors. It was not surprising, therefore, that the jury reached an unjust verdict. Lee Ann is innocent and we are confident that an appellate court will reverse the conviction. We look forward to a fair trial and Lee Ann's exoneration."

King asked Paul about Lee Ann's defense, and Paul described Bruce Barket's strategy as best he could. "I think her defense was that she was having a relationship with this guy. Not that I *think*—she was having a relationship with this guy. As we were trying to reconcile, that he was just jealous and angry and he just came down and did this on his own. I don't know how he could have gotten some of the information he had, like what I looked like and the kind of car I drove."

Along with the revelation that his wife had hired a guy to shoot him, Paul had to deal with the fact that the new baby—the one born in December, Nicholas's little brother, who he presumed was his own, and treated as if he was his own—was actually Salierno's. The baby's father was the guy who shot Alex.

Paul said that he found out after Salierno's arrest. As far as he knew, no DNA tests were ever done. (Paul may not have been aware that a swab of Ralph Salierno's saliva had been taken for DNA comparison purposes during the early morning following his arrest.) Paul did know however that documents were signed to the effect that Lee Ann's latest boy belonged to Ralph Salierno. As far as he knew, Paul said that kid was living with Lee Ann's sister on Long Island.

One of the pleasant consequences of Lee Ann's arrest was that Paul was granted sole custody of Nicholas. He explained to the nation that he was working on being the best single parent he can be.

"Nicholas is my hero," Paul said. "He is just an unbelievable child. I tried to keep him very close to my hip. I don't get a babysitter. I don't get a nanny. My job allows me to do that. I own health clubs and we have a nursery, so we have a very loving relationship. We're very close. He's very busy. Very happy. Of course, I don't know about this stuff, so I go to find out from child therapy. They just think he's doing great. Obviously, there is going to be a time when he is going to know (that his mother is in prison). I'll work on that. I'll do whatever it takes to not allow him to be a victim, as much as I can."

King asked, "Does Nicholas love his mother?"

And Paul answered by changing the tense on him. "He did love his mother. I don't think she was a bad mother. It's a sad, sad situation. I don't know if he's probably not going to see her again. He doesn't ask much about the situation. I don't know why. Like I said, I go to child therapy to find out."

King pointed out that the trial had not been kind to Paul Riedel. The world had learned that Riedel was a violent and abusive man who had dealt cocaine, took cocaine, and was a bookie.

"There seems to be a black cloud around you," King commented.

"I was nineteen years old when I dealt drugs. There's an old saying that any fool can learn from his own mistakes. I made some questionable decisions. Yes, I dealt drugs and I went to prison for six years. It was tough. I was a big kid. I fought a lot. I got stabbed. I almost died. I made it through some tough times. When Nicholas was born, so much changed. It opened up a different side of me."

Then, in a shift of gears that caused nary a ripple in Paul's stream-of-consciousness delivery, he said, "I have never, ever put my hands on my wife." He was defending himself against charges of abuse that had been made by Lee Ann, her brother, and her son Christopher.

"That," Paul said, apparently referring to those charges, "was about a custody battle. That was about a woman who wanted to move to Florida and be with her lover. I wasn't going to allow that to happen. I love my son and I felt— and I feel to this day—that he needed me."

Paul explained that he hadn't been asking for full custody of his son, that he hadn't been asking to take the baby boy away from his mother. "I just wanted what God allows you to have, as any basic parental rights are. I wanted a relationship with my son and I couldn't do that two thousand miles away," Paul said.

Paul made it clear that, along with the birth of his son, the death of his friend also changed him profoundly. He was stricken with guilt that Alex died because of a bullet that was meant for him. He called Alex a "great man."

Paul said that his business was successful, his life was in order, and he was determined to make a positive mark on the world, to pay back for the break he got when *his* killers shot the wrong guy.

"I feel like I have a severe obligation to be a good man

and do the right thing by my son, because I feel I owe that to Alex. I feel that I have a severe obligation to my son," Paul said.

Asked how he felt about his wife, Paul replied, "I don't feel any hatred. I'm confused."

King noted that Lee Ann was angered when she learned that her friend, rather than her husband, had been murdered. He said that this was true, but after the murder he had been more surprised by Lee Ann's lack of emotion over what had happened.

Paul said it struck him as kind of funny at the time, and even more so now that he knew that Lee Ann was responsible, that he had been far more emotional over Alex's death than Lee Ann.

Paul then made sure everyone understood that he was not trying to portray himself as a victim in this situation. He noted that Alex's death was much harder on Alex's family than on him. They were the real victims.

King asked Riedel's opinion of Salierno.

Paul said, "He was just some jerk."

Sal Algeri came on the program at that point. He was asked if, during the weeks following his son's murder, he ever suspected Paul Riedel was the murderer.

"To be honest with you, we did, yes," Sal Algeri admitted.

"Did you think he wanted the whole business to himself?"

"There were some things going on at the time, all right. Minor stuff. They had some differences," Sal said.

King wanted to know if Paul was aware that Sal had suspected him.

"I'm sure he would. That's natural," Paul said, shrugging his massive shoulders.

King asked Sal if he ever confronted Paul with his suspicions, but Paul and Sal both said that they never came into contact with one another during that time. "We had stayed away from each other" was the way Sal put it.

How did Sal feel when he found out that Paul had nothing to do with it?

"I really couldn't believe it. But, as the investigation went along, we started to think that the only thing it could be was a case of mistaken identity. So we were ready for something like that," Sal said. Sal added that he never expected that it would be Paul's wife and lover who were behind the shooting. "We thought maybe it was somebody else who had something against Paul— that they were trying to get him and got Alex by mistake."

Algeri said that the motive, as far as he could tell, was greed. "He wanted money, she wanted money. In a way *she* was selfish because she didn't want to share custody with Paul."

King tried to get Sal to say that he had wished it were Paul who had taken the bullets instead of his son, but Sal wouldn't do it. "You have mixed emotions about stuff like that, it's difficult to say" was all that Sal would admit.

King asked if Sal had ever met Lee Ann Riedel, and the father of the victim seemed unsure. "I was invited to their wedding, so I guess I met Lee Ann. I seen Lee Ann maybe two, three times," Sal said.

Sal said that he had gone to the trial every day and that it was difficult for him. Some days were more difficult than others. The worst were the days when the medical examiner was on the witness stand. "That was when I found out what happened to my son," Sal said. Sal said he felt obliged to attend every day of the trial, no matter how difficult it was. "It was something I had to do for my son," he said.

King asked Paul what his feelings were toward Sal. Paul replied, "I love Sal. I mean, I loved Alex. He was my best friend. I'll go to the grave with him being my best friend."

King asked how Paul felt during the time when Sal and he didn't speak. "It hurt me," Paul said. "But what Sal's going through, I can't even imagine. I can't even relate to what they went through. Even today, you know, Sal and I don't talk much because I'm kind of a reminder of something bad, and that would be selfish. But my heart is with them every day and it will be to the day that I die. Just like Alex's will be."

Paul said that Sal and he had not traveled together to Washington, DC, to talk to Larry King. But they had gotten together after they arrived the night before and they had had breakfast together that morning, which gave them an opportunity to discuss things.

Asked to describe his son, Sal said, "Alex was a very loving person. He had a lot of friends. He was your friend—you had a friend for life. He was very loyal. He would do anything he could for you. If you were in a situation where you needed some help, he would help you out."

Sal said that everyone in Alex's family—his mother, his uncle (Sal's brother), Alex's brother and sister—took his death very hard. "He's always the subject that comes up during family get-togethers when he's not there," Sal said.

"Do you want Alex's killers to die?" Larry King inquired.

"No, I don't want them to die," Sal said. "That would be easy for them. Let them experience the situation over and over again."

King asked Paul the same question and Riedel replied, "She's still the mother of my son, so it's a tough one for me. But I feel that after what happened to Alex, yes, they should pay the consequences. I don't wish death on anybody. That's God's decision, not mine."

Paul said that he last spoke to Lee Ann before she was

convicted. She would call and ask to speak with Nicholas, and he would always let her speak to him.

"Even then, during the trial, I didn't think it was right to take my son's mother away from him," Paul said. He then added that his opinion on the matter had changed since Lee Ann's jury found her guilty of first-degree murder. "Now that's she's convicted, I don't think that it is right for him to talk to her. I don't think he's going to see her ever again. She still tried to call, I haven't allowed her to talk to him. I don't think I am going to allow that."

To conclude the interview, King asked Sal how he goes on.

"Well, you have to go on," Sal said. "I know Alex is with me all the time. I feel him all the time. And, in tough times, I know he's there helping me."

Chapter 57

Sentencing

On Monday, April 26, 2004, Judge Ohlig called to order Ralph Salierno's sentencing hearing. As is customary at such hearings, the judge allowed the friends and family of the victim to have their say. Sentencing hearings always make for an emotional day in court. On this day both of the victim's parents gave statements.

Alex's mother, Lee Ferrari, said that Salierno was a "despicable, cold, calculating person, with no regard for human life, the sort of person who could take another person's life and had the audacity to laugh about it. We want him to suffer every day of his life for what he did."

About Salierno, Sal Algeri said: "He is an evil and cowardly man who robbed from my son life's simple pleasures. Ralph Salierno shot my son in the back and laughed at him as he lay dying. He left us with a hole in our hearts that will never close."

Both Lee and Sal asked the judge to impose the maximum sentence upon Salierno.

Judge Ohlig asked Salierno if he would be willing to

"atone for his deeds" by looking members of Alex's family right in the eye and "asking their forgiveness." Rocco refused. Instead, Salierno's lawyer read a statement.

Seth Muraskin said, "'We would like to express our condolences to the family of Alex Algeri. But we believe the jury made an error in convicting him.'"

Prosecutor Merrifield said, "It is absolutely ridiculous and ludicrous for him to continue to deny he did the murder." She then cited a presentence report by the probation department. The report called Salierno an "unremarkable sociopath" and recommended life in prison.

Judge Ohlig called Salierno's act of gunning down an innocent man in a darkened parking lot as "a dastardly and coldhearted act." Addressing his comments directly to Salierno, the judge said, "It was a cold-blooded killing—for greed and for money and for gain. You had every opportunity to change your mind and not do what you did."

The judge then sentenced Salierno to life in prison without parole for the first-degree murder charge, twenty-five years to life for second-degree murder, and 8½ to twenty-five years for conspiracy, all to run concurrently.

Chapter 58

"I Ask the Court to Tread Lightly"

Lee Ann's sentencing hearing began two days later, on Wednesday, April 28, 2004. It started a little later than scheduled, at about 10:30 A.M., because Bruce Barket was delayed. It was a glorious sun-splashed day. That's a great day for some people, but it's a lousy day for a sentencing. Sentencings should all occur on dreary, drizzly days. Someone was about to be sent inside for a long stretch, and to have the sun shining seemed unnecessarily cruel.

Just as had been the case at Salierno's sentencing, on the day of Lee Ann's sentencing, the friends and family of Alex Algeri were allowed to say their piece. The victim's brother and sister called the defendant "a cold-hearted woman who showed no remorse" for the planning of the murder. They recommended she receive the harshest possible penalty.

"Our brother is gone and the hole in our hearts will never be filled because of [Lee Ann's] greed and hatred of her husband," Christine Stoll, the victim's sister, told Judge Ohlig. "Even though Lee Ann Riedel wasn't there on the night of January 17, 2001, she just as well might have been. Lee Ann Riedel is just as guilty as Ralph Salierno. She came to the funeral, knowing what she did. How do you do that? That's a cold person."

"Does the defendant have anything to say on her behalf?" the judge asked Barket.

"She does not, but I do, Your Honor," Lee Ann's attorney said.

"Proceed," Judge Ohlig said.

Bruce Barket told the court that Lee Ann felt a lot of sorrow over this case. "She misses Alex and she feels badly for the Algeri family. They were friends," Barket said.

Barket then offered a somewhat desperate plea: "Individuals are often convicted of crimes they did not commit. I ask the court to tread lightly in this case, as you are about to send a wrongly convicted person away to prison."

When Barket was done, Merrifield was given the floor. Barket made one last objection about the rules of order at this point, and Judge Ohlig, one last time, overruled him. Merrifield began by reading a letter, a "statement of impact" from the Algeri family. As Merrifield read the impact statement from the Algeris, Barket placed his hand firmly on Lee Ann's back, between her shoulder blades. His palm was flat and his fingers parted. He did not place his hand there so much to comfort her, as to steady her.

Bruce Barket remembered all too clearly how Lee Ann had broken down emotionally when her jury's verdict was announced, and the defense attorney did not want a repeat of that sort of demonstration. But as the sentencing neared, Barket sensed that all efforts to keep his client calm were to be in vain.

Lee Ann's emotions were already starting to bubble to the surface. Hearing what Alex's family had to say about her, she began to turn her head from side to side, as if she were saying "no, no" over and over again. This movement continued and increased in tempo as the sentencing hearing went along. Lee Ann was melting down.

As Lee Ann began showing signs of emotion, her father and stepmother looked forlorn, gripping each other's hands as they had done throughout the trial.

Speaking for the prosecution, Merrifield said that Lee Ann was every bit as guilty as if she had pulled the trigger herself: "Your Honor, Lee Ann provided Salierno a photograph of her husband, and told him when and where he could be found. Even though she was not there at the time of the killing, she aided and abetted the murder. She's just as guilty.

"Justice has been served here, Your Honor. She, because of her own greed and evil heart, wanted her husband dead. This defendant is the most self-absorbed defendant I have ever prosecuted. After Alex was buried, this defendant had the audacity to complain to her inner circle of friends that she had had to stand with the Algeris at the funeral. That shows the depth of her self-absorption. She did not shed one tear. Her motivation was completely selfish. She wanted control of the child. She exhibited sheer unadulterated greed," she said.

Merrifield was impressed with Lee Ann's lack of conscience. She apparently was a complete sociopath as she clung to Paul Riedel in a tight but lethal embrace. The ADA said, "There is nothing more manipulative or coldhearted than a person who would lie in the same bed with a person while plotting his death.

"Your Honor, the only victims in this case are Alex Algeri, who died from a bullet meant for another man, and Nicholas Riedel, Paul and Lee Ann's son, who must now go through life without a mother. The jury found

Lee Ann Riedel guilty of first-degree murder beyond reasonable doubt. This defendant should receive twenty-five years to life."

Justice can be a cold system. Merrifield had neglected to mention that there were two other children, Christopher and Zachary, who were also going to go through life without their mother. However, they were not relevant in these proceedings.

Merrifield had not asked for mercy, that was for sure. But she also had not asked for the harshest penalty, which would have been life in prison without parole.

The judge told Lee Ann to rise. Barket stood at Lee Ann's side, his hand on her shoulder as the moment of truth arrived. She stood before the judge with her head bowed and her hands cuffed behind her.

Judge Ohlig then turned his attention to the speechless woman. His tone was apparent to the court immediately. He was scolding her. He chided her, saying she claimed to know nothing of the murder, yet she had known enough to provide directions and instructions for the excursion to New York in the minivan. She had known enough to provide a photograph of the intended victim. He told her he did not appreciate her refusal to admit her guilt.

"You continue to maintain your innocence despite evidence that you hired, and later had a baby with, a man who was supposed to kill your husband," Judge Ohlig said sternly. "When is this charade going to end? Do you know how many families were affected here? How many lives were affected here? How many lives you have ruined?"

As he spoke, Lee Ann's attention seemed to wander, and she whispered a few words in her attorney's direction. He squeezed a little harder on her shoulder.

She held her emotions in check and did not sob un-controllably as she had when the jury convicted her.

Her hands balled into tight fists. Again her head began to shake from side to side, sending her ponytail flying. In the spectator section her father and step-mother squeezed each other's hands until their knuckles were white.

Judge Ohlig read his sentence: "For the charge of murder in the first degree, I sentence you to twenty-five years to life. For the second charge, murder in the second degree, I sentence you to twenty-five years. For the third charge, conspiracy to commit murder, I sentence you to eight-and-a-third to twenty-five years. All of the sentences are to be served concurrently."

As the judge spoke, Lee Ann was becoming visibly weak in the knees. She swayed back and forth, and Barket held her more firmly to steady her. She dipped slightly. After the sentence was read, she looked back at her father with a panicky expression. Her eyes were bubbling up with tears and her face was flushed. She could be heard gasping. She looked for all the world like a little girl who was looking to her father for help, and her dad couldn't have looked more defeated, because he had no help to offer.

"I am saddened by the lack of respect and discipline in this society," Judge Ohlig said, sighing. "I never cease to be shocked and saddened by the things people will do to satisfy their needs. You went to Florida with the object being to find people who would help you carry out a plot. I'll be frank. The prosecution in this case and I had different ideas when it came to sentencing. I gladly would have given you a harsher sentence, had the prosecutor's office asked for it."

When Judge Ohlig was through reading the sentence, Bruce Barket officially informed the court that there would be an appeal—as if anyone had had any doubts. The judge informed him that the defense had thirty days to file for an appeal.

The hearing over, Lee Ann was led away. Now a thirty-six-year-old mother of three, still slender and attractive, she had not spoken a single word to the court.

An unidentified courtroom spectator—a man about thirty years old—yelled out, "Lee Ann, we love you. You'll be home soon, sweetheart."

That led to a response from the section of court where the victim's family was sitting. "Forget it!" the voice yelled. According to *New York Post* reporter Selim Algar, it was Alex's mom, Leonora, who yelled those words.

Outside the court the principals met the press. Merrifield was asked why she had not asked the judge to give Lee Ann the harshest possible sentence, but the assistant district attorney refused to comment.

The victim's father said, "They chose to give her a lesser sentence. Good for her. Justice has been done. She's going to serve her time. That's good with us."

Algeri's sister Christine said, "If not for Lee Ann, Alex would be home today. She set the wheels in motion. She wasn't there, but she was there. She came to the funeral knowing what she did. Where did he (Salierno) get a picture? Where did he get directions? The evidence shows she was the one."

Outside the courtroom there was a thirtyish man sitting and smoking a cigarette, looking at the ground. He wouldn't give his name, but he said that he was a Lee Ann supporter. He said to a writer, "It is very difficult, her getting twenty-five-to-life, knowing she'll be sitting in a lonely jail cell. She was a mother not only to their son (Paul's son), but to him (Paul). He was a crackhead who abused her—and everyone. She's coming home on appeal."

Experienced courtroom spectators had been surprised to see Denise Merrifield get the last word before the sentence was read. According to law, the victim's family members and the prosecutor spoke first; then the defendant was given a chance to reply. In this hearing, however, the defendant had been given her opportunity to speak before the assistant district attorney spoke.

Once outside the courtroom, Bruce Barket said that the departure from standard order was typical of the trial, which, he said, had been laden with errors and worse.

"This was one of the more unfair trials I have experienced," Barket said. "I am not surprised that the court botched such a simple proceeding. Actually, it would have been ironic if the court had properly conducted the sentence after making so many mistakes during the trial."

Barket said Riedel had retained an appeals counsel and that a notice of appeal had been filed.

The unusual double-jury trial was over. The defendants had been convicted, and all were going to prison for a long time. Later, Judge Ohlig was asked about the difficulty of trying a case with two juries.

He said, "Of course, it was difficult. Juries were constantly being taken out and walked around the corridor, so one side could have their say. Also, there were witnesses being brought up from Florida, so there were a lot of logistical problems, but it worked out OK." As for the heinousness of the crime, the judge added, "I can understand killing someone in the heat of passion. But this was outright 'gun for hire.' The evidence was overwhelming."

Judge Ohlig had displayed genuine anger at Bruce Barket, who had thrown around charges of misconduct during the course of the trial. What did he think of Barket's tactics now that it was all over?

"I kept my composure, and wouldn't let him get the

best of me. I understand he has a job to do, but sometimes he took it too far," he said.

The judge saved his harshest words for Lee Ann: "She had such a cavalier attitude. The only time she broke down was at the sentencing. I think that was when reality hit her. But when somebody cries, I want to see real tears."

Was it wrong to sentence such young people to such long prison sentences?

"That wasn't difficult for me at all," Judge Ohlig said. "I have no problem believing I'm doing the right thing. I have a lot of concern for the families [of the victims]. They don't get to ever see their loved one again. I sleep nights."

Chapter 59

Paget Sentencing

On June 30, 2004—in the same courthouse where Lee Ann Riedel and Ralph Salierno were tried, though in a smaller courtroom—the last of the three defendants, driver Scott Paget, was sentenced for his involvement in Alex Algeri's murder. As he had for all parts of the case, Judge Ohlig presided. Representing the prosecution was Denise Merrifield. Paget's lawyer was Ted Scharfenberg.

As was true at the sentencing hearing for the other defendants, the friends and family got to make impact statements before Paget's sentencing, explaining to the court how Paget's actions damaged their lives in a way that couldn't be repaired.

Denise Merrifield said to Judge Ohlig, "Miss Christine Stoll would like to address the court, Alex Algeri's sister. And Alex's mom, Lee Ferrari, would like to step up with her."

"All right," said Judge Ohlig.

Christine then spoke on behalf of her mother, who

stood at her side. She noted that this was the third time the Algeri family had stood in front of Judge Ohlig at a sentencing hearing. She said that Ralph Salierno was the one who shot Alex, but that he couldn't have done the job by himself. He needed to be driven to and from the crime scene, and for that he paid a few thousand dollars to Scott Paget.

She then turned directly to Paget and said, "Why do this? Why, Scott? Why not go to the police, tell them what you know?" She told him that he had a sense of right and wrong, that it had been woven into his character by his upbringing. If only Scott Paget had listened to his conscience, and she knew he had one, Alex Algeri might still be alive. She noted that although Paget knew what was going to occur, and allowed it to happen anyway, Alex had no idea what was coming. He was at work, trying to make a living like a good, honest man, and he was shot dead—in cold blood.

"Scott Paget could have stopped it—but he did nothing," she said. She said that there was no use trying to explain the family's pain because there were no words for that kind of anguish, that kind of agony. And there was no way for the family to learn to cope with their loss. Alex's murder was going to continue to haunt and sadden those who knew and loved him for as long as they lived.

"Your Honor, we wish that you would impose the appropriate punishment for his involvement in this crime," Christine concluded. Judge Ohlig asked if either lady had anything to add. They did not.

Denise Merrifield then said, "This is a negotiated disposition, which the defendant entered into with the district attorney's office and with the consent of the Algeri family, that he receive eighteen years to life for his participation in this crime.

"While it is true that Mr. Paget did drive all the way

up from Florida and could have, at any moment, turned the car around or stepped out of the car and said, 'I don't want to participate in this any longer'—he did follow through and he did receive money after the fact, when, in fact, Alex Algeri was wrongly shot and killed in this case—and while it is true that Alex Algeri suffered brutally and it is a very tragic end to his life, it is also true that this is also a very tragic end to the life of Mr. Scott Paget.

"The man that stands before you, Your Honor, is an intelligent, articulate man that had his whole life ahead of him, and is now going to be serving eighteen years to life in prison for his participation in the murder of Alex Algeri.

"I would like to bring to the court's attention the amends that Mr. Paget has tried to remedy the situation by doing. He participated fully in the prosecution of Ralph Salierno and Lee Ann Riedel. He gave a full confession to the police regarding his involvement in this crime, which was corroborated by many other sources of evidence produced at trial.

"He also provided the location of the murder weapon in this case, which was located and ultimately produced at court in the trial. For that, the district attorney's office is truly grateful. He was a major assistance in the prosecution against Lee Ann Riedel.

"And for all of those factors, we ask that he be sentenced to eighteen years to life."

Judge Ohlig then said, "Mr. Scharfenberg, would you like to say anything on behalf of your client?"

"Yes, thank you, Your Honor," Scharfenberg replied.

"Or does your client wish to speak?" Judge Ohlig asked.

"He does, Your Honor. But first I have a few brief comments; then I think Scott has a few things that he would like to say as well," Scharfenberg said. "First and foremost, I have spoken to the Algeri family. Scott is truly sorry. I know that sometimes it is even harder to hear something like that at a time like this, because you are so hurt.

"I have been doing this for quite some time and I have represented a number of defendants, and Scott, from day one, wanted to do the right thing after this happened, to try to get the family some closure, and try to resolve this.

"To be honest, I have never had a client that is more remorseful about his actions. And I think worse than the sentence the court is going to impose today is him knowing that he played a part in this, and that someone who was loved has died and he played a role in that.

"Your Honor, the Scott Paget I have gotten to know over almost two years now is almost inconsistent with the person who committed this crime. I cannot, to this day, reconcile the fact that this person who I know was involved in this murder.

"The fact is, however, that he was. I can't reconcile it. I don't think Scott can. He cannot believe himself that he didn't make the right choice, that he made the wrong one, and that he allowed himself to do this, to be an active participant.

"My hope is that, with time, both families can heal. Scott's family is here also. I have talked to them numerous times about Scott, about the case. Their heart goes out also to the victim's family. They also have to, you know, find a way to heal somehow.

"And now, I believe he has just a few words, Your Honor," Scharfenberg concluded.

"Mr. Paget," Judge Ohlig prompted, turning his eyes to the defendant.

Scott then spoke, directing his words to Alex's family: "I just wanted to say that there is not a person in this world that is more sorry for what took place and for my actions. And you know, if there is only one wish I could have, it would be to bring your son back and let me take his place. I am extremely sorry."

Judge Ohlig then said, "Mr. Scharfenberg, is your client ready for sentence?"

"He is," Scharfenberg replied.

The judge continued, "This has been a tragedy here. No parent expects their children to die before them. Mr. Algeri, he didn't die, he was murdered. That certainly is a tragedy. It should never have happened. Mr. Paget . . ."

"Yes, Your Honor."

"I have read this report over several times. I have just come to a conclusion here. The damn drugs that you got yourself involved with got you into this situation. What Miss Merrifield said, the court agrees with. You had an opportunity to reflect on doing the right thing or doing the wrong thing during the long drive up from Florida. I have said for years as a judge that people know when they are in a situation that they shouldn't be in. Bells start ringing in their head, or they get a queasy feeling in their stomach.

"Well, with you it didn't happen—not until after the tragedy took place. Because only then did you come forth as a man realizing your fault and the wrong you did. And I believe you are truly remorseful here. Hopefully, that fact will give some solace to the Algeri family.

"You kept your word with the people as far as testifying truthfully. And I was very impressed with your testimony. I approached the people after your testimony and I asked if they would consider lesser time. I will always remember your testimony and your participation in this case. You testified truthfully and accurately. Your college education came out during your testimony, and I was impressed with that as well. But the people reminded the court that they had an agreement and they must keep the agreement—so I must honor that."

Judge Ohlig then sentenced Scott Paget to eighteen years to life in prison.

The judge added, "Again, I would like to say to the Algeri family that you certainly showed your composure in allowing the trial to proceed in an orderly fashion, notwithstanding your great loss, especially commendable considering the length of the trial. And the court thanks you for that."

The judge then asked Scharfenberg to inform his client officially of his right to appeal, and that was done—and with that, the hearing came to a close.

After the hearing Sal Algeri told the reporter from *Newsday* that he and his family believed Paget when he said he was repentant. "But ours is a family that may never fully heal," Sal told Zachary R. Dowdy, of the Long Island daily newspaper.

There were members of Paget's family there for the hearing, but none had a comment, either inside the courtroom or outside with the press after the sentencing.

Long after he had sentenced Scott Paget, Judge Ohlig told a reporter that he agreed with Detective Anderson, that Paget was not a rotten man, but rather a good man who had been forced into doing bad things because of a drug habit.

"I've recommended to the DA that a few years be shaved off his sentence," Judge Ohlig said. "I told the DA that he testified without hesitation. He was a college-educated man who got whacked-out on drugs, got in with the wrong people, and found himself in over his head."

* * *

On July 8, 2004, responding to a motion filed earlier by Lee Ann's legal team were Judges Fred T. Santucci, J.P.; Gloria Goldstein; Robert W. Schmidt; and Barry A. Cozier, J.J. They declared that the appeal of the trial was to be based on the transcript of the trial as recorded by the court reporters and that Lee Ann's team should be granted a copy of those transcripts in their entirety free of charge.

Just acquiring a copy of a trial's transcript can be a pricey proposition. It is a little-known fact that the transcript of a trial is the property of the court reporters. If journalists or legal firms want copies of the transcript, they are charged by the page. The entire transcript of the Salierno/Riedel dual trial would have cost $28,000, well out of the range of most true-crime writers, or other interested individuals.

The appeal process was ongoing in Salierno's conviction as well. His legal staff had filed to enlarge the time they had to serve and file a brief on an appeal from the judgment made on April 26, 2004, that he was guilty of first-degree murder.

The appeal was before the Supreme Court of the State of New York Appellate Division: Second Judicial Department. The judges hearing the appeal were Sondra Miller, J.J.; David S. Ritter; Reinaldo E. Rivera; and Peter B. Skelos, J.J.

On September 15, 2005, the court decided that since papers had been filed in support of the motion, and no papers had been filed in opposition, that the motion was granted.

The order read, "The respondent's time to serve and file a brief is enlarged until October 17, 2005, and the respondent's brief must be served and filed on or before that date."

Chapter 60

Sitting Down with Sal

On September 30, 2005, Sal Algeri graciously agreed to meet author Robert Mladinich in a diner for an interview. When Mladinich asked if Alex ever had any legal problems, Sal began to cry. Mladinich tried to press him, but he didn't want to talk about it. The writer asked if it was youthful indiscretion, and Sal said that was the best way to describe it.

Mladinich asked if Alex ever went to prison, and he said yes. He would visit him once a month upstate with Alex's stepmother. He still wouldn't divulge what for. Mladinich did not pry further, but a later check revealed that Alex did time for hijacking the Mack truck full of yarn near JFK Airport when he was twenty-two.

Otherwise, Sal was very open when discussing his son. He told Mladinich that Alex was smart, but not a good student, and how he had struggled to find a job he liked during the first few years after he graduated from high school.

He said Alex had been a promising athlete until

mononucleosis during his senior year detoured him, how he had done well as an electrician before and after he went away, and how he had learned his lesson after his release.

Sal said Alex met Paul in a gym. They used to ride their motorcycles together. They went into the gym business together. Alex and Paul had fought during the months and weeks before Alex's death. That's why Paul was the natural first suspect.

He described his son's wake, how Lee Ann had acted nervous there, and how Paul—despite the fact that everyone was looking at him with hatred in their eyes— seemed genuinely upset about Alex's death and shook when he gave Sal a hug.

Sal described how he had found out about Alex's death, and how Detective Anderson was a regular presence in his life after that, dropping by or calling periodically with questions. The questions had started out being mostly about Paul, but as the investigation progressed, Sal noticed that more and more of Detective Anderson's queries were about Lee Ann.

"When the police first started asking me questions about Lee Ann, I thought that maybe Lee Ann's mother and her girlfriend were under suspicion. My first thought wasn't of Lee Ann herself," Sal said. "I got the impression the cops were looking at them—not from anything anyone ever told me, but by the line of their questioning. It seems that they were the main instigators, and they walked away."

"How did Liz and Pat skate?" Mladinich asked Sal.

Sal put his hands up and frowned as if to say, "Who knows?" His best theory was that the mother's girlfriend provided key information in exchange for immunity. "If that's true, I doubt Merrifield would admit that because of confidential informant issues," Sal said.

How did Sal learn that Ralph Salierno had been arrested for his son's murder?

"I don't know what detectives do and I got annoyed by the way I was treated sometimes. It was like I was purposely left in the dark."

Mladinich, a former detective himself, explained to Sal how detectives would be remiss in sharing investigatory progress with family members (good or bad).

Sal responded, "I understand that now, but didn't then. Anderson knows what he's doing. He's a very good detective. He didn't have to go to Florida all those times. He could have put the case on the shelf. I respect and appreciate that he didn't."

What did Sal think of Denise Merrifield and the job she did?

"When Detective Anderson told me she would be the prosecutor on the case, I made a comment about how such a petite, pretty little woman could try such a case," Sal remembered. "But she was terrific, very sharp, very professional. Barket tried to come at her in many different ways, but she always had an answer. The right answer."

What about Bruce Barket?

"Barket put on a good show, but in the end, all it was was a show. Denise was fantastic," Sal replied.

Did Sal believe that Bruce Barket truly thought Lee Ann was innocent?

"Maybe he does, but he has to look at all the people hanging around her," Sal replied. "There are no [angels] in the whole bunch."

And what were his feelings regarding Salierno during the trial?

"I'm not a violent man, but sometimes I felt like just punching him in the head," said Sal.

Like Sal, Lee Ann's father was at the trial every day. Did the two men know one another?

"I met him as the father of the bride at his daughter's wedding," Sal said. "There were times I wanted to say, 'I'm sorry we have to go through this together,' but I never did. I never spoke to him, but he seems like a nice man."

Was it a chore to maintain his perfect attendance record at the trial?

"I never forced myself to go there. I wanted to be there. I wanted to know everything that happened. I see my son all the time. I think about him every day. I work with young guys in contracting and see Alex in those guys. Sometimes I'll daydream and have to slam on the brakes at the last minute. I get chills when I think he's touching me. I'm sure he is."

Were there any court dates that Sal would have preferred to miss?

"I didn't want to be there the day they talked about the autopsy," Sal said. "But I ended up going that day anyway." A group of Alex's friends were going to the trial that day, to show support. As a result, Sal went and was shaken. "The whole thing made me realize that my son never had a chance," he said.

What was the worst moment in the trial, as far as he was concerned? "The worst was when Fiaccabrino testified that Salierno laughed at the noises Alex made after being shot because he couldn't breathe."

A tough question to ask: Did Sal still go to the cemetery to visit his son's grave? "I used to go every weekend. Now I go once a month," Sal said. How often did Salierno, Paget, and Lee Ann cross his thoughts? "They don't pop into my mind very often. Not anymore," he said.

Was he hoping Ralph Salierno would be sentenced to death? "No, but he probably couldn't get it anyway with all of the rules." What about Lee Ann? "I feel Lee Ann should have gotten more prison time," Sal replied.

Everyone mourns differently, said Sal.

Sal said he didn't talk to his daughter about Alex much because they are both very emotional. He didn't want to get her upset "because she's got two children." His other son Paul kept things in. Sal said he was a "big mush" who would sometimes be watching TV, become overcome by feelings, and start crying unabashedly. Sometimes an unexpected thought triggered his emotions—e.g., Alex only had two or three payments left on his bike when he died: tears.

Sal believed that God took Alex because "he needed his work someplace else."

Alex was the "centerpiece of my family's life. He brought so much joy to his parents, his siblings, his sister's children. He never got to celebrate some of the great things in life. He loved kids and would have made a great parent. My daughter's children adored him and he adored them.

"My daughter does a great job keeping him alive," Sal said. "They used to go to the cemetery together, but my grandson said it was too sad."

When was the last time Sal talked to Paul Riedel? "I haven't heard from him since we did *The Larry King Show* together."

Alex Algeri is buried deep within the sweeping St. Charles/Resurrection Cemetery on Conklin Avenue, in Farmingdale, just about five miles from his Dolphin gym. The cemetery is under the guidance of the Roman Catholic Diocese of Brooklyn, and has been serving the Long Island Catholic community for longer than 150 years. It is situated just east of Route 110, behind Republic Airport and the SUNY Farmingdale Aerospace and jetport. When one stands at the grave, the aerial tower—looking similar to a prison-guard tower—is clearly visible on the skyline.

At the grave site Sal planted a memorial tree and put a stone in front of it. Every year at Christmas he and his wife celebrate Alex's life by decorating it.

Chapter 61

Barket Looks Back

On December 16, 2005, author Robert Mladinich visited Bruce Barket at his sixth-floor offices in Garden City, Long Island. Even though, like all lawyers, he hated talking about cases he had lost, he discussed Lee Ann Riedel.

Not being omniscient, Barket gave his opinion as to Lee Ann's innocence as a disclaimer. Barket didn't say so, but he believed that Liz and Pat had had a fight that led to their breakup.

In order to get back at Pat, Barket theorized, Liz had lied to police about Lee Ann's involvement in Algeri's murder—and that she had gotten her criminal friends, the ones who were in trouble, to cut deals by backing up her story.

He explained, "I wasn't there, I don't know exactly what happened, but I certainly don't think Lee Ann participated in, asked for, or did anything to get anybody murdered. The tragedy of this case is it was a clash of two women with two outlooks on life."

He rejected the notion that Lee Ann was scheming and conniving. It didn't fit the pattern. Those types of women hook up with men they can manipulate. Her mating tendencies were the opposite. She sought out men who were absolutely dominant. She was never the one calling the shots. She did not seek out the freedom to make her own decisions. She repeatedly sought out situations where decisions were made for her.

"Lee Ann is in all respects a victim," Barket said. "She's a classic abused woman, who goes from guy to guy, taking their shit. Every guy that was ever in her life had taken advantage of her. It was obvious she was never running the show.

"Her greatest sin was having sex out of wedlock. If she didn't conceive children, she would not be in the situation she is in. She would go from one bad guy to the next. Salierno was sleeping with her and bragging about sleeping with others."

Barket, who has read the latest psychology literature regarding abused women, thought that the prosecution's case against Lee Ann was based on a faulty psychological premise. He explained: "Denise Merrifield looked at the same set of facts and called her manipulative and calculating. She said Lee Ann gets men to do her bidding. That's a throwback to the days when we didn't understand that women stayed with men that abused them. Merrifield says, 'Why didn't she just leave him?' Merrifield's strict conservative views date back twenty years."

Part of Barket's view of Lee Ann's personality is based on her demeanor while dealing with him. A dominant woman will try to gain as much control as possible in all relationships, not just those that are romantic or sexual.

"Lee Ann is anything but manipulative," Barket said. "It is inconceivable that she would have concocted the scenario Denise described. If she were the woman that

Denise described, she would have taken more action in her own defense. She would have tried to manipulate me or get me to believe certain things. She just let me run the show."

Was there anything he might have done differently? Barket said that he had known from the moment he took the case that the evidence against Lee Ann was based on the statements of liars. His job was to hammer away at the credibility of those who said Lee Ann was guilty. In the end, he believed, he had not done that enough, or at least not well enough.

"In the summations I could have spent more time going after Fiaccabrino and Paget's credibility," he said. "Paget's blatant hearsay came in under the guise of the furtherance of a conspiracy."

Some of that hearsay concerned the things Rocco Salierno had told him while they were driving in the van together from Florida to New York and back, and some had concerned things Fiaccabrino claimed he heard Lee Ann say.

Some of his ineffectiveness in discrediting prosecution witnesses had been his own fault, and some stemmed from what he viewed as faulty decisions that were made by Judge Ohlig. Barket had prepared a timeline for his closing argument, a visual aid for the jury that showed that Fiaccabrino and Lee Ann were never in the same place at the same time. Because of the mutual exclusiveness of their locations, it would have been impossible for Fiaccabrino to have heard Lee Ann say anything, much less say things that incriminated her. But, to Barket's extreme disappointment, Judge Ohlig had not allowed Barket to use the visual aid during his closing argument, limiting him to verbal argument only. In the long run, Barket believed, his spoken words had not been nearly as effective as the timeline would have been. Obviously, the jury had not given his words much weight.

Barket admitted that he had been thrown a bit by Judge Ohlig's decision, and it had harmed his closing statement. He had prepared to do it one way and was forced at the last second to do it another way.

"The bottom line was that I didn't go after Fiaccabrino and Paget as well as I had hoped," Barket said.

He had harsh words for Judge Ohlig: "It is a despicable comment on our system when a man *that* divorced from the rules of evidence presides over a murder-in-the-first-degree trial. He was beyond awful. A layperson who watches Court TV knows more about evidence than he does."

In retrospect, the defense attorney saw the soon-to-retire judge's behavior as almost comical—it would have been funny if the consequences had not been so dire. He was certain Lee Ann didn't find it funny. Barket described what he called a "Chevy Chase moment." He said, "The judge wouldn't let me use the charts because they weren't in evidence. My summation wasn't in evidence, because I didn't say it yet. Then he said I could read from the graphs, but I couldn't show them. It was mind-bogglingly stupid and showed an utter lack of basic legal procedure. His courtroom was an evidentiary wasteland. I could not understand what was admissible and not admissible because everything I heard in law school was not there.

"It sounds like sour grapes, but I do think his rulings affected the outcome of the trial. Just look at the transcripts and tell me this guy should be presiding over a murder trial," Barket concluded.

Barket was asked: Was it Big Balls Fiaccabrino who did Lee Ann in?

"Lee Ann lost because of Paget, not Fiaccabrino. Fiaccabrino's tapes were littered with inaccuracies, false claims, and bragging to his buddies. I went through the tapes and pulled out all the boasting and puffing to drug buddies, like guys do."

He implied that, without Paget, he could have discredited Fiaccabrino completely.

"Paget was able to say that Salierno had a photograph and map given to him by Lee Ann. He testified to that on the stand, but nowhere else. He never said it in his statement to police.

"When Fiaccabrino testified that he was there when directions were given and a map picked up by Salierno, Paget filled in the other end. He altered his testimony after Fiaccabrino's arrest to add in the photographs and directions. That information only came from Paget after Fiaccabrino gave information to police."

As for the testimony of Paul Riedel against his ex-wife, Barket noted that he, too, was a known liar, and had even perjured himself in the past.

"Paul said he never took steroids; however, he placed part of the blame for his robbery of the undercover cop on the fact that his behavior was erratic because of steroids," Barket said.

Barket seemed offended that a man like Paul Riedel would have had the audacity to accuse him of breaking the rules. Barket explained, "Riedel said something like, 'You know how it goes, Mr. Barket.' Here he is in the bosom of the prosecutor, a man that has pointed a gun at a cop, lied under oath, and dealt drugs. He implies that the defense attorney (Barket) suborns perjury and doesn't play by the rules."

Afterword

Soon after Alex was shot and taken to Brunswick Hospital Center, where he died, that hospital was converted into a psychiatric-only facility and the emergency room was closed and left empty.

A few weeks after the legal proceedings regarding Alex Algeri's murder were completed, the Honorable Louis J. Ohlig retired from the bench. He is now in private practice on Long Island.

In January 2006, Ohlig declined to allow his photograph to appear in this book. He said that his family was worried about ramifications and he'd rather not have his photo used. He also said that during the court proceedings (he didn't recall if during trial or pretrial hearings), he and Denise Merrifield received death threats.

It was the first time ever he received death threats and he presided over many high-profile cases, including a death penalty case.

He said, "I never got death threats before. I had around-the-clock police protection at my home, as well as a panic button. The neighbors must have thought we had matrimonial problems. My family was more worried than I was. If they're going to do something, they don't tell you. It was still cause for concern. There are a lot of wacky people out there."

As of August 26, 2005, Ralph Salierno's defense team continued to work their way through the appeal process.

* * *

Paul Riedel still owns the gym at which the murder occurred. He has sole custody of the son he had with Lee Ann.

Riedel's matrimonial attorney, Steven Constantino, described this case as *Beauty and the Beast*, adding that it was Lee Ann, a cunningly lethal woman, who was "the beast." According to Constantino, Riedel is now completely off drugs. Once a manic, late-night bodybuilder, Riedel now stays home at night and grows "love handles from eating Devil Dogs while watching television with his son."

Michael "Big Balls" Fiaccabrino, childhood buddy of Rocco Salierno's, who went on to run a marijuana-growing operation, and testify against Rocco and Lee Ann at the trial, was tried for federal drug charges and found guilty. He is currently serving a five-year sentence.

On November 4, 2005, a computer search was made on the Internet for references to the Dolphin Fitness Club address, in Amityville, using a popular search engine. Third among the items found by the search was this:

DOLPHIN FITNESS—Address4Sex—CocksuckerADS— CruisingStops . . . DOLPHIN FITNESS, AMITYVILLE, NEW YORK, BathHouse/Sauna/Gym, Cruising for sex locations. address4sex.com/newpages/s832686.shtml22k

When the Web site was opened, along with advertisements for sex services unrelated to the gym, there was a listing for the gym with its address and phone number, followed by the editorial comment, apparently supplied by those who maintain the *address4sex.com* Web site: "Hot action afternoons & late evenings in Showers." An item added to the Web site in 2004 noted that the club was open twenty-four hours and was great for "cruising."

Today the place looks just like it did when Alex roamed its rooms. The only difference is in the weight room. Now there is a huge sign on the wall that reads BIG AL'S WEIGHT ROOM.

On October 13, 2005, Lee Ann Armanini Riedel wrote a four-page letter, both sides of two sheets of a wide-ruled loose leaf, in her precise parochial penmanship. As she wrote, she sat in her home, a cell in the Bedford Hills Correctional Facility, in Bedford Hills, New York.

She said she was writing to beg for help. She had been sitting in Bedford for two years, in addition to the eighteen months she had spent in the Suffolk County Jail, and she was beginning to feel as if everyone had forgotten her. Being forgotten was, she wrote, "the one thing I always asked to not happen." Her mind was reeling and she didn't know quite what it was she was asking. She wanted someone to discover the truth behind Alex Algeri's murder, so she could be exonerated. She wrote that she didn't have any money—if she was released from prison, she would make sure to pay back all of her debts in full, even if she had to work "a million jobs."

"I did not (the word 'not' was underlined twice) ask Rocco to kill Paul! Please! You have got to believe me! Mike Fiaccabrino lied about everything! I cannot beg you enough!" she wrote.

She hoped that Bruce Barket could help her more than he had. She wrote that she had wished Barket could have helped her more during her trial as well. She still wondered why she had not been allowed to testify. How could the jury believe she was innocent when her lawyer wouldn't even allow her to take the stand and defend herself? She finally had come to believe that Barket's strategy was the smartest, and where had it gotten her? Twenty-five years in stir with no one helping her, that's where.

She noted that the letter's addressee was not a member of her family; then she explained that it was really just justice she wanted. The witnesses against her had lied, she complained, often to save their own skins. People she didn't even know sat on the witness stand and made her out to look like a monster. Something needed to be done.

She agreed that Barket's defense had been, at times, most eloquent, and his words were easy to listen to—but that didn't change the fact that he had failed to convince a jury that an innocent woman wasn't guilty.

"How do you think you would feel? Everyone says the same thing: hang in there, be patient, keep the faith," she wrote. She had been taken from her babies, who were now little boys. She noted that it had been three years since she had seen Nicholas. She lacked the words to communicate her heartbreak. She concluded, "I can't take it anymore. I need to fight for my freedom. I need to fight for my life. I hope and pray to hear from you soon."

Bibliography

Algar, Selim. "25 to life for 'wrong hit' wife." *New York Post*, April 29, 2004, p. 16.

Dowdy, Zachary R. "Accomplice in gym murder gets 18 years to life." Newsday.com. Posted July 1, 2004, accessed October 12, 2005.

James, Carolyn. "Businessman shot to death in Amityville; investigation underway." *Babylon Beacon*, January 24, 2001, p. 1.

Pulitzer, Lisa. "Botch Killer Guilty: Shot wrong man." *New York Post*, March 24, 2004, p. 27.

About the Authors

Robert Mladinich is the author of *From the Mouth of the Monster: The Joel Rifkin Story* (Pocket Books). The book chronicled his college friendship with New York State's most notorious serial killer and the divergent paths their lives had taken. He is a retired New York Police Department second-grade detective who has investigated numerous homicides, and was named NYPD "Cop of the Year" in 1985 for his work as a patrol officer in the South Bronx. He is also a journalist whose reports have appeared in *Playboy, Details,* and *The Ring.* He contributes regularly to the boxing Web site TheSweetScience.com. Visit him there or at www.RobertMlad.com.

Michael Benson is the author of forty-one books, including the Kensington true-crime book *Betrayal in Blood.* He's also written *Who's Who in the JFK Assassination* (Citadel) and *Complete Idiot's Guides to NASA, National Security, The CIA, Submarines,* and *Modern China.* Other works include biographies of Ronald Reagan, Bill Clinton, and William Howard Taft. Originally from Rochester, New York, he is a graduate of Hofstra University and lives with his wife and two children in Brooklyn, New York.

MORE MUST-READ TRUE CRIME
FROM
M. William Phelps